Christlike Acceptance across Deep Difference

Constructive Conversations on Sexuality and Gender

Ronald W. Pierce and
Karen R. Keen, eds.

Baker Academic
a division of Baker Publishing Group
Grand Rapids, Michigan

© 2025 by Ronald W. Pierce and Karen R. Keen

Published by Baker Academic
a division of Baker Publishing Group
Grand Rapids, Michigan
BakerAcademic.com

Printed in the United States of America

All rights reserved. No part of this publication may be reproduced, stored in a retrieval system, or transmitted in any form or by any means—for example, electronic, photocopy, recording—without the prior written permission of the publisher. The only exception is brief quotations in printed reviews.

Library of Congress Cataloging-in-Publication Control Number: 2025014268
ISBN 9781540967596 (paper)
ISBN 9781540969187 (casebound)
ISBN 9781493450060 (ebook)
ISBN 9781493450077 (pdf)

Unless otherwise indicated, Scripture quotations are taken from the Holy Bible, New International Version®, NIV®. Copyright © 1973, 1978, 1984, 2011 by Biblica, Inc.® Used by permission of Zondervan. All rights reserved worldwide. www.zondervan.com. The "NIV" and "New International Version" are trademarks registered in the United States Patent and Trademark Office by Biblica, Inc.®

Scripture quotations labeled ESV are from The Holy Bible, English Standard Version® (ESV®), copyright © 2001 by Crossway, a publishing ministry of Good News Publishers. Used by permission. All rights reserved. ESV Text Edition: 2016

Scripture quotations labeled MSG are taken from *The Message*, copyright © 1993, 2002, 2018 by Eugene H. Peterson. Used by permission of NavPress. All rights reserved. Represented by Tyndale House Publishers.

Scripture quotations labeled NET are from the NET Bible® copyright ©1996, 2019 by Biblical Studies Press, L.L.C. http://netbible.com. All rights reserved. Scripture quoted by permission.

Scripture quotations labeled NRSV are from the New Revised Standard Version Bible, copyright © 1989 National Council of the Churches of Christ in the United States of America. Used by permission. All rights reserved worldwide.

Scripture quotations labeled NRSVue are taken from the New Revised Standard Version Updated Edition. Copyright © 2021 National Council of Churches of Christ in the United States of America. Used by permission. All rights reserved worldwide.

The names and details of the people and situations described in this book have been changed or presented in composite form in order to ensure the privacy of the individuals involved.

Cover design by Paula Gibson

Baker Publishing Group publications use paper produced from sustainable forestry practices and postconsumer waste whenever possible.

25 26 27 28 29 30 31   7 6 5 4 3 2 1

Contents

Contributors v

Introduction: Healing Our Divisions ix
Ronald W. Pierce and Karen R. Keen

Part 1 Biblical Wisdom beyond the Debate

1. Christlike Acceptance and Queer Christians: Romans 14:1–15:13 3
   Ronald W. Pierce

2. Genesis, Discernment, and God's Will 21
   Karen R. Keen

3. From Eunuchs to LGBTQ Christians: Navigating Theodicy, Inclusion, and Holiness 35
   David Bennett

4. The Good News of Romans 1 49
   J. R. Daniel Kirk

5. Excluded from God's Kingdom? (1 Cor. 6:9–10): How to Think about the Threat of Divine Judgment 65
   Wesley Hill

Part 2 Successfully Navigating Divides

6. Navigating Conflict in Community 81
   Tim Otto

7. Speaking Truth in Love: Preparing the Heart to Engage 94
   Tim Muehlhoff

8. Grace across the Divide: Tips for Christ-Honoring Dialogue   109
   Justin Lee

9. Loving through Difference: Navigating Side A/B Friendship   124
   Steven Lympus and Taylor Telford

10. Is There Space at the Table in a Non-Affirming Church?   140
    Brad Harper

Part 3   Ministry with LGBTQ People, Families, and Friends

11. A Shared Pilgrimage   155
    Eve Tushnet

12. Courage Is Ministry   166
    Sally Gary

13. What We Learned from Listening to Sexual and Gender Minorities   177
    Mark A. Yarhouse, Stephen P. Stratton, and Janet B. Dean

14. Evangelism and the LGBTQ Community   191
    Elizabeth Delgado Black

15. Black LGBTQ Ministry   207
    Candace E. Hardnett

16. Cultivating a Shepherd's Heart for the Transgender Community   218
    Amie Scott

17. Supporting Parents of LGBTQ Children   229
    Staci Frenes

18. Christlike Acceptance in Practice: Moving from Enmity to Integrity   241
    Marcus George Halley

Contributors

David Bennett (DPhil, University of Oxford) is a postdoctoral research fellow in the Theology and Religion Faculty at Oxford, associate research fellow at Wycliffe Hall, and a member of the Archbishop of Canterbury's College of Evangelists. He is author of the memoir *A War of Loves: The Unexpected Story of a Gay Activist Discovering Jesus* (2018) and has a forthcoming book with Tyndale Momentum based on his dissertation, *Queering the Queer*.

Janet B. Dean (PhD, The Ohio State University) is professor of pastoral counseling at Asbury Theological Seminary. She is also an ordained elder and serves as associate pastor of pastoral counseling at Lafayette Church of the Nazarene. Dean coauthored *Listening to Sexual Minorities: A Study of Faith and Sexual Identity on Christian College Campuses* (2018).

Elizabeth Delgado Black, a master of theology student at All Nations Christian College, is an evangelist and minister in New York City. She is also cofounder and president of Kaleidoscope, a ministry dedicated to sharing Jesus with those in the LGBTQ community and beyond.

Staci Frenes is a songwriter, author, and speaker with twenty-five years of experience singing and speaking in churches. She authored *Love Makes Room: And Other Things I Learned When My Daughter Came Out* (2021).

Sally Gary (MA, Abilene Christian University; JD, Texas Tech University) is founder and executive director of CenterPeace, a nonprofit ministry building Christian spiritual community for LGBTQ people, supporting parents and families, and equipping ministry leaders. She is the author of *Affirming: A Memoir of Faith, Sexuality, and Staying in the Church* (2021).

Marcus George Halley (DMin, The School of Theology at the University of the South) is an Episcopal priest and the college chaplain and dean of spiritual and religious life at Trinity College in Hartford, Connecticut. He has authored *Proclaim! Sharing Words, Living Examples, Changing Lives* (2020) and *Abide in Peace: Healing and Reconciliation* (2021).

Candace E. Hardnett (MDiv, Liberty Baptist Theological Seminary) is senior pastor of Agape Empowerment Ministries, a church she cofounded in Savannah, Georgia. She also has a podcast called *Godly and Gay* and serves as chairwoman of the board of directors for The Reformation Project.

Brad Harper (PhD, St. Louis University) has served as professor of Bible and theology and as assistant dean of the School of Biblical and Theological Studies at the Multnomah Campus of Jessup University. Along with his son Drew Harper, he coauthored *Space at the Table: Conversations between an Evangelical Theologian and His Gay Son* (2016).

Wesley Hill (PhD, Durham University) is an Episcopal priest and associate professor of New Testament at Western Theological Seminary in Holland, Michigan. Among other books, he authored *Washed and Waiting: Reflections on Christian Faithfulness and Homosexuality* (2nd ed., 2016) and *Spiritual Friendship: Finding Love in the Church as a Celibate Gay Christian* (2015).

Karen R. Keen (ThM, Duke Divinity School) is a biblical scholar, spiritual director, and founder of the Redwood Center for Spiritual Care and Education. She authored *Scripture, Ethics, and the Possibility of Same-Sex Relationships* (2018), *The Jesus Way: Practicing the Ignatian Spiritual Exercises* (2020), and *The Word of a Humble God: The Origins, Inspiration, and Interpretation of Scripture* (2022).

J. R. Daniel Kirk (PhD, Duke University) is a New Testament scholar and author of multiple books, including *Jesus Have I Loved, but Paul?* (2012), *A Man Attested by God: The Human Jesus of the Synoptic Gospels* (2016), and *Romans for Normal People* (2022).

Justin Lee is a speaker and nonprofit executive who founded the Gay Christian Network (2001–2017) and Nuance Ministries (2017–present). He directed the documentary *Through My Eyes*, exploring the struggles of young gay Christians (2009), and authored two books: *Talking across the Divide: How to Communicate with People You Disagree with and Maybe Even Change the World* (2018) and *Torn: Rescuing the Gospel from the Gays-vs.-Christians Debate* (rev. ed., 2024).

Steven Lympus (MDiv, Regent College, Vancouver) has been pastoring in the Presbyterian Church (U.S.A.) for over twenty years. He and his wife, Laura, now serve as directors and house parents at the Alpha Omega House, an inclusive Christian community for students at the University of Montana in Missoula. Lympus also serves as director of community engagement for Revoice.

Tim Muehlhoff (PhD, University of North Carolina at Chapel Hill) is professor of communication at Biola University and codirector of the university's Winsome Conviction Project. He authored *I Beg to Differ: Navigating Difficult Conversations with Truth and Love* (2014) and coauthored *Winsome Persuasion: Christian Influence in a Post-Christian World* (2017) and *Winsome Conviction: Disagreeing without Dividing the Church* (2020), both with Richard Langer. His newest book, coauthored with Sean McDowell, is *End the Stalemate: Move Past Cancel Culture to Meaningful Conversations* (2024).

Tim Otto (MTS, Duke Divinity School) is pastor at the Church of the Sojourners in San Francisco and worked as a registered nurse on the first AIDS ward in the United States. He coauthored *Inhabiting the Church: Biblical Wisdom for a New Monasticism* (2006) and authored *Oriented to Faith: Transforming the Conflict over Gay Relationships* (2014).

Ronald W. Pierce (PhD, Fuller Theological Seminary) is professor emeritus in the Talbot School of Theology at Biola University (1976–2024). He authored *Partners in Marriage & Ministry* (2011) and coedited and contributed to *Discovering Biblical Equality: Biblical, Theological, Cultural, and Practical Perspectives* (3rd ed., 2021).

Amie Scott is senior pastor at Deeper Waters Christian Ministries, a church she founded that serves marginalized populations in Oregon. She attended Calvary Chapel Bible College and is the author of *Deeper Waters: Building Bridges over Cultural Conflict*.

Stephen P. Stratton (PhD, Auburn University) is professor of counseling and pastoral care at Asbury Theological Seminary. For eighteen years, he served as director of the Center for Counseling at Asbury University. He is coauthor of *Listening to Sexual Minorities: A Study of Faith and Sexual Identity on Christian College Campuses* (2018).

Taylor Telford (PhD, University of St. Andrews) is a Presbyterian Church (U.S.A.) pastor who currently serves a congregation in Spokane, Washington, as the associate pastor for imaginative worship. She also serves as adjunct faculty at Whitworth University and the Seattle School of Theology and Psychology.

Eve Tushnet is the cofounder of Building Catholic Futures, which seeks to equip Catholic institutions to serve and share the Gospel with LGBT+ people. She authored *Gay and Catholic: Accepting My Sexuality, Finding Community, Living My Faith* (2014) and *Tenderness: A Gay Christian's Guide to Unlearning Rejection and Experiencing God's Extravagant Love* (2021). She is also editor of the anthology *Christ's Body, Christ's Wounds: Staying Catholic When You've Been Hurt in the Church* (2018).

Mark Yarhouse (PhD, Wheaton College) is the Dr. Arthur P. Rech and Mrs. Jean May Rech Chair in Psychology at Wheaton College, where he also oversees the Sexual and Gender Identity Institute. He has authored multiple books, including *Understanding Sexual Identity: A Resource for Youth and Ministry* (2013), *Understanding Gender Dysphoria: Navigating Transgender Issues in a Changing Culture* (2015), and *Talking to Kids about Gender Identity: A Roadmap for Christian Compassion, Civility, and Conviction* (2023).

Introduction

Healing Our Divisions

Ronald W. Pierce and Karen R. Keen

The idea for this anthology emerged on an otherwise-normal evening, while I (Ron) was listening to a ballad sung by the monastic singer and composer John Michael Talbot:

> . . . I have heard you calling in the night.
> I will go, Lord, if you lead me.[1]

What immediately seemed like a calling from God progressively became clearer that spring semester as I taught my Theology of Gender course against the backdrop of Biola University's[2] announcement of a non-affirming statement regarding gay marriage.[3] During the summer of 2019, I began a series of dialogues with a number of affirming LGBTQ Christians who love Jesus and Scripture as much as I do yet arrive at different conclusions than mine. Although I am not part of the queer community, my heart quickly connected

---

1. Dan Shutte, "Here I Am, Lord" (1981). The song reflects on God's callings to biblical prophets (1 Sam. 3; Isa. 6:8), leading to their willingness to serve as God leads.
2. Biola University's Talbot School of Theology is my alma mater for my MDiv and ThM degrees, and the place I had a career for forty-eight years as professor of Old Testament in the school's undergraduate Bible, Theology, and Ministry division.
3. See Biola's "Statement of Biblical Principles, Section I," accessed October 27, 2022, https://www.biola.edu/about/theological-positions.

with these spiritual siblings in Christ in a way that I had not experienced before.[4]

In that same year, my university colleagues Tim Muehlhoff and Richard Langer were writing *Winsome Conviction: Disagreeing without Dividing the Church*,[5] and our leadership was preparing to launch Biola's Winsome Conviction Project to foster conversations across disagreements with the goal of deepening rather than tearing apart relationships in the church and society.[6] These reconciliatory efforts evoked memories of my roots in the Church of the Brethren peace tradition, and at the same time led me to revisit Barry Corey's 2016 monograph, *Love Kindness*. There, as Biola's president, he is explicitly non-affirming, and yet he advocates for "a third way" that he describes as accepting one another as Christ accepted us (cf. Rom. 15:7).[7] This inspired me to explore a "theology of acceptance" more fully as a kind of theological meeting ground where non-affirming and affirming evangelicals could dialogue, with mutual care and respect, to bring both clarity and charity to our polarized churches and other Christian organizations.

In 2021, I published on the debate from a "non-affirming" perspective,[8] and I vowed then to keep an open mind and heart, to listen carefully and respectfully to new affirming arguments from Scripture, and to show unconditional love to those with whom I disagreed. I became convinced that Corey was on to something, that a "theology of Christlike acceptance" needs further exploration by a group of diverse scholars and pastors united by a commitment to both the authority of Scripture and interpersonal reconciliation in Christ (cf. 2 Cor. 5:17–20). Moreover, such a collection of essays needed to include both affirming and non-affirming Christian writers who had come together to discuss how we might better minister to LGBTQ followers of Jesus by

---

4. *Non-affirming* refers to the view that covenanted same-sex relationships and/or adopting a transgender identity (including possible medical interventions like sex-hormone therapy) are contrary to God's will. *Affirming* refers to the view that both can be ethical for Christians (at least on a case-by-case basis). Other terminology includes "traditionalist" vs. "reformist," "Side B" (non-affirming) vs. "Side A" (affirming), "conservative" vs. "progressive."

5. Timothy M. Muehlhoff and Richard Langer, *Winsome Conviction: Disagreeing without Dividing the Church* (InterVarsity, 2020).

6. Joy Blea, "Biola Launches 5-Year Winsome Conviction Project to Initiate Civil Discourse," *Biola News*, October 7, 2020, https://www.biola.edu/blogs/biola-news/2020/biola-launches-5-year-winsome-conviction-project-i.

7. Barry H. Corey, *Love Kindness: Discover the Power of a Forgotten Christian Virtue* (Tyndale, 2016), chaps. 4–5, esp. xv, 55, 69, 73, 89–90.

8. Ronald W. Pierce, "Biblical Equality and Same-Sex Marriage," in *Discovering Biblical Equality: Biblical, Theological, Cultural, and Practical Perspectives*, 3rd ed., ed. Ronald W. Pierce, Cynthia Long Westfall, and Christa L. McKirland (IVP Academic, 2021), 429–509, esp. 506–9.

accepting them without feeling compelled to pass judgment on them or their standing before God (cf. Rom. 14:1–4).

It quickly became clear to me that I needed a coeditor with a different view than mine, but who would join me in demonstrating Christlike acceptance. To this end, I invited my friend Karen R. Keen to join me as coeditor of this project in the spring of 2022. Karen is an affirming, gay Christian woman who is committed to following Jesus no matter the cost. She has done graduate work in biblical and theological studies and believes the Bible is fully inspired and authoritative. Her testimony of Christian faithfulness is compelling,[9] even though she interprets the relevant Scripture passages differently than I do, according to her understanding of and respect for God's Word. Karen was kind enough to accept my invitation, thereby expressing Christlike acceptance of me despite our differences. I am honored to partner with her and our nineteen other contributors to this book, who represent both sides of the aisle on sexuality and gender.

In September 2019, I (Karen) received an email from Ron, reaching out to dialogue on the topic of sexuality. Having grown up in a conservative Baptist tradition, immersed in the evangelical world, I was well acquainted with Biola, where Ron was teaching at the time. In fact, as a teenager who wanted nothing more than to attend a Christian college, I seriously considered Biola in the early 1990s, though I ultimately settled on a Baptist school in Oregon. So, when a professor from Biola reached out to me, I was delighted to connect. And over the past five years, my friendship with Ron has grown as we've provided feedback on each other's writing projects, shared an appreciation for the practice of spiritual direction (we are both trained in that ministry), and, generally, encouraged each other in life as siblings in Christ.

Like Ron, the increasing polarization in our churches and country concerns me. I have long gravitated toward bringing opposing sides into conversation, beginning in my undergrad days when I signed up for a Christian peacemaker workshop rooted in the Beatitudes. More recently, I served as a dialogue facilitator with the Zeidler Center for Public Discussion, as well as led groups at Duke Divinity School on "Navigating Conflict as a Spiritual Practice." I've been trained in Narrative 4, a compassion-building tool for sharing our stories with one another, and have participated in Peacemaking Circles led by Kay Pranis, a leader in restorative justice. The Holy Spirit keeps guiding me toward connection across differences.

---

9. Karen R. Keen, *Scripture, Ethics, and the Possibilities of Same-Sex Relationships* (Eerdmans, 2018), ix–xi.

My desire to see relational healing persists even when it comes to the deeply personal topic of sexuality. When I realized I was gay in my late teens, it was traumatic. I didn't understand how this could happen to me, a devout Christian. I spent many years trying to make sense of my faith and sexuality, initially attending an ex-gay support group before joining the celibate gay movement and eventually becoming fully affirming in 2016. My journey has been deeply rooted in Scripture, a value instilled in me from childhood. During seminary, postgraduate work, and beyond, I've had many opportunities to dialogue with people holding different views on sexuality, as we discerned this important theological concern together. Some of these conversations have taken place in the public square, as with my dialogue with Wesley Hill, a contributor to this volume. We were both invited by Wheaton College to speak at the Streckert Lecture on the question of sex difference in marriage.[10]

Dialogue and healthy debate on sexuality and gender are essential for the church's theological and ethical discernment. Yet sometimes the debate creates tunnel vision. We lose sight of the bigger picture, including our fellowship in Christ. Our biblical interpretations can easily succumb to myopic dissection of prooftexts, thereby losing the overall message of a scriptural passage. Similarly, dialogue can break down into merely talking past each other, forgetting that we have much in common. This anthology strives to go beyond the debate by bringing together both traditionalist (non-affirming) and reformist (affirming) contributors to share a word that is meaningful across theological positions.

Importantly, this anthology was first birthed out of a real friendship across difference. Christlike acceptance is not theoretical for Ron and me. We have lived it out together. A few years after we first connected, Ron asked if I would join him on this book project, and I readily agreed. We both saw a significant need, even hunger, within the church for resources beyond tired divisions. We believe there is more to say on sexuality and gender that both traditionalists and reformists can affirm with a hearty "Amen." We hope you will find that in this volume.

Who Needs to Read This Book?

The crisis in our public discourse is hard to deny. A staggering 93 percent of Americans feel incivility is a problem and over two-thirds feel it is a major

---

10. "Is Sex Difference Essential to Marriage? A Conversation on Same-Sex Relationships," Strecker Lecture on Christianity, Sexuality, and Gender, Wheaton College, April 5, 2022, https://youtu.be/KWPx7jJy094?feature=shared.

problem.[11] Moreover, incivility is not just a matter of *how* we talk to one another, but at a foundational level it often keeps us *from* talking to one another. As twenty-first-century followers of Jesus, we must consider our role more seriously in healing the divisions that are tearing our churches apart and destroying our witness to the world around us. As Rick Langer, Tim Muehlhoff, and Robert Woods put it in 2019, "We want to offer hope for a more peaceful and productive discourse among Christians that engages honest questions without assuming a single outcome or identical personal convictions. Surely, this kind of engagement is difficult and perilous, but biblical faithfulness demands that we be less concerned with pleasing our echo-chamber audiences than provoking thoughtful, albeit uncomfortable, reflection. If we cannot find a way to speak the truth in love to each other, we will have failed to serve God's purposes in our own generation (Acts 13:36) both within and outside of the church."[12]

So, who needs to read this book? Those who long for a better way of being Jesus's church in our ever-changing world in the twenty-first century and beyond. Those who have a family member and/or loved one who is part of the LGBTQ community. Those within that community who struggle daily to maintain faith in God—or perhaps have already given up on God's people. Those in leadership positions—like pastors, elders, teachers, counselors, and, yes, parents—who exert a great deal of influence and also need resources for guiding God's people. And finally, those who long as we do for a better way, a way of peace and reconciliation amid the current culture war that is destroying the church's witness in this divisive world.

What to Expect

Our anthology has three parts. Part 1 engages biblical texts often used in the debate, exploring these passages in a way that reminds us of Scripture's bigger picture. The debate often truncates the Bible, stripping it of its larger message. Thus, part 1, entitled "Biblical Wisdom beyond the Debate," is designed to shake us out of myopic readings to see what we often miss. When

---

11. "Civility in America 2019: Solutions for Tomorrow," Weber Shandwick, Powell Tate, and KRC Research, June 6, 2019, https://webershandwick.com/news/civility-in-america-2019-solutions-for-tomorrow.

12. Rick Langer, Tim Muehlhoff, and Robert H. Woods Jr., "Introduction to the Theme Issue: Conviction, Civility, and Christian Witness," *Christian Scholar's Review* 51, no. 3 (Summer 2022): 267–70, https://christianscholars.com/introduction-to-the-theme-issue-conviction-civility-and-christian-witness/.

we step back and look at the broader view, we find that both traditionalists and reformists have much to agree on when it comes to the interpretation and proclamation of Scripture.

Part 2 guides us in reflection on the practicalities of having conversations across differences. In "Successfully Navigating Divides," we learn it's possible to have strong convictions while still engaging in meaningful conversation with those who hold different views. These chapters comprise more than step-by-step instructions for dialogue (although there's that too). They contain spiritually rich reflection that faces hard questions head on.

In part 3, "Ministry with LGBTQ People, Families, and Friends," we take seriously the reality that sexuality and gender are not merely "issues"; rather, they involve real people. What does it look like to minister well to and with LGBTQ people? How do we care for parents? What are best practices for pastors? These chapters convey insights from leaders with ministry experience, including the pastoral wisdom of sexual and gender minorities themselves.

In every section of this anthology, the goal is to demonstrate the principle of Christlike acceptance, whether it's in the way we read the Bible, in the way we talk with one another, or in the way we do ministry as Christ's church. We do *not* argue our personal views on this debate. That has been done in a plethora of articles and monographs. Instead, our diverse community of over twenty Christian contributors provides a wide range of substantive-yet-accessible essays that confound the Enemy's attempts to divide us.

Part 1: Biblical Wisdom beyond the Debate

The chapters in this exegetically focused section examine several frequently cited texts in discussions about sexuality and gender, including Genesis 1–3, Romans 1, and 1 Corinthians 6, as well as other relevant passages. But instead of reading them as fodder for debate, we ask, "What is the good news in each passage that is applicable to all of our readers?" And, "What is the biblical wisdom in these texts that goes beyond the disputes?"

Biblical scholar and coeditor Ronald W. Pierce's chapter opens the anthology with Romans 14:1–15:7 to ask whether Christlike acceptance is possible across ethical divides without the need to conclusively settle the debate. Can we treat certain aspects of sexuality and gender as disputable matters within the body of Christ, on which devout Christians can charitably agree to disagree? Ron makes the case that we can, based on Paul's advice to the Romans who were divided on the ethics of eating food sacrificed to idols.

Biblical scholar and coeditor Karen R. Keen follows with an exploration of what the Genesis creation story reveals about discerning God's will. How do we know the right thing to do? Through examining the *imago Dei* and examples of discernment throughout Scripture, Keen demonstrates how different viewpoints need not divide us. In fact, different perspectives are essential to our shared pursuit of truth in Christian ethics.

Theologian David Bennett addresses the dilemma of LGBTQ people's bodies not fitting the created order according to Torah, and how this theodicy lens can address tensions between inclusion and holiness. Drawing on a variety of scriptural texts, including from Genesis, Isaiah, and Romans, Bennett makes the case that LGBTQ people are included in Christ in a way they could not be under the Law.

New Testament scholar J. R. Daniel Kirk brings us back to the heart of Romans 1. For many, this chapter in the Bible has become almost exclusively associated with the wrath of God. But Kirk shows why this misses the very point that Paul is trying to make. Namely, Romans 1 is about God's righteousness revealed, which is humanity made new in Christ. And that's very good news for all of us.

The exegetical section concludes with Episcopal priest and New Testament scholar Wesley Hill's discussion of 1 Corinthians 6. This passage is often cited to threaten people in same-sex relationships with divine judgment. Paul the apostle says certain individuals "will not inherit the Kingdom of God." But what does this mean exactly? Hill explains, from a traditionalist's perspective, why this passage should not be used against LGBTQ people.

Part 2: Successfully Navigating Divides

If you have ever wondered how to navigate differing opinions with family during the holidays or with friends at church, this section of the anthology is for you. These chapters are designed to help us navigate disagreement on sexuality and gender, but they also provide meaningful insights that can be applied to any conversation on controversial topics. If you are tired of divisive arguments and ready to engage across divides in productive ways, then read on.

This section begins with Pastor Tim Otto's guidance on creating a vision for responding to conflict. More than the issues being debated, this also involves the relational dynamics we experience during conflict. Otto describes how our vision of conflict impacts the way we bear witness to Christ's love and proclaim God's grace. Navigating divides is the arena of Christian discipleship and a way we can participate in God's reconciling work in the world.

In the next chapter, communication professor Tim Muehlhoff addresses a frequently overlooked call to engage our own hearts in serious spiritual preparation before dialoguing with people that we disagree with. He provides key areas of reflection and practical heart assessments that equip us to successfully enter into hard conversations.

Author and speaker Justin Lee shares wisdom he has gleaned from over two decades of participating in dialogue across divides, especially on the topic of sexuality. He takes us through seven practical tips that can carry us through difficult conversations, including acknowledging what we have in common, defining our terms, listening well, sharing our stories, and much more.

Pastor Steven Lympus and theology professor and pastor Taylor Telford give us a front-row seat to their friendship across differences. While both authors are gay, they arrived at different convictions on application for the Christian life. So, what does Christlike acceptance look like when two people disagree in significant ways? Lympus and Telford draw from their iron-sharpens-iron relationship to show us how friendship can thrive amid significant disagreement.

Concluding this section, theology professor and pastor Brad Harper explores what navigating differences looks like in a corporate setting—namely, how a non-affirming church might still make room for affirming LGBTQ people. He argues that God shows us by example that accommodation—even for less-than-ideal situations—can be the right thing to do. Harper applies his insights to practical church life, such as LGBTQ people participating in the Eucharist or taking on service roles.

Part 3: Ministry with LGBTQ People, Families, and Friends

The last section of our anthology addresses practical implications of Christlike acceptance when it comes to hands-on ministry. How do we best care for LGBTQ people and their families? What are best ministry practices for leaders? The following essays feature people who have direct experience serving sexual and gender minorities.

The first essay is by Eve Tushnet, cofounder of Building Catholic Futures, who gives us a window into the life and heart of a celibate gay Christian as she reaches across divides. She explores the impact of church wounds on faith, as well as how Side A and Side B sexual and gender minorities can support one another across differences. Tushnet reflects on the possibility and gift of community as the body of Christ.

In the next chapter, Sally Gary, executive director of CenterPeace, describes the ways ministry involves risks and sometimes great costs when it comes to controversial causes. In fact, she says courage *is* ministry. Drawing on nearly twenty years of nonprofit ministry with churches on faith and sexuality, Gary offers a powerful word to pastors, ministry leaders, and any Jesus follower who truly wants to follow the example of Christ. In the end, courage is worth it.

Psychology and counseling professors Mark Yarhouse, Stephen P. Stratton, and Janet B. Dean provide a window into the mental health of Christian sexual and gender minorities. Their research looks at sexual- and gender-identity development, as well as practices shown to reduce distress and foster well-being for LGBTQ people as they wrestle with faith and sexuality.

Elizabeth Delgado Black, cofounder of Kaleidoscope Ministries, provides insights for evangelism. Regardless of what convictions we hold on sexuality and gender, Christians can agree that we are called to share the gospel with all peoples. What does missional outreach with LGBTQ people look like? Black provides real-life examples from her own ministry work.

Candace Hardnett, pastor at Agape Empowerment Ministries, writes from the social location of a Black minister who is also gay. She provides insight into ministry to LGBTQ people in the Black community and the unique concerns at this intersection. Hardnett addresses church hurt and how to create spaces for safety and healing within the church.

Amie Scott, pastor at Deeper Waters Christian Ministries, shares her insights on what a shepherd's heart for the transgender community looks like. As someone who is both transgender and a pastor, she provides a unique perspective on best practices when it comes to outreach to this population. Scott shares her own story, along with ministry tips for making a difference.

Staci Frenes, Christian singer, songwriter, and author of *Love Makes Room*, addresses the frequent concerns of parents with LGBTQ children. How should a Christian mom or dad respond when their child (youth or adult) comes out to them? Frenes shares her own story as a parent of a gay daughter and the wisdom gleaned as she navigated the initial shock of the disclosure and wrestled with how best to support her child. Her insights are helpful for ministry leaders as well.

Finally, this section, as well as the anthology as a whole, comes to a close with the rich spiritual reflections and wisdom of Marcus Halley, college chaplain and dean of spiritual and religious life at Trinity College in Hartford, Connecticut. We intentionally placed Halley's essay at the end because it provides the perfect conclusion to a book on Christlike acceptance. How do we move past enmity when opposing sides believe so much is at stake? Rejecting cheap and sentimental reconciliation, Halley shares a pastoral word on what it really takes to live out Christlike acceptance toward one another.

Final Thoughts and an Invitation

The apostle Paul famously concluded in his First Letter to the Church at Corinth, "And now these three remain: faith, hope and love. But the greatest of these is love" (1 Cor. 13:13). If faith represents *what* we believe to be true from Scripture, and hope represents *where* we would like to see the people of God go, then love speaks to *how* we can best work together to get there. And yes, Paul insists that love is the most important of these three. Elsewhere he declares, "The entire law is fulfilled in keeping this one command: 'Love your neighbor as yourself'" (Gal. 5:14). Love today is not merely a nice sentiment in an overly sentimental age. It is the greatest of virtues by which we fulfill the second greatest commandment next to loving God.

Yes, the challenges of practicing Christlike acceptance within the current climate of Christian discourse are significant, but the rewards can be even greater! Here we can find the reconciliatory middle ground for a better understanding of Scripture, a more respectful dialogue, and a way of ministering together for a better future. The polarized world around us is watching—although it is no longer waiting—for a consistent and convincing Christian witness regarding this, as is the next generation of LGBTQ youth who want to follow Jesus, yet experience the church as a deterrent to doing so.

In the end, we want to demonstrate by the very fact that we are writing this anthology together that "Christlike acceptance" is possible among biblical scholars and pastors—as well as all of Jesus's followers—without the contentious quarreling that currently divides the church and hinders our witness to those around us. We have joined together here as spiritual siblings in Christ with the hope and prayer that the church can find a better way of being Jesus's body in a harshly divided world.

And so, we invite you to join hands and hearts with us in exploring the theological meeting ground of acceptance—Christlike acceptance—so that we can carry forward the work of Jesus peacefully, simply, and together; so that we can obey the final instructions our Lord gave to the "twelve disciples" shortly before Jesus's time of suffering and death on the cross: "A new command I give you: Love one another. As I have loved you, so you must love one another. By this everyone will know that you are my disciples, if you love one another" (John 13:34–35).

We invite you to join us in practicing Christlike acceptance in your sphere of ministry—whether it is formal or informal—so that we can make a difference for the common good of Christ's church in the twenty-first century. We invite you to join us in bringing a balance among Christ's followers that reflects the character of Jesus, who was "full of grace and truth" (John 1:14–17).

The debate over sexuality and gender so far has been 90 percent about clarity and 10 percent about charity. This book seeks to bring greater balance by focusing on charity without sacrificing clarity. The quest for truth has dominated this landscape for decades. Now as the church continues to pursue truth (as best we understand it with our human limitations), we invite you to join us in embracing Christlike acceptance so that we can continue to mature in Christ our Lord in love (Eph. 5:15).

In hope of Christlike acceptance in every church,
Ron Pierce and Karen Keen
June 2024

PART 1

Biblical Wisdom beyond the Debate

1

Christlike Acceptance and Queer Christians

Romans 14:1–15:13

Ronald W. Pierce

When gay marriage was legalized in the United States in 2015, a host of contentious debates followed. During this time, American evangelicals became better known for Christian nationalism than for Christlike love. In contrast, Biola University president Barry H. Corey invited fellow evangelicals to discover the power of the forgotten Christian virtue of "kindness." However, his two chapters on gay marriage do not reference familiar passages like Micah 6:8 (where God requires kindness) or Galatians 5:22 (where the Spirit's fruit includes kindness). Instead, he cites Romans 15:7: "Accept one another as Christ accepted you for God's glory."[1] Then he prays, "Father, you graciously accepted us just as we were, broken and incomplete. May we likewise be accepting of others no matter how unlike us they may be. May we be slow to shun and quick to welcome. May we lean into treating others with Christlike unconditional love and grace. May we have hearts that mirror your loving-kindness. Amen."[2]

---

1. Translations in this chapter are mine unless otherwise noted.
2. Barry H. Corey, *Love Kindness: Discover the Power of a Forgotten Christian Virtue* (Tyndale, 2016), chaps. 4–5; esp. 55, 69, 73, 89–90.

I was pleasantly surprised to read these words by the leader of my alma mater and the university where I taught my entire career—together encompassing over fifty years of my life. In fact, Corey's kind-yet-prophetic words of Christlike acceptance inspired both this chapter and this anthology. Like him, I have longed for a theological meeting ground in the LGBTQ debates,[3] a dialogical space where evangelicals can have respectful and loving exchanges about difficult topics. I envision a reconciliatory roundtable where we can meet to address our failures to reason together in a Christ-honoring way, a place where we work shoulder-to-shoulder, forging a better path forward for Jesus's church in a strife-ridden world.

Naturally, a theology of acceptance will concern some traditional Christians who fear a "slippery slope" toward affirmation, or see this issue as a moral absolute with no room for disagreement, or go so far as to doubt the faith of queer and affirming Christians. In response, I invite both sides of this debate to listen with open hearts and minds as we explore below some fresh thinking on this evangelical stalemate where very little "kindness" is evident.

In short, this essay asserts that we accept other followers of Jesus whose understanding of Scripture regarding sexuality and gender differs from ours without passing judgment on them. To this end, I am revisiting Paul's words in Romans 14:1–15:13 alongside a team of Christ followers who reach differing conclusions about these matters and live their lives accordingly as persons of faith.[4] Indeed, I am advocating for a theology of acceptance to help evangelicals love and serve others better without requiring agreement on this debate. Author and research pastor Caleb Kaltenbach puts it well: "Acceptance means loving people where they are in the moment no matter what (Matt. 5:38–48; Matt. 22:37–40). Acceptance does not mean that we should agree with every decision they've made, opinion they hold, or relationship they're in."[5] I agree with Kaltenbach and believe doing this can make us better witnesses to the polarized world around us and can empower us to minister more effectively to queer people who want to follow Jesus yet experience evangelicals as a deterrent.

---

3. Corey, *Love Kindness*, xv.

4. For my most-recent reflections on the traditional vs. progressive debate, see Ronald W. Pierce, "Biblical Equality and Same-Sex Marriage," in *Discovering Biblical Equality: Biblical, Theological, Cultural, and Practical Perspectives*, 3rd ed., ed. Ronald W. Pierce, Cynthia Long Westfall, and Christa L. McKirland (IVP Academic, 2021), 429–509.

5. Caleb Kaltenbach, "How to Navigate Conversations About Sexual Identity: What Every Pastor Needs to Know," interview by Ben Shin with Scott Rae and Caleb Kaltenbach, *Talbot Magazine* 8, no. 2 (2024): 17, https://www.biola.edu/blogs/talbot-magazine/2025/how-to-navigate-conversations-about-sexual-identity.

Romans 14:1-15:13 in the Context of the New Testament

Three New Testament passages provide a biblical context for my study in Romans 14–15—namely, Acts 15, 1 Corinthians 8–10, and Galatians 2. Although the circumstances differ slightly, these texts address the challenges of a new-covenant theology that radically changes Jew-gentile relationships in the early church's Greco-Roman culture. Acts 15 provides a glimpse into these matters within the Jerusalem church, just a few years before Paul addresses it amid the cultural influences at Corinth (1 Cor. 8–10). Around the same time, this Apostle to the Gentiles opposes the Judaistic legalism in churches scattered across the Galatian province that caused some of these contentious disputes (Gal. 2).

In Acts 15, the first known ecumenical gathering of churches took place in Jerusalem around AD 49 to address a behavioral dispute over what obligations, if any, to place on gentile converts to Christianity. This follows Paul's first journey across Galatia provinces to preach a gospel of freedom in Christ. While insisting on salvation for all who believe, regardless of their ethnicity, Paul met resistance from Jewish leaders and even some gentiles (Acts 13–14). At this same time in Jerusalem, some religious leaders were insisting non-Jews be circumcised in order to be saved. In response, Peter and James support Paul's inclusive theology emphasizing salvation by grace alone. The council only requires converts to abstain from things polluted by idols, sexual immorality, meat from strangled animals, and blood. All agree.

Paul wrote his first (known) letter to believers in Corinth around AD 54–55, shortly after the Jerusalem Council. In chapters 8–10, he addresses their concerns about food sacrificed to idols, those with a weaker conscience and with lesser knowledge, and passing judgment on another's freedom in Christ (cf. 4:1–6). Because he believes idols are only lifeless pseudo-gods created by human hands, Paul asserts that neither eating nor abstaining from meat dedicated to them really matters. Not offending someone weaker in conscience is so important to him, however, that he believes personal liberties must be sacrificed to avoid sinning against other believers—and by extension, against Christ.

The dating of Galatians is disputed. Paul may have written this circulating letter to the churches across the Galatian province before the Jerusalem Council (around AD 48) or after (AD 50 or later).[6] Regardless, he addresses similar concerns to those discussed there, as he also does in 1 Corinthians (AD 54–55) and

---

6. On the dating of Galatians, see Douglas J. Moo, *Galatians*, Baker Exegetical Commentary on the New Testament (Baker Academic, 2013), 1–18.

Romans (AD 55–57). He gives different advice throughout this missive, however, than what is found in Acts 15 or 1 Corinthian 8–10. In a harsh tone similar to that in Acts 13–14, he forbids once-mandatory Jewish laws like keeping special diets and holy days (Gal. 2:16; 4:10), avoiding table fellowship with gentiles (2:11–13), and demanding circumcision for new converts (2:3, 7; 5:2; 6:12).

Circumcision is especially notable because it is the God-given sign of covenantal relationship for all Abraham's descendants—including slaves, even those from gentile nations (Gen. 17:3–14; cf. LXX *ethnos* in Gen. 17:4). Yet Paul goes so far as to call his readers "bewitched" fools (Gal. 3:1), insisting that Christ will be of no value to them if they let themselves be circumcised (5:2). Indeed, the Apostle to the Gentiles (Acts 13:46; 15:7) allows no room for compromise on these matters because the truth of a radically inclusive gospel is at stake (Gal. 1:6–9; 2:5, 14).

To emphasize his point, Paul references an encounter with Cephas (i.e., Peter; cf. John 1:42) as an example of morally unacceptable behavior. Having been explicitly called to extend the gospel to a Roman centurion (Acts 10), Peter once was more inclusive. But now, influenced by religious leaders who want to replace Christian freedom with spiritual slavery, Peter excludes gentiles from table fellowship (Gal. 2:1–14). So Paul opposes him to his face, because this matter has to do with the truth of the gospel. Peter has capitulated to these leaders by qualifying this new-covenant truth in a way Paul never intended when he wrote, "There is no longer Jew and Gentile" in Christ Jesus (3:28). Rather, Paul insists, "Christ set us free to live in freedom, and we should stand firm therein" (5:1).

In summary, circumcision was neither prescribed nor prohibited by the Jerusalem Council (Acts 13–15), and some dietary practices, like eating food polluted by idols, remained off limits. In 1 Corinthians 8–10, one can choose whether or not to eat meat offered to idols as long as those who are "weaker in conscience" are not offended. But in Galatians, circumcision and observance of holy days are strictly off limits, and fully inclusive table fellowship is mandatory. The common thread is to allow personal freedom as long as those weaker in conscience are cared for and the truth of the gospel is preserved. In each case, sexual immorality (*porneia*) remains off limits. Sometimes these behaviors are described in general terms (Acts 15:29; Gal. 5:19), sometimes more specifically (1 Cor. 5:1; 10:8), and in some cases these are in dispute (1 Cor. 6:13–18).

Romans 14:1-15:13 in the Context of Paul's Letter to the Romans

Most New Testament scholars locate Paul's theme for Romans in 1:16–17: "I'm not ashamed of the gospel, which is God's power for salvation to every believer:

Jews first, then Greeks. God's righteousness is revealed in this gospel from faith and for faith, as it is written: 'The just shall live by faith'" (see also Gal. 1:6–9; 2:5, 14). This emphasis is discernable across the letter as Paul prioritizes Israel historically and personally. But Jews had become a minority in the church by now, and gentiles are addressed herein first (Rom. 1:1–6) and frequently (1:13; 11:13–25; 15:15–16). Paul includes his "natural kinfolk" in 9:3b, but gentiles remain his concern.[7] With this in mind, four aspects of the gospel outline this letter:

1. Its Heart: Justification by Faith (1:18–4:25)
2. Its Assurance: Hope of Salvation (5:1–8:39)
3. Its Defense: The Problem of Israel (9:1–11:36)
4. Its Transforming Power: Christian Conduct (12:1–15:13)[8]

In the last section, Paul pens healing words of pastoral care for godly living to believers in Rome.[9] Built on the foundations of sacrificial renewal and transformation (12:1–2), he calls readers to humility and mutual service (12:3–8), to familial love for one another (12:9–21; 13:8–10), to peaceful relationships under pagan rule (13:1–7), to living in the light rather than continuing in darkness (13:11–14), and climactically, to Christlike acceptance (14:1–15:13).[10] This emphasis in the last of these sections is so strong that New Testament scholar and historian Scot McKnight suggests reading the entire letter in its light![11]

1. Accept one another without quarreling over disputable matters (14:1–9).
2. Stop despising and passing judgment on one another (14:10–23).
3. Sacrifice your liberties for those who are weaker in faith (15:1–6).
4. Accept one another as Christ accepted you for God's glory (15:7–13).[12]

Interpretive Questions regarding Romans 14:1-15:13

Keeping in mind the framework described above, four exegetical questions must be asked of this passage.

---

7. C. Marvin Pate, *Romans*, Teach the Text Commentary, ed. Mark L. Strauss and John H. Walton (Baker, 2013), 10.
8. Douglas J. Moo, *Romans*, NIV Application Commentary (Zondervan, 2000), 28–30.
9. Aaron Sherwood, *Romans: A Structural, Thematic, and Exegetical Commentary* (Lexham, 2020), 263, 266, 269.
10. Moo, *Romans*, 30.
11. Scot McKnight, *Reading Romans Backwards: A Gospel of Peace in the Midst of the Empire* (Baylor, 2019), 180.
12. John E. Toews, *Romans*, Believers Church Bible Commentary (Herald, 2004), 233–35.

First, we must ask, *What are the key issues in dispute?* Romans 14 depicts Jesus's followers in disagreement (*dialogismos*)[13] about exercising their freedom in Christ.[14] Some eat anything, including meat and wine, while others restrict themselves to vegetables (14:2); and some treat every day alike, whereas others consider one more sacred than another (14:5). In this context, Paul cites five gentile-related texts from the Old Testament in his concluding remarks to this section (15:7–12), as well as his nearly twenty references to Jews and gentiles throughout this letter.[15] These involve Jewish dietary laws and holy days, the observance of which were exacerbated by the growing number of gentiles in these churches.

It is important to emphasize that "diets and days" are not merely trivial matters of personal opinion for Jews at this time. For example, polygamy and concubinage are presented as acceptable behavior in the Old Testament. But in contrast, breaking the Sabbath (Exod. 20:10–11; 31:14; 35:2; Num. 15:32–36), ignoring dietary laws (e.g., Lev. 3:17; 7:26–27; 19:26), and neglecting to circumcise a son (Gen. 17:9–14; Exod. 4:25–26) could result in one being cut off from God's covenant people—or even being put to death.

Second, we must ask, *Who are the weak and strong in faith, and how should they act?* Paul's reference to being weaker in "conscience" (*syneidēsis*) in 1 Corinthians 8:7, 9–12 finds its parallel in being weaker in "faith" (*pistis*) here in Romans 14:1–2; 15:1–2, suggesting these should be read as synonyms. For the Corinthians, weakness (*asthenēs*) connotes a self-imposed limitation based on conscience, implying personal discernment of right or wrong. For the Romans, similar limitations are called for because of one's faith (*pistis*), or being faithful to what is right. As a result, the "weaker" (*asthenēs*) in conscience/faith are unable to fully live into the degree of freedom in Christ that the "stronger" (*dynatos*) are legitimately enjoying.

Perhaps counterintuitively, this "weakness" is not one's inability to keep these regulations, but rather one's inability to enjoy one's liberty. As McKnight puts it, "Those whom Paul called 'the weak' were Torah-observant Jews, while the predominately Gentile ('strong') Christians exercised freedom from

---

13. Lexical definitions of the Greek terms cited throughout this chapter are taken from Walter Bauer and Frederick William Danker, eds. *A Greek-English Lexicon of the New Testament and Other Early Christian Literature*, 3rd ed. (University of Chicago Press, 2002), commonly known as BDAG.

14. Richard N. Longenecker, *The Epistle to the Romans*, NIGTC (Eerdmans, 2016), 697–98, 700–702.

15. Rom. 1:13; 2:9, 14, 17, 24, 28; 3:1–2, 9, 29; 9:24, 30; 10:12; 11:11, 13, 25; 15:16, 18, 27; 16:4.

following the Torah rituals."[16] Their failure is being too restrictive, not too permissive. Of course, the legalistic and exclusive believers saw it differently, thinking that they were the stronger ones, those with greater faith, and that by keeping certain moral restrictions, they were exercising greater fidelity. In this paradoxical context, Paul calls those who are actually stronger in faith to sacrifice some of their legitimate liberties for the sake of their more legalistic spiritual siblings who are weaker in faith (Rom. 14:1–2; 15:1–2; *asthenēs* in both places creates a double emphasis). The stronger are to bear patiently with those who remain more restrictive, unnecessarily bound by hurtful obligations to the law.

In 1 Corinthians 8:9–13, Paul identifies himself as the stronger, willing to sacrifice his rights so as not to be a stumbling block to the weaker. Further, he insists that failing to do this would be sinning against both them and Christ. Yet, when the truth of the gospel is at stake, he insists that Jewish converts like Peter live fully into their new-covenant liberties and sit at the table with gentiles (Gal. 2:1–14). Paul boldly calls believers to stand firm in the freedom for which Christ has set them free (Gal. 5:1).

Third, we must ask, *What is meant by quarreling, despising, and passing judgment?* In Romans 14:1–3, Paul prohibits three morally related behaviors occurring in these house-churches: quarreling, despising, and passing judgment. First, he calls those stronger in conscience to stop welcoming others into their homes only for the purpose of quarreling (*diakrisis*)—that is, engaging in destructive, verbal conflicts over holy days and dietary laws. Robert Jewett insightfully distinguishes here between a "spirited debate that can lead to greater clarity and understanding for all" and an "intellectual competition aimed at bringing about conformity to the dominant position."[17] The former is helpful; the latter is harmful. In the words of Richard Langer, this kind of quarreling is "the greatest threat to the church today . . . insidiously dangerous because it kills from within" like "a metastasizing cancer."[18]

Paul's second and third proscriptions are linked. The stronger libertarians must not despise the weaker legalists; that is, they are not to show by their attitude or ill-treatment that the legalists' concerns have little-to-no merit or worth (*exoutheneō*). In turn, the weaker legalists should stop passing judgment so as to condemn (*krinō*) the stronger libertarians who eat freely. Each group must do its part to bring an end to this divisive and destructive

---

16. McKnight, *Reading Romans Backwards*, 180.
17. Robert Jewett, *Romans: A Commentary*, Hermeneia (Fortress, 2013), 836.
18. Timothy M. Muehlhoff and Richard Langer, *Winsome Conviction: Disagreeing without Dividing the Church* (InterVarsity, 2020), 17–18.

conflict. The stronger must stop demeaning the character of the weaker, and the weaker must stop condemning the behavior of the stronger. Both must stop insisting that the other agree with them before they can accept them. Instead, they are to accept each other in Christ despite their deeply held convictions regarding what constitutes sinful behavior. As James writes, "Dear family, stop accusing [*katalaleō*] one another. Doing this is like accusing and passing judgment [*krinō*] on the Law itself. It's not 'keeping' Torah, but rather sitting in judgment over it! Only the One who is able to save and destroy can be both Lawgiver and Judge. So, stop passing judgment [*krinō*] on other believers!" (James 4:11–12).

Fourth and finally, we must ask, *What is Christlike acceptance that glorifies God?* Paul frames this pericope with nearly identical calls for a Christlike acceptance that brings glory to God (Rom. 14:1, 3; 15:7) by using the Greek term *proslambanō*. Different translations render this "acceptance" (NASB, NIV), "welcoming" (NRSV, ESV, NABRE), or "receiving" (KJV, HCSB). Paul's use of the verb elsewhere sheds light on its nuanced meaning here.

It appears in Acts 28 where Luke recounts a shipwreck he suffers with Paul while the latter is being taken to Rome to stand trial before Caesar (Acts 26–28). After making it safely to shore on Malta, the islanders show them an "unusual kindness" (*philanthrōpia*) by building a fire to "welcome" (*proslambanō*) them in from the cold rain (Acts 28:2). The first term connotes affectionate concern or compassion for another human being, which is the kind of "welcome" these gentiles give Paul, Luke, and their companions.

The more relevant use of this term appears in Paul's short letter to his friend Philemon, a leader in the Colossian church. Here the apostle makes a polite-yet-direct appeal to his friend regarding Philemon's runaway slave Onesimus, whom Paul befriended while in prison: "I am sending [Onesimus] back to you—indeed, sending my heart. . . . Perhaps he was separated from you for a little while so you might have him back forever—but no longer as a slave; rather, as family. Though dear to me, he is more so to you as both a human being and brother in the Lord. Therefore, if you consider me a partner, accept him as you would accept me" (vv. 12, 15–17; *proslambanō* twice).

Philemon is not merely to "welcome" Onesimus as he welcomed Paul, by preparing his guestroom for Paul (v. 22). Rather, he must "accept" him as a brother in Christ instead of as the slave he once was. This means "accepting" him as a member of the Colossian church that meets in his home (v. 2), including worshiping alongside Onesimus and even washing his feet, as Jesus did for Peter and the other disciples at the Last Supper. Paul's request exemplifies the radically inclusive gospel of Christ that the apostle preached and expected his readers to embrace and model.

These two examples of *proslambanō* shed light on the kind of "acceptance" Paul calls for in Romans 14:1–4 and 15:7. It is more than just "welcoming" as the Maltans did with Paul and Luke. Rather, these believers must "accept one another . . . with all the love and concern that should typify full members of family."[19] This is Christlike acceptance, the kind Jesus exemplifies when he refers to his followers as friends for whom he would lay down his life (John 15:13), accepting them as no less than spiritual family (Luke 8:21).

In sum, Romans 14:1–15:13 is peripheral neither to the message of the larger letter nor to the subsection in which it occurs (12:1–15:13). On the contrary, Paul's call for Christlike acceptance of gentiles is woven throughout both Romans and the other New Testament texts explored here. Although the gospel Paul preaches comes first to the Jews, it reaches its climax in the inclusion of all nations (*ethnos*) in the family of Christ. Though the structuring of Romans may reflect an old-covenant treaty,[20] its heart reveals the new covenant that Jesus foretold on the eve of his crucifixion (Luke 22:20) and that the church celebrates when remembering his atoning sacrifice (1 Cor. 11:25). Paul calls Jesus's followers to go beyond merely "welcoming" outsiders and strangers. They must "accept" (or "receive") other believers as members of their house-churches even as God in Christ accepts them. Moreover, it cannot be for the purpose of engaging them in contentious arguments over disputable behavior that is not essential to the gospel. All are to be accepted in Christ, into God's new-covenant people, by faith alone.

Practical Questions about Accepting Queer and Affirming Christians

Wesley Hill observes that throughout history churches became accustomed to reflecting together theologically on doctrinal disagreements, but they were less certain about moral disputes.[21] Although these two categories are clearly related, doctrinal statements and behavior standards are distinguished in most Christian organizations. With this in mind, I address below four common concerns about Christlike acceptance of affirming LGBTQ Christians in practice.

---

19. Douglas J. Moo, *Letter to the Romans*, 2nd ed. (Eerdmans, 2018), 617.
20. Pate, *Romans*, 13–15.
21. Wesley Hill, "Communion & Disagreement in Acts 15," in *When Churches in Communion Disagree*, ed. Robert Heaney, Christopher Wells, and Pierre Whalon (Living Church Books, 2022).

Are Gay Marriage and Gender Transitioning "Disputable Matters"?

In his chapter on Romans 14:1–15:13, "Disputable Matters: The Forgotten Middle Ground," Richard Langer contrasts "personal convictions," which are disputable, with "moral absolutes," which reflect universal beliefs within the church and for which there should be no room for disagreement.[22] Although he does not state directly where LGBTQ disputes fall, one could easily acknowledge that the church throughout history—like society in general—has been non-affirming. However, the church also long supported slavery and firmly prohibited divorce and usury. These and other so-called "universal beliefs" of the church regarding "moral absolutes" admittedly have changed.

Over the last century, the Western church has been slowly but steadily acknowledging the growing number of queer and affirming people who love Christ and the Bible. This is especially true regarding those who show evidence of being indwelt by God's Spirit and who desire to lead lives of obedience to their Lord as they best understand the Scripture's teaching on sexuality and gender. Prohibiting marriage for gay couples is no longer a universal belief of the church. Moreover, an ever-increasing understanding of sexual development, intersexuality, and brain science continues to contribute to softening older, more rigid correlations between birth sex and gender identity.[23] Therefore, honesty and humility require evangelicals to acknowledge that LGBTQ concerns have become disputable matters among Bible-believing, Spirit-filled Christians.

It is also important to remember—as was argued above and as Langer acknowledges—that the holy-day and food disputes Paul confronts in Romans 14:1–15:13 were not trivial differences of opinion, as we might consider disagreements over days and diets today.[24] For devout Jews in Paul's day, sinning against God by breaking laws regarding holy days, diets, and circumcision could result in the offender being cut off from God's people or even killed. These were moral, behavioral disputes about what was sin and what was not, indeed matters of great spiritual concern for Paul, not merely preferences.[25]

In the light of these complexities, evangelical ethicist Scott Rae has rightly observed that contemporary arguments over the plausibility of affirming

---

22. Muehlhoff and Langer, *Winsome Conviction*, 20–21.
23. See the recent, must-read monograph by Vanguard University's professor emeritus Vincent E. Gil, *A Christian's Guide through the Gender Revolution: Gender, Cisgender, Transgender, and Intersex* (Cascade Books, 2021).
24. Muehlhoff and Langer, *Winsome Conviction*, 20.
25. Sarah Heaner Lancaster, *Romans: A Theological Commentary on the Bible* (Westminster John Knox, 2015), 130. Also, Longenecker, *Romans*, 707.

Christian, monogamous, covenanted, same-sex marriages today continue to remain inferential.[26] Building on his conclusion, it seems reasonable to apply Christlike acceptance to disputes regarding both marriage and the more complex challenges of gender dysphoria.[27] Doing so does not trivialize the importance of our disagreements, but instead demonstrates that followers of Jesus can disagree on deeply held convictions regarding what should be labeled "sinful behavior," but do it with civility, kindness, and Christlike grace.

Can Queer and Affirming People Really Be Christians?

Usually, this concern is raised with 1 Corinthians 6:9–10 in mind, where one finds a list of people whose persistent and willful sin suggests they "will not inherit God's kingdom." This text is referenced by Christian apologist Sean McDowell, who states unequivocally that a person who affirms monogamous same-sex marriage cannot be a faithful follower of Jesus.[28] To defend this harsh judgment, he cites Paul's condemnation of two groups identified by the Greek nouns *malakoi* and *arsenokoitai* in 1 Corinthians 6:9.

In response, it should be noted that the translation of these terms is itself a disputable matter. Are these "men who practice homosexuality" (ESV), or are they "male prostitutes" and "men who engage in illicit sex" (NRSVue)? Moreover, there is an honest debate among evangelicals about what Paul condemns as "sexual immorality" here and elsewhere in the New Testament. Could this be exploitative or excessively lustful sexual practices like pederasty, incest (1 Cor. 5:1–13), prostitution (1 Cor. 6:12–20), or sex with slaves (class/status) and/or pagan orgies (Rom. 1:18–32)? Moreover, is Paul even aware of loving, same-sex relationships between people of equal class and/or status? And since the biblical texts are not explicit regarding these questions, on whose shoulders should the burden of proof lie: those who are affirming or those who are opposing? Finally, the question of consistency needs to be addressed. For example, the list in 1 Corinthians 6:9–10 includes adulterers, and Jesus said that anyone who divorces his wife to marry another commits

---

26. Scott B. Rae, *Moral Choices: An Introduction to Ethics*, 4th ed. (Zondervan, 2018), 325. Scott also serves as both dean of faculty at the Talbot School of Theology and senior advisor to Biola's president Barry Corey on matters of missional faithfulness.

27. See James K. Beilby and Paul Rhodes Eddy, eds., *Understanding Transgender Identities: Four Views* (Baker Academic, 2019).

28. Sean McDowell, "Can You Faithfully Follow Jesus and Affirm Same-Sex Unions?," *Sean McDowell Show*, March 1, 2024, https://www.youtube.com/watch?app=desktop&v=fUh-MwkuPF4&t=33s. McDowell is associate professor of Christian apologetics at Talbot School of Theology.

adultery (Matt. 19:9). Are all divorced and remarried Christians living in adultery? Increasingly, a majority of evangelicals see the latter discussion as more complex than this.

Looking at this from another perspective, the legal descriptions in Numbers 15:22–31 distinguish between a sin committed in error (*shagah*) and a sin committed with a high hand (*beyad*). Is it not possible that affirming, queer Christians who love Jesus and respect the authority of Scripture yet interpret the key passages differently than traditionalists do *may* be guilty of sinning unintentionally, rather than willfully disobeying God's will? If so, this does not disqualify them from being Christian any more than it would disqualify others who struggle with their own unintentional sins.

Is Accepting a Person the Same as Affirming Their Behavior?

Acceptance sits at the center of the welcoming-accepting-affirming spectrum. Although welcoming can be a step toward accepting, and possibly affirming, the three are not the same. I can welcome a stranger into my home, but such a guest may never be accepted as part of my family. And I can accept them as family without affirming their behavioral choices. Multnomah professor of theology Brad Harper and his wife, Robin, demonstrate this well by accepting their gay and affirming son Drew. He is fully included as a dearly loved member of their family on the basis of his birthright, even though they do not support all of his behavioral choices. Brad and Drew tell their story together in their coauthored book, *Space at the Table*.[29]

What is true of biological family can also be true of spiritual family when it comes to LGBTQ disagreements.[30] For example, when I am asked if I would officiate a gay wedding, I reply, "I would attend and participate in the wedding as a friend or family member, but could not in good conscience officiate it." By signing the marriage certificate, I am explicitly endorsing the marriage, which I cannot do in good conscience. I hope my affirming LGBTQ siblings in Christ can respect my conviction; but I also realize this kind of respect goes both ways. We all answer to God for our reading and application of Scripture, and when wrong, that error is on each of us respectively. Meanwhile, affording one another dignity of conscience is part of being family. We are spiritual

---

29. Bradley Harper and Drew Harper, *Space at the Table: Conversations between an Evangelical Theologian and His Gay Son* (Zeal Books, 2016). It should be noted that this is not always the case. Sometimes an affirming LGBTQ child in a family is disowned by their Christian parents. In contrast, sometimes an LGBTQ child will not accept a parent who is accepting, but not affirming, of them. For them, Christlike acceptance is just not enough.

30. See Joseph H. Hellerman, *When the Church Was a Family: Recapturing Jesus' Vision for Authentic Christian Community* (B&H Academic, 2009).

siblings not because we agree but because we share a saving relationship with the same Creator, Redeemer, and Sustainer.

Is Acceptance the Same as Condoning Sexual Immorality?

Two New Testament passages are often cited in response to those who choose to be accepting of affirming, queer Christians. In 1 Corinthians 5:9–12, Paul forbids associating with sexually immoral people who claim to be Christians (v. 11). And in Romans 1:26–32, he condemns those who engage in lustful, shameful, unnatural, same-sex sex, insisting that they deserve death along with those who approve of their behavior (vv. 28–32).

Regarding these texts, two factors must be taken into consideration. First, these lists include also those who are envious or greedy, those who slander, gossip, disobey a parent, or drink excessively (1 Cor. 5:11; Rom. 1:29–30). If all these kinds of people deserve death, and all should be expelled from today's churches, our congregations would shrink considerably.

Second, the kind of lustful and idolatrous people described in Romans 1 do not resemble any LGBTQ Christians that I know. Are we to read into these contexts today's faithful, covenanted, Christian, same-sex marriages? This is an ongoing debate that calls for intellectual humility on the part of people who are not afraid to say, "I could be wrong, and therefore am willing to abstain from passing judgment on others" (Rom. 14:1–4). Perhaps we who are more traditional might someday come to discover that God has accepted LGBTQ Christians all along.

It is clear that a number of traditional evangelicals will still have hesitations about a theology of acceptance. After all, no one wants to condone what God condemns. But we should be able to agree that the debates are not as cut-and-dried as they seemed to many of us a couple decades ago. We have a clearer understanding of both same-sex orientation and gender identity than we could have possibly had a generation ago. And the exegetical arguments are being better refined for both sides—not just the traditional viewpoint. Therefore, it seems prudent to proceed with great caution and humility.

What Might Accepting Queer and Affirming Christians Look Like?

For a topic as important and sensitive as this, interpretation alone is never enough. We must move from right thinking to right living in the light of God's Word and in the power of God's Spirit. To this end, I close with some questions about applying a theology of Christlike acceptance to the church's queer and affirming children.

Acceptance in Personal Relationships

Barry Corey's account of his experience with an affirming, gay Christian friend illustrates Christlike acceptance on a personal level as well as anything I can imagine. He was privileged to be the first person she came out to regarding a same-sex relationship that eventually led to marriage. Upon hearing this, Barry responded with grace instead of judgment, continued to worship with his friend, to minister alongside her among the poor in Bangladesh, and to visit in the home of her and her wife. Essentially, he remained the same friend he had been before she came out to him. What he did *not* do was react by doubting her faith or questioning her commitment to Christ, even though he disagreed with her theology and personal choices. This is Christlike acceptance in practice.[31]

Now, some will insist that Corey's theology and behavior are equal to affirmation—despite his frequent and explicit statements to the contrary. These twice-removed separatists will likely distance themselves even from non-affirming Christians who accept their queer and affirming siblings. This fundamentalist[32] practice can extend several degrees until there are only a few "true believers" left in an exclusive inner circle. To borrow from the words of Pope Francis, we need to "remain vigilant against rigid ideological positions" expressed "under the guise of good intentions" that often lead to this type of distancing behavior.[33] As an academic who has taught in a fundamentalist context for nearly fifty years, I have experienced this treatment personally from colleagues who have distanced themselves both relationally and positionally simply because I am explicitly accepting—even though I remain non-affirming. No doubt, this will be a challenge for many who choose to explore this theological meeting ground of Christlike acceptance.

---

31. See Corey, *Love Kindness*, 53, 55, 58–59, 60–65, 70.

32. Lyman Stewart's *The Fundamentals: A Testimony to the Truth* (Testimony, 1909–15) was the basis for establishing the Bible Institute of Los Angeles (B.I.O.L.A., now Biola University) and the source for what became known as the American fundamentalist movement. See Paul Rood, "The Untold Story of *The Fundamentals*," *Biola Magazine*, September 2, 2014, https://www.biola.edu/blogs/biola-magazine/2014/the-untold-story-of-the-fundamentals.

33. Courtney Mares, "Pope Francis to Roman Curia: Rigid Ideological Positions Prevent Us from Moving Forward," *Catholic World Report*, December 21, 2023, https://www.catholicworldreport.com/2023/12/21/pope-francis-to-roman-curia-rigid-ideological-positions-prevent-us-from-moving-forward/.

Acceptance in Christian Organizations

It seems self-evident that applying Christlike acceptance is more difficult in religious organizations with doctrinal statements, policies, governing boards, and donors than it is in personal relationships. The complexity involved is significant, and the process will vary. With this in mind, I will suggest a few questions for thought while we work together as Christ's church in the twenty-first century to establish guidelines that are both workable and biblical.

Leaders in Christian organizations and churches teach by way of example both explicitly and implicitly. Moreover, if the organization has a doctrinal statement, then as a matter of integrity the teaching of its leadership should be consistent with that statement. But must such statements, when they exist, address the progressive vs. traditionalist debate over sexuality and gender? After all, this disputable matter is more about behavior than doctrine. Further, different church members have different degrees of influence and responsibility. Might not adhering to whatever the official position is be less important for someone on the maintenance staff than for someone who leads a Bible study, or less important for someone who leads a Bible study than for an elder or teaching pastor?

The same holds true in other Christian organizations, like global-outreach ministries, colleges and universities, publishing houses, and so forth. At which levels of responsibility do varying commitments to a doctrinal statement need to apply? To revisit the family analogy, What might a loved and trusted member of your biological family who is gay and married be allowed to do within the family, even if you as a family leader hold non-affirming views? Should they not be permitted to do the same in a church-family community that holds non-affirming views?

Additionally, a church community must make clear up front any restrictions on LGBTQ members rather than "welcoming" queer people in the church door, waiting until they are comfortably committed, and then breaking the bad news to them—a bait-and-switch tactic. Also, there should be consistency between how a church handles these matters and how it handles other aspects of behavior, such as divorce (Matt. 19:9), care for the poor (James 5:1–6), temperance, self-control, hospitality, gentleness, contentiousness, and the love of money (1 Tim. 3:1–4).

Whatever the circumstances, the process requires mature, spiritual discernment within the leadership of Christian organizations and inclusion of queer followers of Jesus as participants in the process. This should include times of discussion and prayer in a safe context committed to asking good questions and doing no harm, with the burden resting on those feeling compelled to restrict the freedom of others—as it was with Paul's advice to the early churches in Rome.

Modeling these attributes at various leadership levels sets an example of accepting others as sacred siblings in Christ without requiring agreement. Or as the apostle Paul puts it so poignantly, "Accept them, but not for the purpose of engaging them in quarrelsome disputes or in order to pass judgment on their spirituality or behavior" (Rom. 14:1–4). In this way, the Cooperative Baptist Fellowship (CBF) has endorsed the idea of Christlike acceptance by allowing for greater diversity among individual congregations within the organization by accepting one another, as well as practicing respect and love for others as members in good standing, regardless of one's view on sexual orientation and/or gender identity.[34]

To implement a different kind of acceptance, both the Church of England and the Catholic Church have explored "blessing but not affirming" same-sex unions. At the time of this writing, Anglicans are moving in this direction more cautiously, on a "trial basis."[35] In contrast, Pope Francis has officially permitted priests to bless gay people in same-sex relationships, emphasizing that they should not be subjected to "an exhaustive moral analysis" in order to receive God's love and mercy. But he also qualified this by insisting this practice not be confused with the ritual of marriage, making it clear that his intention is not to "legitimize" anything but "to open one's life to seek God's help to live better, invoking the Holy Spirit to live out Gospel values more faithfully."[36]

Finally, I must return to the statements of Biola University's president, who inspired this chapter. In 2020, just three years after Barry Corey's *Love Kindness* was published, he secured funding for and launched Biola's Winsome Conviction Project (WCP) to "foster conversations that deepen—rather than tear apart—relationships, help to heal a fractured church and nation, foster civility and bring biblical compassion to a warring public square."[37]

---

34. See the CBF Executive Coordinator Report in the 2024 General Assembly Plenary Session, delivered by Paul Baxley, June 20, 2024, 17:20–22:49 min., https://vimeo.com/963325194.

35. Madeleine Davies, "Church of England Advances Plans to Bless but Not Affirm Same-Sex Couples," *Christianity Today*, October 26, 2023, https://www.christianitytoday.com/news/2023/october/church-of-england-general-synod-same-sex-blessing-lgbt-coup.html.

36. Nicole Winfeld and David Crary, "Pope Approves Blessings for Same-Sex Couples That Must Not Resemble Marriage," Associated Press, World News, December 19, 2023, https://apnews.com/article/vatican-lgbtq-pope-bfa5b71fa79055626e362936e739d1d8.

37. Winsome Conviction Project's vision statement: "Utilizing public conversations, deeply held convictions will meet honest disagreements in a virtuous communication climate in which participants care deeply, think clearly, speak graciously, and listen patiently. Change will only happen when we approach differences at the intellectual and heart levels. We take seriously the Scripture's admonition that just as a 'harsh word stirs up anger' a gentle word has the potential

Since then, on campus and through scores of WCP podcasts,[38] faculty have engaged a diverse group of divisive topics ranging from American politics to human sexuality, frequently inviting widely differing voices to participate in positive and healing discussions about important issues. Regrettably, however, the WCP has not yet invited a queer and affirming Christian to join them to demonstrate "winsome conviction" on this controversial topic. The WCP's work has been a good step in the right direction that is consistent with a theology of Christlike acceptance, but it needs to go further in the spirit of both Corey's book and its own underlying philosophy. This will take courage and risk.

Final Reflections

Christlike acceptance is expressed in four ways in Romans 14:1–4 and 15:7: "Be accepting of one another" (imperative), "because God has accepted you" (past tense), and "accept one another" (imperative), "as Christ has accepted you" (past tense). God's historical work through Christ on our behalf is our model, whereas our collaborative work with one another is our ongoing obligation and challenge. Paul sets his call to acceptance in the context of substantive behavioral disagreements about what constitutes right living under God's new covenant in Christ, as a people called to live differently than either the Jewish or Greco-Roman world around them. The weaker in faith still cling to old-covenant rituals and live in fear of moral contamination from Rome, while despising and passing judgment on those stronger in faith, who live more fully into their freedom in Christ. Both must accept each other into their fellowships without the contentious quarreling and judging that has, until then, characterized and divided them.

As followers of Jesus today, we too have been engaged in divisive disagreements over the exegetically reasoned views and behaviors of some LGBTQ Christians, which has led to our despising and passing judgment on others regarding their understanding of the Bible's teaching on sexuality and gender. Although I have arrived at my own exegetical conclusions, evidence from both Catholic and Protestant circles suggests the proverbial jury is still out on who is right in the progressive vs. traditionalist debate: the libertarians or the legalists. And this significant behavioral dispute will no doubt continue for

---

to turn 'away wrath' (Prov. 15:1)." "About the Winsome Conviction Project," Biola University, accessed April 17, 2024, https://www.biola.edu/blogs/winsome-conviction/about.

38. See *Winsome Conviction* podcasts, Biola University, accessed April 17, 2024, https://www.biola.edu/blogs/winsome-conviction/articles/category/podcast.

the foreseeable future. In such a tumultuous time, personal and intellectual humility require us to respect the plausible arguments of Christian advocates on both sides while at the same time faithfully living out our respective understandings of Scripture. I firmly believe that a theology of acceptance is a workable solution to this current dilemma, a critical meeting ground that is at the same time both biblical and Christlike.

On a personal note, my own spiritual roots remain firmly planted in the peace traditions of the Church of the Brethren, where we still understand our calling as continuing the work of Jesus—peacefully, simply, and together.[39] Accomplishing this with regard to the present discussion by adopting a theology of acceptance will certainly require what Quaker sociologist Parker Palmer calls taking "bigger risks on behalf of the common good."[40] But is this really too much to ask of Jesus's followers, who are supposed to be known by our unity (John 17:21) and love for others (John 13:34–35)? We must demonstrate better the love of Christ for those whose behavior we may deem outside the biblical norm. In this light, it is tragic that so much hate speech has been generated by evangelical professors, pastors, and leaders against their more progressive neighbors.[41]

Finally, Paul makes it clear in his admonition to the Corinthians that three things remain in the end: faith, hope, and love (1 Cor. 13:13). Faith includes the doctrine and dogma we believe to be true, and hope is what motivates us to stay faithful as God's witnesses in a troubled world. But love—explicitly highlighted as the greatest of the three—is what we are called to do every day as ministers of compassion and kindness to others. We must take more seriously Jesus's assertion that the entire Law and the prophets are fulfilled in loving God and neighbor as much as we love ourselves (Matt. 22:37–40; Mark 12:29–31), echoed in Paul's bold claim that all of the Torah is fulfilled by loving our neighbor as much as we love ourself (Gal. 5:14).

---

39. "About Us," Church of the Brethren, accessed September 16, 2024, https://www.brethren.org/about.

40. Parker J. Palmer, *On the Brink of Everything: Grace, Gravity and Getting Old* (Berrett-Koehler, 2018), xiv. Those of us who embrace a theology of acceptance while employed at a conservative Christian organization know altogether too well the risks involved in, and the price that may need to be paid for, promoting Christlike acceptance.

41. See Kate Shellnutt, "Evangelicals Are the Most Beloved US Faith Group among Evangelicals: And among the Worst-Rated by Everybody Else," *Christianity Today*, March 15, 2023, https://www.christianitytoday.com/news/2023/march/evangelical-reputation-negative-us-survey-religious-groups-.html.

2

Genesis, Discernment, and God's Will

Karen R. Keen

Genesis features prominently in debates on sexuality and gender. But often overlooked is how the biblical story of human origins can shape our understanding of discernment when it comes to ethics. Both traditionalists and reformists on LGBTQ matters care about God's will for humankind. Indeed, devout Christians on either side of the debate have engaged in prayerful study. In other words, we have in common the pursuit of truth and desire to conform our lives to the ways of God, even if we disagree on particularities. Given this common goal, it's worth exploring what Scripture reveals about discerning God's will, including insights from the Genesis creation story. What we learn is that good Christian ethics are best determined *because* of our differing perspectives, not in spite of them. Rather than being a biblical text that divides us, Genesis can offer hope that traditionalists and reformists are better together.[1]

---

1. In previous writings, I have used the terms *traditionalist* and *progressive* to distinguish between those who reserve marriage between a man and a woman and those who believe gay people can participate in marriage. But the term *progressive* can be too easily misunderstood because of other theological and political connotations. A more accurate term is *reformist* to describe those who believe reform is warranted when it comes to understanding marriage, in line with other Christian movements of reform over the centuries.

Imago Dei (God's Image) and Human Agency

In Genesis 1, the first living things depicted are vegetation and animals, and the biblical author emphasizes their reproductive capacity. The plants and trees are seed-bearing, reproducing according to their kinds (vv. 11–12, 29). Similarly, when sea creatures and birds are created, "God blessed them and said, 'Be fruitful and increase in number'" (v. 22).

But when the creation narrative arrives at human beings, the first attribute emphasized is the *imago Dei*, which comes with unique agency. God makes humankind "in our image, in our likeness, *so that they may rule*" (v. 26; emphasis added).[2] This places human beings in a unique relationship with God, as well as with other creatures. Namely, human beings become God's representation and governing hand on earth. God gives human beings unique power to make consequential decisions.

The second creation story, in Genesis 2, highlights the need for humankind's agency, for "there was no one to work the ground" (v. 5), and so God made the human being (or the earthling) "to work it and take care of it" (v. 15).[3] The biblical author provides an initial example of this rule when God introduces the human being to animals to see what the earthling will name them (vv. 19–20). The exercise makes clear God's intent for human beings to engage in discernment and decision-making pertaining to earthly governance.

Humanity's role in governing all of creation is reiterated, even after humankind shows itself to be evil and God responds with a flood. In a replay of creation, God starts over with human beings after the flood, and familiar creation themes are reiterated (9:1–3). Humanity's governance is reassured when God instills a submissive disposition in the animals so that they will respond to human rule, and all the earth's living things are "given into [human] hands" (9:2). Importantly, humanity's evil does not remove their existence as the *imago Dei*.[4] Even after the flood, this unique feature of human beings is asserted and affirmed (v. 6b).

---

2. For more on the translation "so that," connecting the *imago Dei* to the human capacity to rule, see Ian Hart, "Genesis 1:1–2:3 as a Prologue to the Book of Genesis," *TynBul* 46 (1995): 319–20. I also discuss the *imago Dei* in my article "Cultural Influences on the Hermeneutical Frameworks in the Debate on Same-Sex Relationships," *Interpretation* 74 (2020): 253–64, https://doi.org/10.1177/0020964320921961. In "Cultural Influences," I also discuss the new, problematic trend that associates the *imago Dei* with God creating "male and female," which is not the view of Jewish or Christian tradition.

3. *'Adam* is connected to the word *'adamah*, meaning the ground/earth.

4. In the past, I might have said we reflect the image of God, but I agree with Carmen Imes's language of "being" the image of God. See her book *Being God's Image: Why Creation Still Matters* (IVP Academic, 2023).

In the ancient Israelite mind, an "image" (*tselem*) had associations with idolatry. A statue (image) of a god would be placed in a temple to represent the deity's presence. But the Israelite temple had no such statue. Human beings are the "statue" that conveys the presence of God in the world. The problem with nonhuman images of God is that "they have mouths, but cannot speak, eyes, but cannot see. They have ears, but cannot hear, noses, but cannot smell. They have hands, but cannot feel, feet, but cannot walk, nor can they utter a sound with their throats" (Ps. 115:5–7). In other words, they are inanimate objects devoid of power or action.

At this point, someone might say, But what about animals that share a sensate experience with human beings and rule their own roosts in the animal kingdom? Or what about people with disabilities who might not be able to see or hear? Wanting to preserve the dignity of every person, some have suggested that we shouldn't think of the *imago Dei* in terms of governance, since some people don't have the intellectual or physical capacities to rule.[5] But while it's true that the *imago Dei* comes to mean more than governance in the New Testament (as we will see), it's important to read Genesis 1 from the perspective of the original author.

The writers of the human-origin narratives were making general observations about how the world works. Even John Calvin made this point, asserting that Genesis 1 relays what is visible to the naked eye. He drew this conclusion after comparing the science of his day with what he read in Scripture. Noticing that Genesis does not reflect advanced scientific understanding, Calvin concluded that the biblical author was accommodating his audience's limited knowledge by describing what ordinary people can know through simple observation.[6]

The Genesis origin stories reflect what is plain to the naked eye—sprouting seeds and agricultural cycles, birds swooping through the air, women crying out in childbirth, sweat dripping from the brow while tilling, light from moonbeams on a sleepless night, and rays pouring forth the dawn. Similarly, the biblical writers observed that human beings (as a species) possess certain abilities that other animals do not, resulting in human beings having the upper hand. The writers attributed this greater possession of power to God's intentional plan for humanity. Psalm 8 praises this reality:

---

5. Anna Maliszewska, "*Imago Dei* in People with Profound Intellectual Disabilities," *Theologica Xaveriana* 69 (2019): 1–26.

6. See John Calvin's discussion of Genesis 1, particularly verse 16 in *Commentaries on the First Book of Moses Called Genesis*, Commentaries on the Book of Genesis, vol. 1, trans. John King (Eerdmans, 1948). See also Calvin's *Institutes* 1.14.3.

> You have made them a little lower than the angels
> and crowned them with glory and honor.
> You made them rulers over the works of your hands;
> you put everything under their feet:
> all flocks and herds,
> and the animals of the wild,
> the birds in the sky,
> and the fish in the sea,
> all that swim the paths of the seas. (vv. 5–8)

The earth has been put under the authority of human beings—for better or for worse. One example of how this plays out in a biblical narrative, as it relates to ethics, is when Moses is overwhelmed by all the particular cases that people bring to him on matters of daily life (Exod. 18:13–26). His father-in-law, Jethro, asks why Moses is taking on all this responsibility by himself. Moses says, "Because the people come to me to seek God's will" (v. 15). Jethro replies that this savior complex is "not good" and recommends sharing responsibility among a wide number of capable, trustworthy, and god-fearing leaders. Moses agrees this is a better way to help the community discern God's will in daily life.

The story implies that discerning the divine will is made complex by the infinite number of everyday scenarios that arise, and that determining the best course of action involves human agency in decision-making. Human beings have some say in the practicalities of human flourishing.[7]

And yet, we also know that human agency can go awry. Going back to the early Genesis narratives, things did go wrong. But we find a curious set of circumstances when it comes to Adam and Eve, suggesting the story is about discernment. God intentionally places a forbidden tree within arm's length in the Garden of Eden. God also allows the snake to have access to the human beings, not unlike the adversary's permission to engage Job. What is God doing? This narrative is often preached as a lesson in obedience, and while it encompasses that, if God only wanted compliance, God could have created the conditions for rote obedience. Instead, the story conveys the importance of learning and practicing discernment.

---

7. We might also consider examples of the saints negotiating with God, arguing that idol-worshiping Israelites shouldn't be destroyed (Exod. 32:11–14) or wrestling with the Lord until a blessing is given (Gen. 32:22–31).

Human Agency, Discernment, and God's Law

Interestingly, when God starts over with human beings after the flood, and familiar creation themes are reiterated, a new "Garden of Eden" moment occurs (Gen. 9:1–4). Again, God says, "Do not eat . . ." Only this time, instead of fruit from a particular tree, the instruction is "You must not eat meat that has its lifeblood still in it" (v. 4). Significantly, this directive alludes to Israelite law (e.g., Lev. 17:10–14; 19:26; Deut. 12:16, 23–25; see also Acts 15:20, 29). Scholars have long noted that the writings of Genesis incorporate Israelite law, having been compiled after the establishment of Israel.[8]

Thus, law is one lens that frames the Israelite narrative of early human history. In other words, ethics, and not merely a theological origin story, are in the minds of those who shaped the canonical form of Genesis.[9] In addition to the law against eating meat with blood, the first several chapters of Genesis allude to other Israelite statutes, including Sabbath practice (Gen. 2:2–3; Exod. 35:2; Lev. 23:3; Deut. 5:12–14), distinguishing clean and unclean animals (Gen. 7:2, 8; Lev. 11), and offering acceptable sacrifices (Gen. 8:20; Lev. 27:11).

The Old Testament authors are clear that following Mosaic law is imperative, being closely connected to God's will.[10] So, what is the relationship between human agency, discernment, and God's law? Even as the biblical authors express clear concern for obeying God, we find them exercising surprising freedom when it comes to discerning what constitutes righteous application of law. Even biblical laws are subject to discernment, thereby actualizing the agency human beings have been given to govern, including to judicate situations.[11] And while those decisions are to be congruent with

---

8. Even evangelical scholar Bill T. Arnold dates the composition history of Genesis to after the rise of the state of Israel. He proposes sometime between the tenth and eighth centuries BC. See his commentary *Genesis*, New Cambridge Bible Commentary (Cambridge University Press, 2009), 12–18. For more on the origins and when the biblical texts were written, see part 1 in Karen R. Keen, *The Word of a Humble God: The Origins, Inspiration, and Interpretation of Scripture* (Eerdmans, 2022).

9. The Israelite creation story retells the origin of the universe and humanity by playing off older Babylonian stories. Compare Genesis with *Enuma Elish* and *Atrahasis*.

10. Some scholars believe Genesis may have been compiled and edited after the sixth century BC, following the exile, given themes of expulsion and scattering in Genesis (e.g., Adam and Eve, Cain, and the Tower of Babel). Ezekiel, the prophet who wrote during the exile, frequently blames failure to adhere to Mosaic law as the reason for exile. If so, ethical reflection in Genesis is entwined with theodicy, an attempt to make sense of national tragedy and trauma. Numerous studies on the legal rhetoric in Ezekiel are available. As one example, see Eric X. Jarrard, "A Legal Allusion: The Correlation of Law and History in Ezekiel 20," *Vetus Testamentum* 73 (2023): 645–82.

11. I also discuss legal deliberation in my book *Scripture, Ethics, and the Possibility of Same-Sex Relationships* (Eerdmans, 2018). See esp. chaps. 4–6.

God's good character, the way that happens is not through God's overpowering or controlling human beings, but rather through God's shaping human beings' character, including giving opportunities to try and fail, as we see in the Garden of Eden story.

Importantly, laws in the Old Testament are not comprehensive, nor were they ever intended to be. In fact, they are part of what is called mixed genre. The legal collections (such as the Covenant Collection or Holiness Collection) are embedded in narrative, serving the biblical authors' storytelling purposes. In addition to not being comprehensive, the laws sometimes change or conflict. This is the result of legal deliberation, as well as different textual traditions being placed together in what comprises the biblical anthology.

While some scholars argue that these revisions reflect outright rejection of previous tradition, I see a respect for tradition in the fact that earlier laws are left side by side in the scriptural texts with the new applications, instead of being deleted. Joshua Berman summarizes a perspective similar to mine: "Indeed, as authors revised the collections, they certainly intended to invalidate former normative practices. But that did not entail a rejection of the authority of that text. Rather the earlier prescription was seen to be fulfilled through its reapplication to meet a new challenge."[12] With that in mind, let's look at a few examples of discernment from ancient Israelite and early Jewish and Christian engagement with biblical law.[13]

Discernment on Consecrated Bread

Original Mandate: Only Levitical priests may eat consecrated bread (Lev. 24:5–9).

New Application: David and his men, who are not eligible, are given permission to eat the consecrated bread (1 Sam. 21:3–6; Matt. 12:3–7).

The Holiness Collection takes seriously the sacredness of worship. Certain rituals conveyed respect for the holiness of God. One of these rituals had to do with consecrated bread, also called "showbread" or "bread of Presence." For a non-priest to eat the bread would have been an act of desecration. Twelve

---

12. Joshua Berman, "Supersessionist or Complementary? Reassessing the Nature of Legal Revision in the Pentateuchal Law Collections," *JBL* 135 (2016): 211.

13. The following examples are not intended to be exhaustive. For example, in my book *Scripture, Ethics, and the Possibility of Same-Sex Relationships*, I discuss cases like slave-law revision (Exod. 21:1–11 vs. Deut. 15:12–18) and expectations regarding permanency of marriage (Deut. 24:1–4 vs. Matt. 19:1–9 vs. 1 Cor. 7:12–15). You can also find examples of these kinds of shifts in Michael Graves, *How Scripture Interprets Scripture: What Biblical Writers Can Teach Us about Reading the Bible* (Baker Academic, 2021).

loaves of bread were placed "on the table of pure gold before the LORD" in the sanctuary as an offering (Lev. 24:6–7). And only the blood descendants of the priest, Aaron (Moses's brother), were permitted to eat this bread because of the holiness of the offering (v. 9). In violation of this law, a priest gave the showbread to David and his men upon request because the men were hungry. Jesus acknowledged David broke the law, but he taught that David was innocent anyway because "I desire mercy" (Matt. 12:7). That is, breaking the law was the right thing to do because people were hungry, and the whole point of the law is to serve the common good of human beings (Mark 2:27).

Discernment on Inheritance

Original Mandate: Land inheritance goes to males, who are counted in the census (Num. 26:4, 52–56).

New Application: Daughters can inherit land (Num. 27:1–8; see also Josh. 17:3–4).

Like most ancient Near Eastern cultures, Israelite society was patricentric, giving males greater authority. As heads of their households, men were the ones counted in the census and allotted land according to their tribe. Inheritance passed down to descendants through patrilineal lines (i.e., from fathers to sons). Sons received inheritance, but daughters did not—that is, until five sisters (Mahlah, Noah, Hoglah, Milcah, and Tirzah) challenged this system. They made a case to Moses that daughters should be allowed to inherit their father's land if there are no sons, and the case was determined in the women's favor. This change benefitted the plight of women in a system that offered them little economic safety net if they had no male authority, even as it allowed their father's (and, therefore, the family's) name to endure.

Discernment on Interfaith Marriage

Original Mandate: Interfaith marriages are not allowed (Deut. 7:3–4; Ezra 9–10).

New Application: Interfaith marriages can remain intact (1 Cor. 7:12–14).

Israelite law emphatically denounces interfaith marriages. While Israelites could marry a *convert* to Israel's God (e.g., Ruth), they could not marry someone actively practicing another religion. In fact, after the return from exile, Ezra required men married to pagan women to divorce them, sending them away along with any children born to them. Why such severe resistance to interfaith marriages to the point of tearing families apart? The concern was that such marriages would lead God's people astray into idol worship. In contrast, Paul rejected divorce as the best solution for interfaith couples. In fact, he encouraged the couples to stay together because he had the opposite perspective of previous biblical authors. Whereas the Old Testament writers believed remaining in such marriages would lead believers to apostatize, Paul thinks staying in the marriage could result in believers sanctifying their non-Christian spouses. It's not that he isn't aware of potential spiritual pitfalls—he discourages entering interfaith unions in the first place (2 Cor. 6:14–18). But Paul decides to gamble in favor of keeping families together.

Discernment on Association with Pagan Culture

Original Mandate: Do not eat food sacrificed to idols (Exod. 34:15–16; Acts 15:19–29).

New Application: It's okay to eat food sacrificed to idols (1 Cor. 8:4–8).

For obvious reasons, Israelite law forbade eating food sacrificed to idols. The biblical authors sensed God telling them to have nothing to do with anything associated with another religion. After all, such food was prepared during the very act of worship. To eat it was tantamount to participating in the worship of that god. Even the early church ruled that not only Jews but also gentile converts to Christianity could not eat food sacrificed to idols. The Jerusalem Council upheld the law for the church—that is, until Paul, who initially signed off on the Council decision, later decided to teach a contrary view. Eating food sacrificed to idols is okay because idols aren't really gods. For the Christian who knows there's only one true God and holds that allegiance in her heart, the meat is just meat. Thus, Paul leans toward freedom of conscience, as long as the decision doesn't harm one's own faith and precautions are taken not to be a stumbling block to others.

Having considered a few examples of discernment, leading to new applications of law, one might ask, How is it that the biblical authors deliberated concerning scriptural directives? Weren't the original commands straightforward? Isn't God the same yesterday, today, and forever? This could be answered in different ways, including noting that Scripture was not meant to be read and applied as codified legislation. But perhaps even more overlooked is the reality that a law is not virtuous in and of itself. That's why Rahab's act of deception in hiding spies was considered righteous, when deceit is normally condemned (Josh. 2; James 2:25–26). A similar example from modern times is Corrie ten Boom, who lied to Nazis to save Jews hiding in her house. To *always* follow the commandment "Do not lie. Do not deceive one another" (Lev. 19:11) would actually lead to great evil in certain circumstances.

Being the *imago Dei* with its God-given ruling agency involves employing discernment. Jesus taught that when David or his own disciples violated the law, they could still be innocent because in certain situations the law was leading to harm (e.g., preventing people from eating; Matt. 12:1–8).[14] That defeats what the law is supposed to do. Doing "no harm to a neighbor" is the fulfillment of the law (Rom. 13:10).

Repeatedly, Scripture describes the importance of discernment when it comes to knowing and applying God's will to a situation, whether it's discerning between two prostitutes fighting over a baby (1 Kings 3:16–28), or trying to decide when it's right to answer the fool and when it's not (Prov. 26:4–5), or discerning between which spirits are of God and which aren't (1 Cor. 12:10; 1 John 4:1), or simply having to discern because *God made it necessary to do so*. As Paul says, we know only "in part" because prophetic revelation is through a glass darkly (1 Cor. 13:9, 12).

There's no getting around discernment. Even if we wanted to rely solely on Scripture for every decision, as though it were legislation, it's not even possible to do that. The directives that are included don't come anywhere close to being comprehensive. We are still forced to make ethical decisions apart from explicit directives in Scripture. For example, should Christians use in vitro fertilization (IVF)? There's no discussion in the Bible of IVF or innumerable other ethical concerns. And, as we have already seen, even applying a specific biblical directive can result in evil if done without consideration of circumstances. So there's no getting out of discernment.

Discerning Truth Together across Divides

If being the *imago Dei* involves responsibility to practice discernment and decision-making, how do we know that we aren't making wrong decisions? One of the most important, yet often overlooked, biblical principles is found in Proverbs 18:17: "The first person to make his case in a dispute seems right (*tsadiq*), until another person comes to thoroughly examine (*haqar*) him" (my trans.). In other words, we cannot arrive at truth without coming together across differences. Discerning God's will, including

---

14. I write in more depth on Jesus's teaching regarding David eating consecrated bread and the implications for biblical interpretation in my book *The Word of a Humble God*. See especially the last chapter, although the whole book is ultimately about how to interpret and apply Scripture to the Christian life.

by interpreting and applying Scripture, requires hearing perspectives from all sides and weighing the evidence. When we study ethics in homogenous echo chambers, we never have our assumptions cross-examined. We think we are right, but our conclusions have not been tested. This principle of cross-examination remains true even when it comes to spiritual gifts. Paul instructs that a prophetic word spoken at church should be weighed by others (1 Cor. 14:29).

If we are reluctant to listen—truly listen—to our opponents in a debate, to seriously contemplate their arguments on a matter, we reveal ourselves to be less interested in the pursuit of truth than we are in "being right." And that's simply pride posing as godly devotion. If we go through life never changing our mind on any theological or ethical concern, there's a good chance we're not practicing the biblical wisdom of Proverbs 18:17. The pursuit of truth requires being open to evidence, including opposing perspectives and insights we have yet to sincerely wrestle with.

In the discussion on sexuality and gender, the lack of true cross-investigation is evident, especially when it comes to Genesis. Traditionalists focus on the creation narrative's mention of "male and female" and "be fruitful and multiply," but rarely consider theological implications of other details such as "It's not good for the human being to be alone" or the God-given drive to "leave father and mother" to create one's own kinship unit. Similarly, reformists write extensively on diversity in creation, including the Genesis 1 merisms encompassing all the things existing between two extremes (binaries)— "heavens and the earth"; "there was evening, and there was morning"—and they also note the patricentric culture in which Genesis was written, but they rarely engage with the theological implications of sexual differentiation or procreation.

We are often too afraid, tired, and frustrated to really open ourselves up to opposing evidence, worried about what might happen if we concede a point made by the other side. But what if we can arrive at more truth by acknowledging the best evidence that each side brings to the table? What if it's not the zero-sum game we often think it is? Paradoxically, our distinct perspectives actually enhance our ability to pursue truth. Each of us only has the ability to see part of the whole, given our social contexts and human limitations. But when we look at the whole from the various angles that diverse voices provide, we have more evidence to work with.

Let's consider what this looks like on the ground, especially how our respect for the *imago Dei* can help us break through our resistance to working together.

Oneness vs. Uniformity

Scripture uses the metaphor of a human body to describe how diversity participates in oneness. We are Christ's single body—his arms and legs and hands. Important for discerning God's will across differences, we are collectively Christ's body. There's no getting away from one another. With all the divisions in the church, including thousands of denominations, we might forget Christ has only one body, not multiple bodies. No amount of splintering off into our preferred camps changes that fact. The hand cannot say to the foot, I have no need of you (1 Cor. 12:15–26). For "as a body, though one, has many parts . . . so it is with Christ. For we were all baptized by one Spirit so as to form one body" (vv. 12–13).[15]

Our oneness does not require uniformity. Our oneness is a spiritual reality given by God in the same way that God created human beings as the *imago Dei* at the original creation. It's God's work that molds and fashions us into a single body—only this time not from dust of the ground but through baptism by the Spirit. Through baptism, God shapes us into "the image of his Son" (Rom. 8:29).[16] Collectively, we become the "statue" (body/image) of the Son.[17] While Genesis emphasizes ruling the earth as the key feature of the *imago Dei*, the New Testament emphasizes our glorification. We "are being transformed into his image with ever-increasing glory, which comes from the Lord, who is the Spirit" (2 Cor. 3:18).

It's worth repeating that last line—our oneness as the image of the Son "comes from the Lord." That's why we can disagree and still be members of Christ's single body. Oneness is achieved not by agreement but by God's work. The early church disagreed on food sacrificed to idols (1 Cor. 8) and on how to do ministry (Acts 15:36–40), but they were still the limbs and eyes and ears of the same body—Christ's. Neither does oneness require uniformity on every ethical question. On the one hand, Paul says getting circumcised is a rejection of the gospel itself (Gal. 5:1–12); on the other hand, he takes Timothy to be circumcised (Acts 16:3).

---

15. For more on the theology of church divisions, see Eugene Schlesinger, *Ruptured Bodies: A Theology of the Divided Church* (Fortress, 2024).

16. In his humanity, Jesus was made as the image of God, and the Son is also "the exact representation" of God (Heb. 1:3; see also Col. 1:15; John 1:1–3; Phil. 2:6). In this way, Christ is the image of God in a more direct way than human beings because of his deity. Scripture connects this to the Son's preexistence and role as creator of the earth.

17. Jesus had his own physical body, and that physical body is now resurrected. So how is it that we are, collectively, Jesus's body? Paul calls this a spiritual mystery brought about by the profound union of Christ and humanity. To explain, Paul uses a metaphor from human experience: "one flesh" oneness of marriage. So also, it's possible to experience a kind of spiritual marital oneness with Christ/God (Eph. 5:29–32; see also 1 Cor. 6:16–17; Rev. 21:1–3).

When it comes to discernment across differences, recalling that Christ's body cannot be dismembered helps us resist the delusion that we can live without one another. Since we are stuck together, we might as well listen to one another about the ethics that matter most to us.

Imitating God's Generosity

It was generous of God to make human beings as the divine image, giving them ruling power to make decisions concerning how life on earth unfolds. And it was generous to affirm human beings' agency even after their wickedness was on full display (Gen. 9:2). But God's generosity is even more remarkable than that. Whereas the Israelite understanding of *imago Dei* referred to rule over the material world, the New Testament adds *spiritual* rule. Now, the *imago Dei* includes being enthroned with God. That's a mind-boggling reality.

We have been seated (enthroned) with Christ in the spiritual realm (Eph. 2:6). Christ says, "To the one who is victorious, I will give the right to sit with me on my throne, just as I was victorious and sat down with my Father on his throne" (Rev. 3:21). We will judge even angels (1 Cor. 6:2–3) and reign forever and ever (2 Tim. 2:12; Rev. 22:5).

Being conformed to the image of the Son means we become like God in a way akin to the Second Person of the Trinity. This involves not only conformity to God's good character as displayed in Christ (Col. 3:9–10) but also inheriting the riches of the Son (Eph. 1:3–5; Heb. 2:5–11). That's true for slaves, women, gentiles, and other people often left out of privilege granted to an elite son (Gal. 3:28). Now, those who are crucified, buried, and risen with Christ are *all* the one body of the Son, sitting on the throne.

If we are tempted to dismiss our opponents as sinners, disqualified from discerning God's will, it's worth remembering that God gives us a voice and responsibility even when we don't have it all together. When we sin, God doesn't give up on us. God *comes relationally near*, walking in the Garden to find us (Gen. 3:8–9), giving us covering for our shame (v. 21), and protecting us from eternal consequences (vv. 22–24). God's response to sin is Immanuel, "God with us" (Matt. 1:23). God comes near *while* we are sinners, *while* we are enemies (Rom. 5:7–8, 10). For as Jesus said, "If you love those who love you, what credit is that to you? Even sinners love those who love them . . . but love your enemies, do good to them . . . *just as your Father*" (Luke 6:32–36; emphasis added). Even if we make mistakes, God's mercies are new *every* morning (Lam. 3:22–23).

God's generosity is the model for all of us, whether we are traditionalists or reformists. Do we take what God gives us, and all the privileges that come with that, and yet have the audacity to refuse to offer the same to others?[18] If the Master of the Universe is willing to *share a throne* with you, a sinner, are you not willing to work together with someone across the aisle?

Listening to Outsiders

Even if we think our opponent in the debate can't possibly be a Christian, we would benefit from listening. Why? Human beings in general, and not merely Christians, are the *imago Dei*. That was established at creation. That means even atheists and people who practice other religions have God-given agency to make contributions to the earth's governance. More than that, even nonbelievers can have an impulse to follow the virtues of God, apart from baptism (Rom. 2:14–15; see also Acts 10).

Some of us have been taught that outsiders have nothing to teach us. In fact, some of us have been raised in churches that "protected" us from anything written or spoken by outsiders, with warnings we might be led astray. But this actually makes it *more likely* that we will be deceived. Proverbs 18:17 teaches that withholding information thwarts the pursuit of truth. Cross-examination between two sides with different perspectives fosters the pursuit of truth. Similarly, studies suggest lack of educational access contributes to a person's susceptibility to deception.[19] Withholding access to (outside) information, which is so common in some church circles, impedes our ability to discern God's will. In contrast, Scripture invites us to weigh opposing views. This implies that outsiders *can* have a perspective worth weighing.

In his book *Stranger God*, Richard Beck also notes that God can show up in people and places we don't expect, and by practicing hospitality toward outsiders, we open ourselves up to encountering God. He gives the example of the Midianite Hobab, who became the Israelites' guide into the Promised Land (Num. 10:29–33). God used a non-Israelite to share wisdom and insight with God's people—the very path to the Promised Land. Similarly, Beck sees a theme in Scripture where God shows up incognito, as when Jesus can be found in the prisoner or homeless person (e.g., Matt. 25).[20]

Importantly, we can be mistaken in our negative assessment of someone. Jesus's disciple John complained, "Teacher . . . we saw someone driving out demons in your name and we told him to stop, because he was not one of us."

---

18. There's a parable about this attitude (Matt. 18:23–35).
19. E.g., people with higher education levels are less susceptible to conspiracy theories. See K. M. Douglas et al., "Someone Is Pulling the Strings: Hypersensitive Agency Detection and Belief in Conspiracy Theories," *Thinking and Reasoning* 22 (2016): 57–77.
20. Richard Beck, *Stranger God: Meeting Jesus in Disguise* (Fortress, 2017).

And Jesus replied, "Do not stop him . . . for whoever is not against us is for us" (Mark 9:38–41). Even though John observed that the person was acting in the name of Jesus, he still didn't want to recognize him as legitimate. In other words, we can dismiss others as not "real Christians" or as outsiders, but in doing so, we may miss what God is doing.

Conclusions: Being the Image of God

Genesis is significant in the debates on sexuality and gender, but what is often overlooked is what Genesis teaches us about how to discern God's will. Being the image of God has significance for all human beings, as creatures to whom God has given responsibility for the earth's flourishing. As a human race, we are to work together for the common good. For the ancient Israelites and early Christians, this included discerning biblical law and revising its application, according to context, to ensure "no harm to a neighbor" (Rom. 13:8–10).

Even more than that, we are being conformed to the image of the Son and given a role in governing in the spiritual realm. We have been enthroned with Christ. Such generosity from God invites us to be generous with one another across differences, just as God has been generous with us. In fact, how we treat one another is truly how we fulfill what it means to be the image of God. John 1:18 states, "No one has ever seen God, but the one and only Son . . . has made him known." The same language is used of us: "No one has ever seen God; but *if we love one another*, God lives in us and his love is made complete in us" (1 John 4:12; emphasis added). In other words, like Jesus, we make God known by how we treat one another.

While we may not always know the right answer, because we discern through a glass darkly, we can be assured that "love never fails" (1 Cor. 13:8). Love is always right. And "there is no law" against the fruit of the Spirit (Gal. 5:22–23). Perhaps making God visible by holding fast to one another across our differences is more vital than being right. For even if we are confident in our own position on sexuality and gender and have "all knowledge," still, if we "do not have love, [we] are nothing" (1 Cor. 13:2). Our charity toward one another makes God known (1 John 4:12), and that's the greatest knowledge of all.

3

From Eunuchs to LGBTQ Christians

Navigating Theodicy, Inclusion, and Holiness

David Bennett

In this chapter, I argue for why we need to have humility in our ethical responses to the interpretation of the ethics of the New Testament when it comes to LGBTQ people. The central argument of the chapter consists in a constructive, biblical theology of how the notion of natural or created order from the Torah or Jewish Law generates a theodicy dilemma for LGBTQ people, who do not inhabit notions of created good or moral normativity as easily as heterosexual, cisgender people. Such a dilemma can be responded to in a distinctly theodicean and Pauline fashion that helps us to navigate the tension between inclusion and holiness. LGBTQ people are included and justified through the new righteousness given in the person of Jesus Christ in a way they could not be under the Law due to the way creation was submitted to decay and frustration by God.

Since LGTBQ realities are first linked to our bodies and desires, they are linked to human affirmation and dignity as creatures of God. In this sense, sexual orientation or aspects of gender identity are linked to the created goodness of our humanity and yet are also part of the larger cosmic drama of the fall.¹ A theodicy-based lens can be applied to the differences of embodiment that LGBTQ people experience in their bodies, lives, and desires.² In this way, I chart a theological way forward for radical LGBTQ inclusion and acceptance without compromising one's convictions and commitment to radical holiness.

A Radically Inclusive First-Century Church

Imagine for a moment that you are a Jewish person of the first century living around AD 40. You are living about seven years after the death of Jesus Christ. You learn of a strange set of events that has happened: A seemingly righteous man, but perhaps another failed messiah figure, died on a cross. His followers claim that he rose from the grave three days later. Not long after, people outside Jerusalem in an upper room were baptized with God's Holy Spirit because of their new faith in Jesus Christ. A devout Jewish man, Peter, claims to have seen the risen Jesus, as do five hundred others. You learn that the crucified one is the ultimate Messiah of God who rose from the grave, vindicating his true identity as the Danielic "Son of Man," "Son of David," the "Son of God."³ Moreover, those baptized with the Spirit are not just Jewish believers, but people from all over the known world. Your mind fills with all sorts of prophecy from the Hebrew Scriptures, reminding you that one of the signs of the Messiah coming is that the gentiles will be grafted in and many will be made righteous through a greater new covenant.

Suddenly, all of the categories of unclean people under the Jewish Law, or Torah, who were barred from full access to God's presence in the temple—like Samaritans, gentiles, women, and eunuchs—are receiving the Holy Spirit

---

1. For the notion of moral or created "order," see Oliver O'Donovan's works on creation and moral order, particularly *A Conversation Waiting to Begin: The Churches and the Gay Controversy* (SCM, 2009), esp. chaps. 4–6; and *Resurrection and Moral Order: An Outline of Evangelical Ethics*, 2nd ed. (Apollos, 1994). See also a recent reappraisal of O'Donovan's retrieval of creational ethics by Samuel Tranter, *Oliver O'Donovan's Moral Theology: Tensions and Triumphs* (T&T Clark, 2020).

2. I acknowledge from the outset that I write from a Side B position as a celibate gay Christian, accepting the catholic, or traditional, teaching derived from Scripture, which affirms that marriage between a man and a woman is the only faithful place for sexual expression. With this comes the affirmation of the universal way we are called to express a broader erotic friendship or nonsexual intimacy, which will fill all of creation in the future and has started now in Jesus. I prefer to delineate this from the outset as it will help the reader understand my perspective and reading of these texts, without shutting off a precious co-wrestling and solidarity with those who share different stances. I share my own views, albeit from a time before my doctoral work, in the book *A War of Loves: The Unexpected Story of a Gay Activist Discovering Jesus* (Zondervan, 2018).

3. Matt. 21:9; 26:64; Mark 14:62; Rev. 1:7.

and becoming full members of this new-covenant *ecclesia*, or community, all across the world. Similarly, Paul affirms the inclusion of same-sex-attracted people in 1 Corinthians 6:9–11 when, after describing those who will not inherit the kingdom of God, he writes: "That is what some of you were. But you were washed, you were sanctified, you were justified in the name of the Lord Jesus Christ and by the Spirit of our God."[4] This new gospel is for all people, without distinction, through faith. The leaders of this new *ecclesia* start claiming that now that the Messiah has fulfilled the Torah, there is a new way for the world outside of Israel to be made right with God apart from the Law, or Torah. A whole new creation project that upholds but surpasses this Law has come.

You hear of an Ethiopian eunuch being baptized. Gentiles all over the Roman world start getting baptized, or being baptized with the Holy Spirit, and come to faith in God through this Messiah. Miraculous events break out to confirm their faith. A highly educated Pharisee called Saul suddenly turns from persecuting these Messiah followers to becoming one himself and advocates this new way of including the gentiles. The very people who could not fully participate in the temple system start to become inheritors of this new-creation life everywhere.

You then hear that this Messiah likened himself to a new temple and to a eunuch for the sake of the kingdom. He was single and childless when he died. This is not the Messiah you would expect in any sense. Surely God's Messiah would marry, have a family, and pass on the redemptive seed of Abraham through procreation. God has come to confound a certain kind of superficial human wisdom with a more divine, paradoxical wisdom: this Jesus who looked like he was defeated on the cross was actually the seed of Eve, which was stricken and yet crushed the head of the serpent of death under his feet by rising again and liberating creation from its bondage.

It is hard to overstate how difficult it would have been to come to the point of recognizing this Jesus as the Messiah. It would require a marked shift in thinking. The question of God's goodness in the light of a new covenant and new creation evokes the question of how God could allow those who are unclean or impure under the Law to become righteous apart from it through

---

4. It is important to note that 1 Cor. 6:9, before this verse (1 Cor. 6:11), refers to an action, not an orientation. Paul's words have often been used harmfully to cover over the dilemma LGBTQ Christians face by inferring that Scripture requires a change in orientation. This displays a dangerous lack of compassionate awareness of the distinction between acts and orientation and of the fact that Paul refers to same-sex acts and not an unchosen orientation.

faith in Jesus Christ. Paul grounds his argument for gentile justification and inclusion in Jesus Christ by asserting *all* of humanity, Jew or gentile, is outside of the righteousness of the Law (Rom. 1–5). And by extension of Paul's universalizing of "all" in Adam (5:12), so also LGBTQ people and cisgender heterosexual people.

This question of law versus inclusion is essential to the current Christian crisis surrounding LGBTQ questions in the church and the differences of approach. Three major responses have formed around the status of LGBTQ people in today's Christian church and whether they can be truly righteous, in a way that is very similar to the first-century crisis over gentile justification in Jesus Christ. The first view sees any LGBTQ *identity* or sexual *orientation*, as well as same-sex *behavior*, as instantly incompatible with the gospel that offers universal justice, or justification, to all through repentance and faith in Jesus. The second view holds to the holiness of the Law, which teaches us what sin is and denies gay marriage (behavior) but understands that sexual orientation or LGBTQ identity should not in any way bar anyone from being made righteous with God through the faith of Jesus Christ and our faith in him. The third view sees all human sexuality and experience of gender as now being made clean despite the Law and embraces gay marriage and gender transition as holy possibilities before God.

I do not try to "solve the problem" of these three views, but point to a way forward for how we can walk together without harming or oppressing one another across theological differences.

Soteriology, Inclusion, and Holiness

Hidden in the morass of questions, I believe, is a fundamental root or strand that has been lost in the reading of Scripture because of the culture-war mentality of the late-Christian, or post-Christian, West. This strand I call "theodicy." *Theodicy* refers to the Greek words *theou* (God) and *dikaiosynē* ("righteousness" or "justice"), relating to the question of how God can be righteous despite the existence of evil and suffering.

The Epistle to the Galatians was addressed to the region of Galatia, from which migration to Rome was particularly intense. Notably, worship of the emperor was most concentrated in Rome and the region of Galatia, which connected the Eastern world to Rome.[5] Thus, Paul's magisterial epistle to the

---

5. Justin K. Hardin, *Galatians and the Imperial Cult: A Critical Analysis of the First-Century Social Context of Paul's Letter* (Siebeck, 2008), esp. 120–45.

church in Rome shares similarities with his Letter to the Galatians. Under the emperor's power and in an area of significant Jewish migration, Paul established his authority as an apostle of the gospel, of which he is unashamed because it is the power to save the (gentile) world. Paul writes to address and undo the arguments of his attackers who object to the notion that the nations can be reckoned right with God apart from Torah.

This created a theodicy crisis surrounding the status of the Law and gentile inclusion. This crisis centered on how God could be righteous or just if the immoral gentiles are included in God's people without living under the Law. The crisis around the status of Jesus Christ and his claim to messiahship reached its height in Rome, where Emperor Claudius had recently forced all Jews to leave by edict. The edict was likely spurred by infighting over the significance of Jesus Christ and the claim that God was now engrafting gentiles through this crucified Jewish Messiah. This was right at the heart of the conflict between Paul and his attackers, who were undermining his apostleship due to his inclusive stance on justification of the gentiles by faith in Jesus Christ.

Paul carefully sets up his argument to rhetorically wedge those who are denying that gentiles can be made righteous apart from the Law. They seem to be arguing, as implied by Romans 9–11, that it is not just of God to do so, for the Law is binding for the Jewish people and cannot be undermined. Paul's agitators argue that the gentiles must become Torah observant. But Paul's rebuttal takes into account sin's entry into the world and the sacral destruction of creation by people worshiping it rather than the Creator (Rom. 1).

In Galatians, Paul rehashes this argument with his own gloss, not disagreeing with the Law but disagreeing with its use by these "agitators" or "imposters" who are resisting his gospel, which teaches that all can be justified by faith: male and female, Jew and Greek, slave and free (Gal. 3:28–29). He reminds those who judge the immorality of gentiles, including same-sex activity, that they themselves do not live according to Torah.[6] For this reason, Paul writes in Romans that these agitators are blaspheming the name of God among the gentiles (2:24). By confronting their own lack of innate righteousness in the Law, Paul defends those who are gentiles or same-sex attracted from the condemnation of the Law through the theology of the Law. He teaches his enemies that while grace is not a license to sin, the Law is not a license to condemn (vv. 1–12). All have fallen short of the glory of

---

6. William Loader, "Paul on Same-Sex Relations in Romans 1," *Interpretation* 74, no. 3 (2020): 242–52; see also Loader, "Homosexuality and the Bible," in *Two Views on Homosexuality, the Bible, and the Church*, ed. Preston Sprinkle (Zondervan Academic, 2016); and E. P. Sanders, *Paul: The Apostle's Life, Letters and Thought* (SCM, 2016), esp. the appendix on "homosexuality."

God (3:1) and are in need of this deeper justification, which comes through Jesus Christ alone (v. 25).

Romans 1 is written not so much to instruct gentiles as to trap those who are condemning those outside the bounds of the Law, especially those engaging in same-sex activity and who find themselves oriented in desire to this end. The picture of this corrupted sexuality involves an echo of the Genesis account where God creates human beings in two sexually differentiated bodies, male and female. Paul turns this claim to righteousness under and through the Law and this creational ordering on those who are excluding gentiles. In Romans 2, he reminds these imposters that they do the same things as those they are condemning and are equally in need of the grace of the gospel through Jesus as are the gentiles.

Some commentators, like Douglas Campbell, have tried to argue that Paul is quoting his enemies in Romans 1 and disagrees with the Law altogether.[7] I think Paul's rhetorical strategy is far richer than that, requiring an appreciation of the fact that Paul is constructing a theodicean response to explain why justification by faith is necessary apart from the Law through (the faith / faith in) Jesus Christ. As Tom Holmén asserts:

> At the beginning of Romans 3, Paul affirms theodicy in different ways as if to ensure that his readers will understand what is at issue. He uses theodicean language known, on the one hand, exclusively from Jewish theology and, on the other, from the common theodicean way of reasoning. . . . In Paul's view, Jesus's death on the cross is *the* solution to the theodicy problem. One should, however, observe that with the contention that everybody is a malefactor Paul has radically redefined the problem. The question that was universally experienced as the gist of the theodicy problem, namely, why bad things could happen to good people and good things to bad ones, is not, according to Paul, relevant anymore! In Paul's view, all people should be considered "bad" and should therefore, in principle, only reap misfortune. Paul would thus rephrase the question: Why is God not visiting his doom on everybody. Judgement and revenge, tools of God's righteousness, lie idle. This is what now, according to strict logic, threatens God's justice and poses a theodicy problem. Paul's solution to such a problem is thus the cross of Christ, but the presupposition for accepting that solution is that one adopts the view that all people deserve punishment and suffering alone. The Pauline theodicy solution is intended to solve the Pauline theodicy problem.[8]

---

7. Douglas A. Campbell, *The Quest for Paul's Gospel: A Suggested Strategy* (T&T Clark, 2005), 233–61. Compare this with the critical response to Campbell's reading of Romans 1:12–27 in Joel Thomas Chopp, "Unearthing Paul's Ethics: Douglas Campbell on Creation, Redemption, and the Christian Moral Life," *Journal of Theological Interpretation* 11, no. 2 (2017): 259–76.

8. Tom Holmén, *Theodicy and the Cross of Christ: A New Testament Inquiry* (T&T Clark, 2019), 100.

In a similar way to Tom Holmén's argument for the cross as a theodicy, I suggest that Jesus's death on the cross as a eunuch (celibate for the sake of the kingdom) forms part of the theodicy, which allows gentiles and eunuchs (and, by extension, sexual and gender minorities broadly) to be rendered righteous in God's sight through the greater *hilastērion* (expiation), Jesus Christ (Rom. 3:25).

In the first two chapters of Romans, Paul addresses his enemies who sought to counteract his position on the inclusion of gentiles. His enemies sought to circumcise gentiles and to use the presence of sexual immorality in the gentile world as evidence against their justification through Jesus alone (1 Cor. 6:5–12; Rom. 1:18–2:20). The apostle Paul upholds the moral integrity of the Law in the Letter to the Romans when he clearly states that the Law still reveals what sin is but cannot justify sinners (Rom. 3:20; 4:15). He sharply condemns his enemies' belief that the Law was a source of righteousness in God, using their own lack of righteousness within the Law to illustrate the universal need for salvation in Jesus Christ (2–3:1).

Paul's theodicean wrestle with God's election of both gentile and Jew is also the quandary of those who engage in same-sex acts. For the diasporic Jewish context, as E. P. Sanders has argued, same-sex acts were associated with gentile immorality and out of bounds for Jews.[9] Paul recapitulates this ethic through his letters for the gentiles in Romans 1 and 1 Corinthians 6:9, but he does not deal with the constructive dilemma: If this is true, what about the status of people who are oriented toward this behavior, particularly Christians attracted to the same sex?

Porneia, or sexual immorality, was a distinctly Jewish concept for the early church and involved much more than sex outside marriage; it meant any form of sexual activity that transgressed the Torah or Jewish stipulations, which Paul sought to teach the gentiles—but with the empowerment of grace and faith, rather than with the condemnation of the Law. Notably, there were both exploitative and consensual forms of sexuality that were seen as outside of the bounds of the Law's teaching, and not only same-sex acts (Acts 15:29; Lev. 18).[10] *All* people need to be made righteous apart from the Law through Jesus Christ, partly because sin weakens our capacity for sexual righteousness (Rom. 3:21). It can be inferred, then, that people attracted to the same sex can definitely be justified by faith like everyone else.

---

9. Sanders, *Paul: The Apostle's Life, Letters and Thought*, 245–51.

10. Craig A. Williams, *Roman Homosexuality: Ideologies of Masculinity in Classical Antiquity* (Oxford: University, 1999), 245–53 (appendix on "marriage between males"), 161 (erotic vs. priapic models of [same-sex] sexual intercourse).

Christ as Eunuch: Jesus's Identification with LGBTQ People

If soteriological inclusion of gentiles outside of the Law, including LGBTQ people, does not compromise God's righteousness, we are still left with the question of what these Christians do with their desires and LGBTQ sanctification. This is where the figure of the eunuch can be constructively appealed to in order to construct a biblical analogy to the question of LGBTQ inclusion and sanctification. The prophetic words of God to eunuchs in Isaiah 56:3–6 address the problem of how God can be good to eunuchs while retaining God's holiness among his people.

Deuteronomy 23:1 states, "No one who has been emasculated by crushing or cutting may enter the assembly of the Lord." This text stipulates that eunuchs could not enter the assembly or gathered people of God in the temple and were perceived by ancient cultures as impure or unnatural or contrary to God's law.[11] The category of the eunuch became a problem during the exilic and post-exilic time, when eunuchs were disbarred from the "holy" people of God. Such a disbarring produced a deep problem of exclusion for a group of people who did not choose to be eunuchs, which is addressed in Isaiah 56:3–6 and later by Jesus in Matthew 19:12. Such a dilemma could be framed as a theodicy-based dilemma, present in post-exilic Israel.[12]

The question of God's goodness to eunuchs, and how they could be fully included in the worship of God, was clearly an issue that the author of Isaiah needed to address. N. T. Wright describes the relationship between the Sabbath and the eunuch in Isaiah 56:

> [Isaiah] chapter 54 is about the renewal of the covenant and chapter 55 rounds it off with a picture of all creation renewed. "Instead of the thorn shall come up the cypress; instead of the brier shall come up the myrtle; and it shall be to YHWH for a memorial, for an everlasting sign that shall not be cut off." . . . The prophet insists it's vital that they [eunuchs] keep the sabbaths. Why? What's going on? . . . The answer is that once new creation has been launched all sorts of things look different. . . . The picture of Eden restored in chapter 55 will be an everlasting sign that shall not be cut off. Now the new name, given to the previously excluded eunuchs, will bring that everlasting sign into fresh reality. The powerful rescuing love which sent the Servant of the Lord to die for us will now reach out to welcome in the excluded

---

11. Katherine E. Southwood, "The 'Foreigner' and the Eunuch: The Politics of Belonging in Isaiah 56:1–8," *Biblical Interpretation* 30, no. 4 (2022): 438.
12. Southwood, "The 'Foreigner' and the Eunuch," 440–45.

and outcasts, as a sign in the present time of the ultimate new creation still to come.[13]

In Isaiah 56:3–6, God addresses the problem of exclusion by promising a name better than sons and daughters to those who cannot as easily procreate, marry, or be involved in "righteous" sexual activity leading to these ends as described by Torah.

This theodicean reading of Isaiah, as Katherine Southwood and N. T. Wright suggest, provides a basis for solidarity with those we disagree with on sexual ethics. At the same time, these texts issue a more radical call to holiness that sacramentally orders the vocations of all people, particularly those like the eunuch, who are socially marginalized in a way similar to LGBTQ people. The church is called to live in this "christological" tension of radical inclusion and holiness, which abstains from immorality and yet reaches out in "incarnational" solidarity to the other with whom we disagree.

In Acts 8:36, we see the eunuch theme carried over, as part of the early church's identity, with one of the first non-Israelites adopted into the church, an Ethiopian eunuch: "As they traveled along the road, they came to some water and the eunuch said, 'Look, here is water. What can stand in the way of my being baptized?'" In such a way, the church can be conceived of as part of an eschatological Israel now realized in Jesus Christ into which sexual and gender minorities like eunuchs can now be justified and embraced and called to holiness through Jesus Christ. They are identified with Jesus Christ, who in Matthew 19:12 curiously describes celibate people as those who become "like eunuchs for the sake of the kingdom of heaven." The acceptance of eunuchs in Isaiah 56:3b–6 can be a foundation for how the New Testament approaches the topic of sexual identity and chastity and those identities that exist outside an easy or direct sexual dimorphism of male and female within marriage.

God deals with the theodicy dilemma of the eunuch by offering eunuchs a present reward for faithfulness to the Sabbath and by giving a monument to eunuchs within God's house—an eschatological reward of a name better than sons and daughters. God responds to the eunuch's incapacity to participate directly in the procreative element of marriage. Such a name is interestingly and christologically applied in the New Testament to the Ethiopian eunuch, who reads the prophetic text of Isaiah 53:8, including "Who can speak of his descendants?" (Acts 8:33), referring to the suffering servant's dying before having fathered offspring. The Isaiah 53 prophecy is linked to Jesus's sacrifice

---

13. N. T. Wright, "A Sign of New Creation Isaiah 56:4–7: A Homily at the Service for the Consecration of David Bennett to a Life of Celibacy," Pusey House, Oxford, November 11, 2023.

on the cross in the Gospels, where it could be understood that on the cross Jesus became a "[eunuch] for the sake of the kingdom of heaven."

This christological hinge not only meets the theodicy dilemma of the Law's exclusion but promises a name for those beyond the sex binary who honor the Law and its Sabbaths. Through this brief biblical theology, I suggest that eunuchs receive the rectifying name of Jesus, which is better than sons and daughters as Isaiah promised, and become a site of inclusion for people who do not easily fit within the male and female creational differentiation and ordering.

It was no mistake that the eunuch in Acts 8 was reading the Isaiah 53 suffering servant song, which outlines Jesus's own sacrificial death and speaks of this servant's lack of children ("Who can speak of his descendants?"). On the cross, Jesus incarnationally identifies with the "eunuch," who is barred from entry into the temple under the stipulations of the Torah and considered unnatural by Jewish teachers.

In Second Temple Judaism, eunuchs were commonly understood not only as unnatural but often as effeminate or questionable in terms of their gender. According to Josephus, eunuchs are "'monstrosities' which must be completely shunned on account of their unnatural effeminacy and lack regenerative capacity."[14] In a similar way, Philo of Alexandria denounces eunuchs as men who "belie their sex and are affected with effimination, who debase the currency of nature and violate it by assuming the passions and the outward form of licentious women."[15] Eunuchs, then, had a similar status to LGBTQ people in the church today. They queered, or disrupted, binary views of gender and sexuality. They also wrestled with dehumanizing prejudice and theodicy questions related to creation, procreation, and gender.

In the prophetic promise and hope of a new name, the eunuch becomes associated with Sabbaths and the coming renewal of creation and provides one of the intertestamental echoes of how celibacy comes to be given such a high status in the New Testament.[16] This can be extended to LGBTQ people. Their bodily difference and incapacity to easily access the created good of marriage generates a theodicy dilemma that God addresses by providing a better name in the future through Jesus Christ. Such a name is different, odd, or queer to heterosexual people who do not, in most cases, face or wrestle

---

14. F. Scott Spencer, "The Ethiopian Eunuch and His Bible: A Social-Science Analysis," *Biblical Theology Bulletin* 22, no. 4 (1992): 157; see also Josephus, *Antiquities of the Jews* 4.290–91.

15. Philo, *Special Laws* 1.324–25, trans. F. H. Colson, Loeb Classical Library 320 (Harvard University Press, 1937). See also Philo, *Special Laws* 3.37–42; cf. Philo, *On the Contemplative Life* 57–63 ("disease of effeminacy").

16. Wright, "Sign of New Creation."

with the questions of procreation or their moral or legal status, as they can more easily participate in and access the created ordering of marriage. The eunuch receives the name of Jesus Christ, a nonprocreative form of generation, a name better than sons and daughters.

Through the lens of the eunuch, we are given new insight that can be applied to how marriage, gender, embodiment, and same-sex desire interrelate as a theodicy question. This question can be met by the grace and free justification given in Christ. Like the eunuch, LGBTQ people can be made right with God "apart from the Law" and are given a name better than what they lacked (marriage and procreation). Their obedience to the Law and the temple system is no longer required in Christ for salvation. The good news is that the salvation of Christ meets us in the difficulty of being included and so that we might worshipfully offer up our bodies as living sacrifices.

The greater inner holiness the Law points to is a grace-wrought fruit of sanctification in Christ, not extrinsic or "Pelagian" obedience. The theodicean differentiation of embodied questions like the eunuch, or LGBTQ experience, means we are called to inhabit an intensely difficult tension. The tension involves living into the radical inclusion of the gospel in which we humbly recognize that we all fall short of the glory of God and are outside of the Law's righteousness. Justification provides a stable ground for a Christlike solidarity with those we disagree with ethically on gay marriage, as well as forming a radical holiness in us where we are called to flee and forsake *porneia*, or sexual immorality, described by the Law in holiness of fellowship.

Returning to Grace and Law

Living in the difficult tension of inclusion and holiness is where Jesus formed his own ministry and approach to similar dilemmas in his time. Seeing through the lens of the Pauline dialectic of grace and law and the apocalyptic promise of inclusion of eunuchs in Isaiah 56 helps us to identify the theodicy of celibate asceticism, same-sex desire, and queerness. Questions of sin and sexual immorality are not removed but remain for all Christians. Since LGTBQ realities are first linked to our bodies and an unchosen orientation of desire, they harken back to the created goodness of our humanity and yet are part of the larger cosmic drama of the fall.

The tension between the beauty and goodness of creation and the Creator's subjection of creation to the fall's drastic effects of decay and frustration (Rom. 8:27) is another layer of the theodicean element with which LGBTQ people wrestle. The Law teaches us what sin is, and yet we are confronted with the fact that sexual orientation, gender dysphoria, and intersex embodiments are not chosen identities but unchosen differences that God has allowed in his mysterious purposes.

In 1 Corinthians 15, Paul discusses how there are different bodies with different glories (vv. 35–49), and perhaps the prophetic future of enquiry into these questions is to search out that glory without losing or erasing the creational nature of the moral order and sexual difference. The resurrection can, in this sense, meet the theodicean dilemma of being LGBTQ without fully answering the dilemma faced by each person as they wrestle with God to find the gift and carry the difficulty of why God has allowed them to have a particular difference of embodiment.

I am convinced that the ethics of how one lives out one's embodiment faithfully before God is absolutely essential. I do not proffer theodicy as a way to lessen the moral or ethical calling of obedience in the gospel to chastity, but perhaps to open a space of generosity to siblings in Christ who may be, understandably but mistakenly, different as they wrestle with the theological mystery of human sexuality and gender and its pastoral implications. Paul does not undermine the Law, given that it teaches us what sin is, and yet the way that God meets the theodicean dilemma of the eunuch in Isaiah 56 gives us a paradigm from which we might adjudicate and approach the question of sexual orientation and gender dysphoria, particularly in relation to how the eunuch dilemma is met in the Old and New Testaments.

We are invited to wrestle at the deeper point of mystery that lies at the center of our human sexuality and gender, just as the Jewish world had to wrestle with the problem of eunuchs, gentiles, and the Law. At this point we can proffer a grace-filled generosity to those who disagree with our ethical convictions and, in turn, receive such generosity back. We do not lump LGBTQ questions in the same category as sins, which do not have this theodicean dilemma at their heart. Instead, we recognize that we are standing on sacred territory, which involves a thicker texture. Such mysterious territory requires pastoral grace toward those with whom we disagree and yet prophetic witness to them of our own convictions. We must live in the tension of the Jewish temple halakhic concern for holiness, being unstained from the world and sin, yet live in the call to radical incarnational solidarity with those within these theodicy dilemmas.

We are permitted a solidarity with those with whom we disagree, even if we may wrestle with how, if at all, fellowship is possible. For Paul, to undermine the full inclusion of gentiles *and* to undermine the righteousness of the Law and its teaching on sexuality and gender were both causes to withdraw fellowship (Acts 15; 1 Cor. 6:8–11; Rom. 2:1–10). And yet Paul also circumcised

Timothy and maintained relationship with Peter when, it seemed, for a moment they may have disagreed on how this new righteousness should be ethically worked out in the church (Acts 16:1–5; Gal. 2:11–17).

What these tensions in Paul's experience invite us into is a life of radical inclusion and incarnational solidarity with all human beings, particularly LGBTQ people who have to face this intense difficulty of wrestling with the Law, which describes sin, and discerning where the bounds lie, as they pursue radical holiness and the imperative to flee from sexuality immorality. Pivotal to this solidarity is the need to compassionately recognize LGBTQ people's particular theodicean dilemma, which the heterosexual church does not experience. Equating the LGBTQ wrestle with sexual immorality tout court has brought incalculable damage to those who would discover the greater righteousness of grace in Jesus Christ. If we live obediently to the call of radical holiness and radical inclusion, which we find engendered in the life of Jesus Christ, we can proceed in confidence that we are living in faithfulness to the New Testament teaching on human sexuality and gender.

Overall, I hope this chapter has shown how those occupying various positions might be invited into this gospel-based tension between the radical holiness of the early Christians and the radical inclusion of Jesus and Paul, who embraced the world with love and truth and, above all, grace through the Spirit's manifold power and wisdom, which can reach and embrace even those we are tempted to dismiss.

Conclusion

I hope I have shown a way, informed by my reading of Scripture, for readers to be generous toward those with whom they disagree through a recognition of the theodicy dilemma faced by LGBTQ people, while maintaining their conviction regarding the ethics of human sexuality and gender. A removal of the creation-based ordering of sexual difference risks undoing the difference and difficulty with which LGBTQ people wrestle, while a recapitulation of the Law risks oppressively covering this difference over by reconstructing a moral law, or law of Adam and Eve—the letter of the law, which kills (2 Cor. 3:6). There is much to learn from LGBTQ Christians who straddle the irreconcilable ethics on this question from both Side A and Side B convictions, and beyond. Only through wrestling with Scripture, tradition, and experience—which are often complex and, at times, baffling—can we humbly approach those with whom we disagree to build friendships and solidarity without compromising our deeply held convictions.

The theodicean lens I have outlined provides a rationale for practicing this solidarity with those from whom we might ethically differ. Christ followers are called to live in the fellowship of light that keeps itself unstained from the world and yet practice this incarnational solidarity with the world. Living faithfully in this tension, I hope, can constitute a profound step toward dismantling the culture war through a recentering on both friendship and a Jesus-shaped holiness. Equally, the pathway I have described calls us to recognize the mystery of the gospel, which does not provide easy answers but powerful revelation to assist us as we seek to love God and neighbor as ourselves in the way of Jesus.

I hope this chapter may open a pathway for readers to be generous toward those with opposing views, while upholding a moral theology of the created order and the original goods of sexual difference and marriage. Such an affirmation must privilege the greater righteousness and beauty of a Christ-shaped love, which reaches across the current divides around LGBTQ inclusion in the church. Such an incorporation of theodicy-based elements of the gospel, which have often been harmfully eschewed, can help us reapproach the current crisis. It will lead us not only to obey the highest part of Jesus's law and teaching, which is to love God, neighbor, and our enemies as ourselves, as well as those who are fundamentally different from us, but also to call the world to a more beautiful love, which Christ followers are called to embody through this deeper incarnational holiness, which can attract the world to Jesus's radically inclusive offer of salvation to all.

4

The Good News of Romans 1

J. R. Daniel Kirk

To the attentive eye, Romans 1 provides a richly textured introduction to Paul's letter. Debates about same-sex relations have often kept readers too narrowly focused on a few contentious verses, causing us to miss how the chapter serves as an entryway to all that comes after. To articulate the good news of Romans 1—and, indeed, how it is good news for all who follow Jesus—we will need to explore the manifold ways that this chapter's themes are echoed across the letter. Here are a few examples:

- Paul states that the gospel was promised in the Scriptures (Rom. 1:2)—what Christians today might refer to as the "Old Testament"—and goes on to include over fifty biblical citations and allusions in this letter, approximately half of all such scriptural references found in the entire thirteen-letter Pauline corpus.
- He describes Jesus's descent "according to the flesh" and his enthronement "according to the Spirit" (1:3–4),[1] which previews the flesh-Spirit dichotomy that shoots through chapters 6–8.

1. Biblical translations in this chapter are my own unless otherwise noted.

- The resurrection of Jesus (1:4) becomes a theme in its own right, appearing in nearly every section of the letter, and often at critical junctures.[2]
- Paul's own mission to the gentiles, and to the Romans as part of that designation, not only frames concerns for Jew and gentile inclusion (1–4; 9–11; 14–15) but also delineates gentiles as the audience of the letter—a reminder that Paul makes at several points.[3]
- The great theme of faith (or faithfulness: "the obedience of faith") is broached as it marks the manner of gentile inclusion (1:5).

And all of this is before we arrive at what is often thought of as the thesis statement of the letter: Paul's proclamation that he is not ashamed of the gospel, due to its salvific power that goes to both Jews and Greeks, a gospel that puts on display God's righteousness from faith to faith (Rom. 1:16–17).[4] Examples of the reach of Romans 1 could be multiplied. But I trust that what has been laid out above is sufficient to make the case that any attempt to do justice to a passage in the chapter must account for its place in the larger flow of the letter's argument.

This essay builds on these observations as it looks to the latter half of Romans 1. Starting with verse 18, Paul appears to be using language that suggests the disordering of creation as he articulates a stereotyped condemnation of gentile rejection of God.[5] In chapter 2, Paul turns to a somewhat different depiction of Jewish disobedience in order to draw a global portrait of humanity's need for salvation. In the light of anti-creation, Paul develops new-creation theology as God's response to this unraveling of the created order.

New creation is a phrase that Paul uses twice (2 Cor. 5:17; Gal. 6:15) when describing our reality as people who belong to Christ. Paul understands Jesus as the one who makes right the work of Adam (Rom. 5; 1 Cor. 15), putting to death the old humanity so that a new humanity might emerge through his

---

2. Cf. J. R. Daniel Kirk, *Unlocking Romans: Resurrection and the Justification of God* (Eerdmans, 2008).

3. A. Andrew Das, "The Gentile-Encoded Audience of Romans: The Church outside the Synagogue," in *Reading Paul's Letter to the Romans*, RBS 73, ed. J. L. Sumney (Society of Biblical Literature, 2012), 29–46.

4. The language of these verses reverberates through Paul's proclamation of God's faith (Rom. 3:1–5), the display of God's righteousness through Christ's faithfulness in going to the cross (3:21–26), the faith of Abraham (4), the discussion of saving faith (5:1–11), Christ as second Adam figure (5:16–21), the contrast between the gospel proclamation and Mosaic law (10), and holding fellowship across lines of theological difference (14:17, 22–23).

5. Stanley K. Stowers, *A Rereading of Romans: Justice, Jews, and Gentiles* (Yale, 1994), 83–125.

resurrection (Rom. 6). Because new creation has begun with Jesus's resurrection, those who are in Christ also experience a new family. New creation also means there is hope for the nonhuman universe to be renewed along with the full restoration of humanity (Rom. 8).

As we will see, a critical piece of this restored world is humanity's being rightly subservient to God and therefore free from the enslaving powers of sin and death (Rom. 6–8). In short, new creation, for Paul, reaches from the dirt below to heaven above, wrapping up everything in between. Such a vision of new creation is what we express our hope for in these lines from the great hymn "Joy to the World":

> No more let sins and sorrows grow,
> Nor thorns infest the ground;
> He comes to make his blessings flow
> Far as the curse is found.[6]

Importantly, this new creation is not a reinstatement of Genesis 1 and its vision of humanity—namely, male and female as the image of God, authority given to rule, and, especially, the purpose and power to reproduce. Rather, as we will see throughout this essay, the gospel of Paul (and Jesus!) reframes every facet of this primal vision. New creation means that the image of God and the task of rule are reconstituted around Christ. Christ is not simply a restored Adam; by entering resurrection life through the Spirit, he becomes a completely new type of Adam. Being part of this new humanity, even bearing the divine image, is no longer a matter of physical progeny but, instead, the work of the Spirit.

"For": The Solution to God's Wrath Revealed

Readers often experience a significant shift between Romans 1:16–17, where Paul summarizes the gospel as the "revelation" of God's righteousness, and Romans 1:18–32, where Paul elaborates on the "revelation" of God's wrath on the gentiles. The Nestle-Aland Greek New Testament has a blank line between verses 17 and 18 as if to underscore that a completely new line of thought is starting to be traced. But Paul connects these two verses in the same way he had connected verses 16 and 17, which is the same way he had connected verses 15 and 16, with the Greek conjunction *gar*, meaning

---

6. Isaac Watts, "Joy to the World," Hymnary.org, accessed January 7, 2025, https://hymnary.org/text/joy_to_the_world_the_lord_is_come.

"for."[7] Thus, while Romans 1:18–32 certainly shifts focus from God's acts of salvation to a stylized narrative of human decline, the reader of Romans must take seriously that these latter verses somehow form the ground or reason for what preceded.

There are (at least) two ways to interpret this. One is a minimal view, which simply says that the reason ("for") God displays saving power in the Christ event is that humanity had gone badly astray. This is no doubt true, as far as it goes. But it is also possible to go further. Paul here sets one "revelation" on top of another. The ongoing "revelation" (*apokalyptetai*) of God's wrath in Romans 1:18–32 (esp. v. 18) is the reason for the "revelation" (*apokalyptetai*) of God's righteousness in 1:17. As we turn our eyes toward the human failures enumerated in the latter half of the chapter, we should be having our sight sharpened to see the good news of God's righteousness revealed, which is unpacked as the Letter to the Romans unfolds.

Paul invites us to read gentile decline not only as the backdrop but even more as the reason for the revelation of God's righteousness, the good news with which he has been entrusted. In other words, God's righteousness revealed (Rom. 1:16–17) is calculated to address and overcome the problem—namely, the holistic disordering of creation, wherein humanity cedes its role as the image-bearing rulers of the earth, with the potential and obligation to recognize and worship the Creator (1:18–32). In the larger context of Romans, the gentile decline lays the groundwork for salvation—a new creation with a new humanity. The image of God is renewed in people who are faithfully serving God together and extending God's reign as humanity submits to the lordship of Jesus and the ongoing march of the Spirit.

This gospel that reveals God's righteousness (Rom. 1:16–17) is the story of new creation—of which the first creation is but a pale shadow.

How Romans 1 Is Often Read

In debates on sexuality, Romans 1 is often read as a passage centering on God's wrath. The problem that Paul reports in Romans 1:18–32 is that gentiles are turning the created order on its head. They are ignoring the Creator God and the ways that this God has been made known through the created world (Rom. 1:19–21). Their failure manifests in not worshiping God as they should

---

7. For a wide-ranging assessment of how Paul uses the conjunction *gar* here and elsewhere, see Sarah H. Casson, *Textual Signposts in the Argument of Romans: A Relevance-Theory Approach*, ECL 25 (Society of Biblical Literature, 2019), 207–45.

(vv. 21, 25). Instead, they worship images of creatures (v. 23). In describing idolatry, Paul participates in the Jewish tradition of evoking the creation narrative with its depiction of images, humans, and various animals (v. 23; see also Deut. 4:15–20). Ironically, humans, who are themselves the image and likeness of God (Gen. 1:26–28), fall prey to the temptation to create images in their own likeness (Rom. 1:23; Deut. 4:16).

In their errant attempt to play God, humans lose their connection with the true divinity. Three times in his depiction of humanity, who have rejected the worship of God, Paul states that God "handed them over" (Rom. 1:24, 26, 28). Thus, humans who were created in God's image and likeness for the purpose of ruling the world on God's behalf (Gen. 1:26) cede that rule and find themselves under the thrall of enslaving, sinful powers.[8] Romans 1 then culminates with a litany of sins practiced by those enslaved to depraved minds (vv. 28–32). Verse 28 is the third time that Paul says the people were "handed over" by God, underscoring through the list of vices that follows that the primal human purpose of exercising dominion over the earth has been stripped and that rule has been replaced with servitude.

Paul conveys the truth of creation undone. But the problem of reading Romans 1 as merely God's wrath on the gentiles is that we miss Paul's primary point. Recall that Paul has already told us that the revelation of God's salvation in Christ is couched specifically to answer the problems depicted here. We cannot just start with the problem and project into the future; instead, we must allow Romans itself to show us how best to understand not only what went wrong but also what God intends to do about it. In other words, we must start with God's solution to the unraveling of creation.

Starting with the Solution: Reading "Backwards"

For the better part of the past fifty years, New Testament scholars across the ideological spectrum, from the more conservative Herman Ridderbos to the mainline/secular E. P. Sanders, have recognized that Paul reasons

---

8. When reading these passages, modern readers should be aware that today's consensual coupling of same-sex partners is not typically the sort of same-sex relationship that the ancients either approved or critiqued. In ancient Greece and Rome, it was generally understood that an acceptable same-sex sexual encounter was one in which a person with higher standing and greater power, such as a master, was the active (penetrating) partner in a coupling with someone of lesser standing, such as a slave. These are also the relationships that Jewish readers would critique. See Craig Williams, *Roman Homosexuality*, 2nd ed. (Oxford University Press, 2010).

"backwards."⁹ That is to say, his theology develops from the solution that God has provided in Jesus's death and resurrection to the problem that this solution resolves. Others, such as Richard Hays, have built on this to demonstrate that Paul's reading of Scripture itself works backwards—Paul (and, indeed, the rest of the New Testament authors!) provides interpretations of Scripture that are possible or credible only after someone already believes that the crucified Messiah is the resurrected Lord over all.¹⁰ Christ comes first; then, after that, comes understanding why Christ was necessary.

This means that for our study of new creation, as with everything else, to know what we are to believe, what we are to do, or even what Scripture means, we must begin with the answers given in the death and resurrection of Jesus and the community that formed around him in the first century.¹¹ Such an approach to Scripture and ethics, a radically Christ-centered approach to interpretation, has revolutionary implications for discovering the "good news" of Romans 1. When attempting to articulate how the revelation of God's righteousness (Rom.1:16–17) answers the revelation of God's wrath (Rom. 1:18–32), we have to start with Christ. To know God's "answer" to the "problem" Romans 1 lays out, we must look to the full-orbed picture of salvation that Romans goes on to depict.

God Handed Over

The good news is the reversal of the story of primal failure in ways that are often unpredictable and that can be known in truth only through what God has actually done in Christ. The first unexpected reality is God's pivotal role in the gentiles' predicament. With a threefold repetition of "God handed them over" (*paredōken autous ho theos*, Rom. 1:24, 26, 28), we discover how gentile humanity becomes enslaved to the depraved minds and passions that marked lives of disordered service.¹²

---

9. Herman Ridderbos, *Paul: An Outline of His Theology*, trans. J. R. de Witt (Eerdmans, 1975); E. P. Sanders, *Paul and Palestinian Judaism: A Comparison of Patterns of Religion* (Fortress, 1977).

10. Richard B. Hays, *The Conversion of the Imagination: Paul as Interpreter of Israel's Scripture* (Eerdmans, 2005).

11. See Richard B. Hays, *Moral Vision of the New Testament: Community, Cross, New Creation; A Contemporary Introduction to New Testament Ethics* (HarperOne, 1996).

12. Cf. Beverly Roberts Gaventa, "God Handed Them Over: Reading Romans 1:18–32 Apocalyptically," *Australian Biblical Review* 53 (2005): 42–53. Similarly, Paul describes the predicament of both Jews and gentiles in Romans 11 by saying that God "bound everyone over to disobedience" (v. 32).

But equally unexpected is the way the gentiles' degradation is mirrored by the Christ event, on which the history of humanity pivots. Launching into the climactic exultation that culminates Romans 8, Paul describes the God who is "for us" as the one who did not spare his own son but "handed him over [*paredōken auton*] for us all" (8:32). Here is a saving reversal in the gospel, the "revelation of God's righteousness" that offsets the act of God in the "revelation of God's wrath." In Paul's rendition of the good news, God sent Jesus and gave him as a sin offering (8:3). Using the same language previously deployed to refer to the gentiles' predicament, we discover, God *handed over Jesus* to be subject to the powers of sin and death.

If the revelation of God's wrath is found in God's handing over humanity to enslaving powers of disordered hearts and minds, the revelation of God's righteousness is found in God's handing over Jesus so that all might be free of such tyrannical lords. And perhaps we can infer from this a salvific intention even in the primordial "handing over" of gentiles.

Attend carefully, and we discover a narrative texture to Paul's theology. The movements of God, the movements of the Spirit, track with the story of Christ from death to resurrection. In a paradoxical way, the life of rebellious, gentile humanity participates in the story of salvation that Jesus establishes. The gentiles are first "handed over" and then given new life against all hope, against all deserving. Jesus himself is "handed over," which Paul sometimes depicts as Jesus's own great act of faith (Rom. 1:17; 3:22), trusting against all hope that God would give him, too, new life. We even see this in Paul's vision for unbelieving Israel. His hope is that those who have, for the time, been rejected (11:15), like the gentiles and even Jesus before them, will be accepted and thus receive "life from the dead" (11:15).

This movement from handing over, rejection, and death to freedom, acceptance, and life from the dead is itself the good news that shines through every dark and apparently hopeless situation on earth. God is none other than the one "who gives life to the dead" (Rom. 4:17). It was Jesus himself who fulfilled the promise of Habakkuk 2:4: "The righteous one will live from faith." This is the good news, the story of salvation that the rest of humanity can hope for as well.

This, then, brings us full circle to the "good news" that so many readers rightly see articulated in Romans 1:16–17, immediately before the bad news of gentile disobedience. That good news is God's power: the power to free humanity from its bondage to sin and death, the power to raise Jesus from the dead. It is good news for Jew and gentile alike. God is faithful to Israel, God fulfills what was previously promised in the Scriptures, and God sees to it that the death of which the gentiles are worthy (1:32) is fulfilled in Christ even as they are freed from their enslavement to sin and death. That good news promises life to all who are faithful, even as Christ's own faithfulness in going to the cross is met with resurrection life by the power of God's spirit: "The righteous one will live from faith" (1:17; cf. Hab. 2:4).

Gentiles Included in the People of God

To ask what God might do in light of such a negative depiction of humanity as we find in the latter half of Romans 1 is to ask what might be the revelation of God's righteousness (1:16) that comes about because (gentile) humanity has gone astray in precisely this way. The answer comes from what God has done in Christ. So we search Romans. In doing so, we discover that gentiles' worshiping God is at the heart of the gospel story (15:6–9). As the book of Acts shows in some detail, and as we can see mirrored in Galatians, the welcoming of non-Jews—without their having to keep Torah—was a tremendous surprise to the early church. In retrospect, however, Paul can see that it is not only necessary but even a fulfillment of Israel's Scriptures (15:9–12). The good news of Romans 1 is a revelation of God's righteousness that includes a new family of Jews and gentiles worshiping God together (15:8).

Paul himself acknowledges that the way in which the gentiles are included in the people of God is unexpected. In talking about gentile sexual practices, he describes something that he calls "contrary to nature" (*para physin*, Rom. 1:26). What a shock it is, then, to find him claiming in Romans 11 that gentiles are, as a whole, grafted "contrary to nature" (*para physin*, 11:24) into the olive tree that is the family of God. Being part of the new-creation people of God does not demand a universal return to first creation, "natural" practice, or Jewish identity (which is to say, faithfulness to the Law). This is good news for gentile humanity. Gentiles do not have to embody Jewish identity and practices (e.g., Sabbath keeping, food laws, and circumcision) in order to be part of God's family.

Inclusion of the gentiles among those who are saved by Israel's Messiah is in Romans, as in all of Paul's letters, the specific context in which "justification by faith" comes to the fore.[13] After showing that God's righteousness is put on vivid display in Christ's faithfulness in going to the cross (3:21–26), Paul will turn to Abraham as a forerunner of trust in God (4:1–25). In both instances, we see Jesus and Abraham both entrusted themselves to God. They had faith.

---

13. Krister Stendahl, *Paul among Jews and Gentiles and Other Essays* (Fortress, 1976), 1–77, esp. 23–40.

In his urgency to demonstrate that full participation in the family of God is not by means of physical descent, Paul goes to great lengths to distance God's blessings, even for Jews, from a physical line. Richard B. Hays has convincingly argued that Romans 4:1 asks a rhetorical question to which the answer, given throughout the chapter, is no: "What shall we say then? Is Abraham found to be our forefather according to the flesh?"[14] No, indeed—instead, he is forefather by faith. Removing physical descent (and, hence, procreation) from the equation both allows the Spirit to take center stage in propagating the people of God and enables full and equal participation of Jews and gentiles in the family of God.

This undermines every attempt in the history of the church to tie God's special blessing to procreation. This is good news for a childless young couple, single person, or someone who marries after menopause. For Paul, Genesis 1:26–28 is, in fact, no longer the core depiction of human relationships. This is why he says in Galatians 3:28 that in Christ there is no longer "male and female," in clear echo of Genesis 1:28. New creation is not a return to first creation. In the new creation (i.e., in Christ), family is determined by sharing in Jesus's sonship such that all of us are siblings with God as Father. We are one another's family. And we are heirs together of the new creation that God has as the inheritance for all God's children. This is the good news, taking root in the ground of Romans 1, that the church has too little explored or embodied.

Paul's rendering of the Abraham narrative has been received, read, and accepted in Christian churches for nearly two thousand years. But familiarity has the power to blind us to the extraordinary interpretive moves Paul makes to include gentiles in the Abrahamic promise. Here is a classic case of Paul "reading backwards," providing an interpretation that is only compelling after a person shares the conviction that Jesus is the fulfillment of the promise to Abraham. To begin with, Paul makes much of the timing of Abraham's vindication: he was justified (Gen. 15:6) before he was circumcised (Gen. 17:23).

This Paul interprets as an indication that Abraham can be father of all who trust God without being circumcised (Rom. 4:9–11). An alternate, perhaps more obvious, reading is that when God tells Abraham in Genesis 17 that any uncircumcised male will be cut off from among the people as a covenant-breaker, this cements circumcision as an unvarying requirement. But for Christian readers, the revelation of God's righteousness commends Paul's preferred reading—circumcision is not required to be a child of Abraham.

---

14. Richard B. Hays, "'Have We Found Abraham to Be Our Forefather according to the Flesh?' A Reconsideration of Rom 4:1," *NovT* 27 (1985): 76–98.

No less striking is Paul's interpretation of Abraham's faith such that it matches perfectly with the movement from death to resurrection, which is, itself, the shape of Paul's gospel. After describing God as the one "who gives life to the dead" in Romans 4:17, he goes on to describe Abraham's receiving the promise of a seed and then considering his own body, which had already died ([*ēdē*] *nenekrōmenon*), and the deadness (*nekrōsin*) of Sarah's womb (4:19). In other words, Abraham's faith is faith in the resurrecting God.[15] We believe as Abraham believed when we believe in the God who handed over Jesus and raised him again (4:24–25). The story of salvation has reached back and reshaped the story of Abraham and Sarah.

Understanding the good news of Romans 1 entails recognizing that God has wrapped gentiles into the saving work of Christ. This is one of Paul's most fundamental convictions. Acts, Romans, 2 Corinthians, Galatians, and Philippians show us that this conviction and its implications were hotly contested. This is the good news we see coming to light in Romans 4: the Scriptures in which God has prepromised the gospel (1:2), when rightly read, will testify to the surprising inclusion of those whom God has, in fact, saved—even in passages that seem most obviously designed to keep them out. The story of gentile decline (1:18–32) is undone by including gentiles in the heretofore Jewish promises of Abraham.

Of course, the salvation God provides is not just for gentiles. In Romans 2:1–3:20, Paul argues that Jews, too, have been faithless to God and are therefore in need of the saving work of Christ. This means that all of humanity stands in need of the salvation God has provided—God's righteous act in Christ (1:16–17; 3:21–24). The solution that includes both Jews and gentiles, without the gentiles having to become Jewish, is a new humanity that takes its place as ruler of a new creation.

"Sonship": God's Reigning Children

The language of "image of God" means, in part, being a child of God (see Gen. 5:1–3: Adam is to God as Seth is to Adam). In Romans, Jesus is the child of God who also bears the image of God (1:4, 8:29). Being part of God's family has been transformed from being a physical descendant of Adam or Abraham to being a recipient of the Spirit of adoption who unites us to Jesus's sonship through being joined to his death and resurrection (8:14–17).

---

15. Cf. Kirk, *Unlocking Romans*, 72–74.

The first intimation that Romans provides of adoption is 1:4, where we read that Christ was "appointed son of God with power according to the Spirit of holiness, by the resurrection from the dead." By calling Jesus "son of God," Paul is not invoking the later Christian meaning of the Second Person of the Trinity; he is drawing on older biblical precedents in which humanity, or its special representatives, are God's sons and daughters. Genesis 1:26–28 describes human creation as in the "image" and "likeness" of God, which is to say God's children, with the task of ruling the world on God's behalf.

Humanity is God's progeny, God's sons and daughters on the earth; when we look at humans, we come as close as we are able to seeing the face of God. Moreover, this relationship comes with the task of rule. In one important strand of Israel's royal theology, Israel's kings are invested with both sonship and rule upon their enthronement ("You are my son—today I have begotten you"; Ps. 2:7). Paul places Jesus into this nexus of sonship, royalty, and rule. The resurrection is his enthronement, the restoration of the humanity to its place of ruling the created order on God's behalf (Gen. 1:26–28)—a fitting answer to the problem of people serving creatures as though they held the power of the Creator (Rom. 1:23, 25).

Once being a child of God in the image of God and the task of rule are reconstituted around Christ, there is no longer a command or blessing of physical progeny for the purpose of continuing these roles. The good news that grows in the ground of Romans 1 is that, as the Spirit cries out from each of us, "*Abba*, Father" (Rom. 8:15), joining our cry to Jesus's own prayer (Mark 14:36), the word of God spoken over Jesus at his baptism echoes to us as well: "You are my beloved child" (Mark 1:11).

That Paul means to depict Christ as the firstborn son of a new humanity becomes clearer in Romans 5:12–21, where he extensively contrasts Christ with Adam.[16] Adam represents all humanity in sin, death, and condemnation. Christ represents humanity in obedience, grace, and vindication before God. The hinge on which the fate of humanity turns is "one righteous act": Jesus's faithfulness in obedience to the point of death (v. 18). Importantly, those who receive the benefits of Christ's work will "reign in life" (v. 17). The primal human calling to rule the world, the rule into which Christ himself is ushered at his resurrection, is also the destiny of humanity that is in Christ.

In the Adam-Christ parallel we see that Christ's death and resurrection overcome the problem of sin and death as powers that rule over humanity ("sin reigned in death," v. 21) no less than the problem of sin as guilt

---

16. Cf. James D. G. Dunn, "Adam and Christ," in *Reading Paul's Letter to the Romans*, RBS 73, ed. J. L. Sumney (Society of Biblical Literature, 2012), 125–38.

("condemnation," v. 18). In Romans 6, Paul tackles the problem of enslavement to sin head-on. Christ as the embodiment of old humanity is crucified to sever the rule of sin (v. 6). Once again, we see that Christ delivers from both sin's guilt and its power. This is carried forward in chapter 8, as we read in 8:1–4 of the death of Jesus as a sin offering that removes condemnation (the consequence of guilt) from those who are in Christ, even as they are set free from the law governing sin and death (liberated from sin's power).

Delivery from sin and death as guilt and power takes place under the rubric of Jesus as God's "son." In conjunction with the argument that Jesus offsets the work of Adam, the language of sonship underscores that Jesus embodies the primal role of image-bearing son of God, the one who is empowered to rule the world on God's behalf. The anti-creation story of humanity being handed over to depraved minds and degrading passions (Rom. 1:24, 26, 28) is undone by the new Adam, the first human of the new creation. How, then, is this story of new humanity good news for us?

God's Resurrected Children

The gospel of the resurrected Christ in Romans 1:4 prepares the reader for what will ultimately be the antidote to humanity's decline: the Spirit.[17] As Jesus enters his new-resurrection life by the power of the Spirit, so too are those in Christ marked by the Spirit as the animating power in their lives. In Romans 8, resurrection life joins with the pairing of sonship, new humanity, and freedom under the reign of Christ, introducing a cosmic sweep that, all told, is God's answer to all humanity's sin in Adam. Even as Jesus's resurrection inducts him into a new life of sonship by the Spirit (1:4), so too those who receive the Spirit are God's children, joined to the turning of the ages in Christ's death and resurrection (8:14–17).

Paul himself leaves us a verbal linkage, connecting Jesus's resurrection sonship in Romans 1:4 to those (both male and female) whose "sonship" is derivative of Christ's own. The gender-specific language of "sonship" helps underscore that people of any gender are included in the rights, privileges, inheritance, and even rule that is conferred upon the firstborn son in the patriarchal power structure that Paul envisions.

Romans 8:29's deployment in various theological schemas has often prevented important aspects of the verse from coming to light. There we read,

---

17. Cf. L. Ann Jervis, "The Spirit Brings Christ's Life to Life," in *Reading Paul's Letter to the Romans*, RBS 73, ed. J. L. Sumney (Society of Biblical Literature, 2012), 139–56.

"Those God foreknew God appointed beforehand (*proōrisen*) to be made into the form of the image of God's son (*eikonos tou huiou autou*) so that he might be the firstborn (*prōtotokon*) among many siblings." The verbal connections between Romans 1:4 and 8:29 are rooted in the word that is often translated "predestined" (*proōrisen*). This is the joining of the *pro-* prefix to the verb *horizō*, meaning "to appoint" or "set aside"; *horizō*, in turn, is the verb that Paul deploys in 1:4 when speaking of Christ being appointed (*horisthentos*) son of God.

The sonship to which God appoints Jesus at his resurrection is the same sonship to which God has pre-appointed those who are joined to Christ by the Spirit. Romans 8:29 itself, as well as the larger context, point to this "sonship" as the re-creation of humanity. New humanity bears the image of the resurrected Christ (Rom. 8:29). Moreover, Romans 8:19–23 paints a picture of the created order having its hopes tied to the resurrection of those in Christ: creation waits with anxious longing for the revelation of God's children, "our bodily redemption" (esp. vv. 21, 23). New humanity finds its consummation at the general resurrection of the dead, a moment that will spell new life for the entire created order.

The good news is not simply about humanity's relationship to God (overcoming the guilt and power of sin), or our relationships with one another (especially the rift between Jews and gentiles); it is also about restoring the world in which we live and the fruitfulness of our relationship to it. The wrath of God revealed upon and through a disordered creation in Romans 1:18–32 is met with the cosmic good news of new creation with a new humanity at its head.

We Are Family

Having seen that the image of God to which humanity aspires is now found in the resurrected Christ, seeing further that this humanity is marked by the same filial relationship to God that was humanity's at the time of creation in Genesis 1, and also having seen that the primordial task of rule has been transformed as Christ is Lord and those who receive his gift of life will reign in resurrection life through him (Rom. 5:17), what are good-news implications?

For Paul, no less than Jesus (e.g., Mark 3:31–35), family is redefined around God the father and the siblings who identify with the firstborn son, Jesus. For Paul, this is a key component to universalizing the gospel, allowing it to transcend the boundaries marked by physical descent from Abraham. As noted above, these rhetorical and theological moves allow us to leave aside concerns about procreative bloodlines. Reproduction "according to the flesh" is taken out of the equation as Romans systematically locates all three of the Genesis 1 blessings (rule, image-bearing filial relation to God, and reproduction) in the work of the Spirit.

The blessing of rule is given through the Spirit by the resurrection of Christ, first, and then by raising other people with and in Christ (Rom. 1:4; 5:17). The blessing of bearing God's image is no longer passed by physical propagation as it was from God to Adam to Seth (Gen. 5:1–3); instead, it is given by the Spirit joining people to the crucified and risen Christ (Rom. 8:14–17, 29). Image of God has been relocated from physical descent to the spiritual family that comprises the followers of Jesus or those who are in Christ.

This reconfiguration of the identity of God's family is reflected in the final exhortations of the letter body of Romans (14:1–15:12). As this section concludes, it navigates the wonder of gentile inclusion in the people of God, while insisting on the ongoing inclusion of Jews.[18] God had made good on the promise of a savior to Israel (15:8), and gentile inclusion is an act of mercy (15:9). The decline of gentile civilization is reversed not only through personal transformation and incorporation into the family of God, generally speaking, but also through inclusion within the people of God on earth. Those who had previously failed to glorify God or give thanks (1:21) now glorify God for God's mercy (15:9). The gentiles are glad alongside the people of God—the Jews (15:11). Paul envisions the family being visible and tangible, as Jews and gentiles gather in one congregation to raise one, united voice in praise to God (15:6).[19]

All this, of course, is good news for the majority of Christians today, who do not share Jewish ancestry. But the implications should push us all toward more uncomfortable discoveries about just how big the good news of Romans 1 might be. Romans 1:18–32 is a stylized condemnation of the culture of the consummate outsiders, the ones whom everyone "knows" do not belong to the family of God. The reason they're judged to be outsiders is simply that they do not fall within the sphere demarcated by the prime identity markers of God's people: they don't have the Law, they don't have circumcision, and they don't keep food laws. Yes, they are accused of behaving in a much more sordid manner, but Paul goes to great lengths to say that their behavior is not, in fact, categorically different from Jewish, insider behavior (2:1–3:20).

---

18. See J. Brian Tucker, *Reading Romans after Supersessionism: The Continuation of Jewish Covenantal Identity* (Cascade Books, 2018), esp. chap. 9, "A Doxological Social Identity," 221–43.

19. Tucker, *Reading Romans after Supersessionism*, 221–43.

But the most shocking part of all this is that when gentiles are brought in, they are not made to conform to the standards that had previously existed for demarcating the people of God. The same people whom Paul seemed to condemn as acting contrary to nature (*para physin*) in Romans 1:26 he celebrates as being grafted contrary to nature (*para physin*) into the stock that is the people of God in Romans 11:24. They were brought into Christ, not into the Law.

Rigorous application of the good news of Romans 1 to a modern context will demand that we and the communities we are part of take stock of what we "know" is required to belong to the people of God, and to ask if it just might be that God's good news is bigger than the box we have drawn by such boundary-marking lines. Such lines may pertain to theological distinctives, church government, practices, creeds or confessions, ethics, or politics. If Romans is any guide to the good news, then the conversions God requires are likely to differ considerably from the ones that we would demand. Put positively, the good news that grows in the soil of Romans 1 should have us guided by the principle that anyone who comes through our doors should hear one message above all: "You are God's beloved child"—our own echo of God's pronouncement spoken over those who have received the Spirit of the resurrected Son.

Conclusion

In Romans 1:18–32, Paul presents a problem that is pitched to find its solution in the good news he proclaims. He calls this the revelation of God's wrath (1:18). But if we attend carefully, we discover that the ground he lays enables an all-encompassing depiction of salvation to take root—a salvation that is, itself, the revelation of God's righteousness (1:17). In fact, human disobedience is framed by a "good news" that is much bigger than what is carried by common gospel presentations. Too often we think of sin requiring forgiveness as the sum total of the good news. We imagine the goal of God's work to be, at heart, providing us a way out of condemnation so that we can share in justification. But the scope of God's righteousness, revealed in the gospel, is infinitely more. It's an entirely new creation. God's handing over of Jesus, not sparing God's own son, unleashes a power that will transform the world from the earth below to heaven above.

The good news is that anti-creation decline is remedied, not by a return to the Genesis 1 vision, but by an unpredictable new creation with a new humanity whose identity has been transformed by the Spirit who raised Jesus from the dead. God incorporates us into Jesus's resurrection-sonship, marking us as free from enslaving powers and depraved minds. It reaches out to wrap up even the quintessential outsiders into the family of God—all of us get to hear God's declaration that we are God's beloved children as we cry out, "*Abba*, Father." This family is the new humanity—the ones destined to rule the world in the age to come even as Christ is Lord, now. It is a family that holds in trust the renewed image of God. We are fruitful by embodying the fruit of the Spirit. We are the diverse family who enact in our regular worship the reversal of the gentiles' quintessential failure: refusing to honor God as God or give thanks.

All of this is God's doing. The One who did not spare the gentiles in their disobedience, but handed them over to enslaved minds, the One who did not spare God's own son but handed him over for us all—this is the God who will "freely give us all things" (Rom. 8:32). "All things" begins now, for those who have been joined to Christ, as the hostile powers of sin, death, and law give way to the lordship of the Messiah and as those who are in him share in a reign of life and love, of grace and peace.

5

Excluded from God's Kingdom? (1 Cor. 6:9–10)

How to Think about the Threat of Divine Judgment

Wesley Hill

Toward the end of her book *Scripture, Ethics, and the Possibility of Same-Sex Relationships*, Karen Keen recommends that Christians with differing convictions on the morality of same-sex sexual relationships should hold space for one another in the church: "The best thing that traditionalists and progressives can do is to walk alongside each person with reassurances of God's unconditional love. Paradoxically, it is freedom that allows us to hear and surrender to the will of God."[1] By not making agreement on sexual orientation and gender identity a test of Christian fellowship, Keen suggests, Christians of all stripes can offer one another room and time to discern God's leading in their lives without fear of ostracization or spiritual manipulation.[2]

---

1. Karen R. Keen, *Scripture, Ethics, and the Possibility of Same-Sex Relationships* (Eerdmans, 2018), 107.
2. Other recent writers have emphasized that there is ample precedent in the New Testament for this posture of mutual welcome. Where there are disagreements about how to relate to the law of Moses, now that the Messiah to whom the law had pointed had appeared and inaugurated

Many Christians who continue to believe that same-sex sexual behavior is sinful, however, find that there is one major obstacle to adopting this posture of freedom in disagreement and charity, and it is a textual obstacle: Paul's warning about the consequence of unrepentant sin in 1 Corinthians 6:9–10. In a list of various vices and sinful practices, including same-sex sexual ones, Paul says, "Wrongdoers will not inherit the kingdom of God." How then can we agree to accommodate a "progressive" or "LGBTQ-affirming" Christian, with their conviction, if we believe that holding that conviction will ultimately lead to their disinheritance from God's kingdom of salvation?[3]

Prominent evangelical Christian leaders have taken 1 Corinthians 6:9–10 to mean that if one holds an "affirming" position and acts accordingly, then one should fear eternal judgment. The late Anglican theologian J. I. Packer describes the vices in 1 Corinthians 6:9–10 this way: "They are ways of sin that, if not repented of and forsaken, will keep people out of God's kingdom of salvation."[4] Likewise, the Calvinistic Baptist preacher John Piper has said, "The point is not that one act of homosexual or heterosexual experimentation condemns you, but that returning to this life permanently and without repentance will condemn you. 'Men who practice—who give themselves over to this life, and do not repent—will not enter the kingdom of God.' They will perish."[5]

Reformed theologian Michael Horton concurs: "These passages [such as 1 Corinthians 6:9–10] do not threaten believers who struggle with indwelling sin and fall into grievous sins (see Rom. 7 for that category); rather, they threaten professing believers who do not agree with God about their sin."[6] And the current president of the Council on Biblical Manhood and Womanhood,

---

the new age of redemption, believers are not to judge one another but instead to accommodate those with whom they differ (Rom. 14:1–15:13). Reciprocal recognition and hospitality, rather than mutual recrimination and condemnation, is the way forward for Christians who disagree. For two recent articulations of this point using Rom. 14–15, see Justin Lee, *Torn: Rescuing the Gospel from the Gays-vs.-Christians Debate*, rev. ed. (Worthy, 2024); and Christopher B. Hays and Richard B. Hays, *The Widening of God's Mercy: Sexuality within the Biblical Story* (Yale University Press, 2024).

3. The question may also be framed from the other, "progressive" side: How can affirming Christians continue to accommodate "traditionalists" or "conservatives" if the latter are viewed as stubbornly impeding the inclusive work of the Holy Spirit? Eugene Rogers forcefully raises this question in his *Sexuality and the Christian Body* (Blackwell, 1999), pointing to Jesus's dire warnings about those who refuse to celebrate with those whom Jesus has welcomed (Matt. 22:11–12).

4. J. I. Packer, "Why I Walked," *Christianity Today*, January 2003, 48.

5. John Piper, "Let Marriage Be Held in Honor: Thinking Biblically about So-Called Same-Sex Marriage," Desiring God, June 16, 2012, https://www.desiringgod.org/messages/let-marriage-be-held-in-honor. Italics removed.

6. Michael Horton, "Let's Not Cut Christ to Pieces," *Christianity Today*, July 12, 2012, http://www.christianitytoday.com/ct/2012/julyweb-only/lets-not-cut-christ-to-pieces.html.

Denny Burk, has drawn the ecclesial conclusion: "[A church member's] settled commitment to the [LGBTQ] 'affirming' position would in fact compel us to treat the 'affirming' member as an unbeliever and set them outside of the church."[7] In short, interpreters from across the evangelical spectrum agree that Paul's warning of eternal exclusion from God's kingdom prohibits us from recognizing "affirming" Christians as genuine believers.

My goal in this chapter is not to offer an ironclad rebuttal to this evangelical position. Mainly, I want to demonstrate that there are too many ambiguities and complexities in the Pauline text for it to be pressed and wielded in the way traditionalists have done, often to the spiritual harm of gay Christians.[8] In what follows, I offer a fresh engagement with the text, first emphasizing how poorly it has been served by a proof-texting approach and then concluding with a reflection on a more theologically responsible use of the text in our current discussions.

1 Corinthians 6:9-11 in Context

The text we're considering is a part of what the New Testament calls "First Corinthians," though it is not Paul's initial letter to the churches in Corinth that he had founded a few years before writing to them (see 1 Cor. 5:9 for reference to a previous letter). On his so-called second missionary journey (recounted in Acts 15:36–18:21), Paul evangelized the teeming port city of Corinth and then departed for Ephesus, across the Mediterranean in Asia Minor. On his third missionary journey (Acts 18:22–21:17), Paul returned to Ephesus and stayed there for three years. It was during that time that he received at least one written communication from the Corinthian churches, as well as an oral report from people associated with Chloe, probably a leader in one of the assemblies (1 Cor. 1:11; 16:17). In response to these communications, Paul penned what we now call First Corinthians, either as a single letter or perhaps as a string of letters that later editors strung together as the canonical edition.

The portion of 1 Corinthians we are considering reflects the third item of concern that Paul addresses. In the first four chapters, he speaks to the

---

7. Denny Burk, "Why Churches Might Need to Excommunicate 'Affirming' Members of the Congregation," November 29, 2016, https://www.dennyburk.com/why-churches-might-need-to-excommunicate-affirming-members-of-the-congregation/.

8. For a painful account of an excommunication gone awry, see "Steve's Story, Part 1," ACNAtoo, accessed October 18, 2023, https://www.acnatoo.org/diocese-of-the-upper-midwest/steves-story-part-1; and "Steve's Story, Part 2," ACNAtoo, accessed October 18, 2023, https://www.acnatoo.org/diocese-of-the-upper-midwest/steves-story-part-2.

divisions and factionalism that have riven the Corinthian Christians. In the fifth chapter, he turns to address a matter of sexual immorality, in which a man is sleeping with his father's wife (5:1). Then, in chapter 6, he responds to a situation in which one of the Corinthian believers, having been the victim of fraud perpetrated by another member of the church, has taken his brother to a civil magistrate, rather than agree to a process of reconciliation within the Christian community (6:1–8).

Paul's response is fourfold.[9] In the first place, Paul highlights the tragic, incomprehensible irony of a believer's willingness to sue another believer in a secular court—when in fact believers are the ones who, in their glorified eschatological state, will be declared competent to pronounce judgment even on angels! (6:2–3). Though the picture Paul holds of the future kingdom is somewhat obscure, it seems that he expects God will exercise his final assessment of the world and its history through the glorified agency of resurrected believers themselves. If such is our destiny, Paul reasons, why would anyone dream of appealing to unbelievers to try a case of fraud?

Second, Paul incredulously asks whether it can really be the case that the Corinthian church is so dysfunctional as not to be able to adjudicate between believers who are at odds with each other: "Is it possible that there is nobody among you wise enough to judge a dispute between believers?" (6:5). Paul probably intends sarcasm here, since it seems that the Corinthian believers styled themselves as wise and spiritually mature (3:18; 4:8). If you really are so wise, Paul seems to say, then surely you are competent to adjudicate a relational fracture.

Third, Paul argues that it would be far better to endure wrongdoing than to go through the very public (6:6), acrimonious process of going to court: "The very fact that you have lawsuits among you means you have been completely defeated already. Why not rather be wronged? Why not rather be cheated?" (6:7).

Fourth and finally, Paul returns to the scandal of the presenting issue in the first place: "You yourselves cheat and do wrong, and you do this to your brothers and sisters" (6:8). Will not a lawsuit, while offering some redress for the initial fraud, simply underscore the unresolved ruptures in the Corinthian churches rather than repair them in any deep and lasting way?

The next section—the focus of this chapter—then returns to the identity of the "ungodly" whom Paul has already said in 6:1 are not worthy to pass judgment on disputes between believers: "Or do you not know that wrongdoers

---

9. Andrew J. Wilson, *The Warning-Assurance Relationship in 1 Corinthians*, WUNT 2, 452 (Mohr Siebeck, 2017), 67.

will not inherit the kingdom of God?" (6:9a).[10] From there, Paul goes on to list various kinds of "wrongdoing" or "unrighteousness" that characterize the lives of those "ungodly" persons: "Do not be deceived: Neither the sexually immoral nor idolaters nor adulterers nor men who have sex with men nor thieves nor the greedy nor drunkards nor slanderers nor swindlers will inherit the kingdom of God" (6:9b–10).[11]

For many traditionalists, the meaning of this warning is that anyone—regardless of whether or not they are baptized—who persistently, unrepentantly engages in any of the listed behaviors should not enjoy assurance of salvation but rather fear exclusion from God's kingdom. But in order to appreciate the full weight of the warning, we need to understand how traditionalists understand the phrase "men who have sex with men."

An Ambiguous Vice?

The NIV translation quoted above includes the phrase "men who have sex with men." This English phrase attempts to translate two Greek words.[12] One of them is *malakoi*, which is a loan word from Latin meaning "soft." It is used elsewhere in the New Testament to refer to clothing (Matt. 11:8; Luke 7:25), though here in 1 Corinthians 6:9 it is used as a plural noun. This was not unusual: multiple Greek authors from Paul's milieu indicate that *malakos* was a typical way to designate a man who flouted traditional male gender norms and behaved in ways that showed passivity or "effeminacy."[13] The term could be used as a descriptor of men who wore feminine garments, were castrated (voluntarily or not), or who lacked sexual self-control from the perspective of the critic. It was also a term used to refer to men who were penetrated in sexual intercourse with other men.[14]

The other Greek word that Paul pairs with *malakos* is *arsenokoitēs*. Unattested in any extant Greek texts prior to Paul, it appears to be a word that Paul himself might have coined. It is composed of two words—literally, "male"

---

10. The Greek word *adikoi*, which the NIV translates as "ungodly" in 6:1, is the same word translated as "wrongdoers" in 6:9.
11. There are a number of these so-called vice lists in Paul's letters. In the undisputed letters, see Rom. 1:29–31; 13:13; 2 Cor. 12:20–21; Gal. 5:19–21. In the disputed letters, see Eph. 4:25–32; 5:3–5; Col. 3:5, 8; 1 Tim. 1:3–11; 4:1–3; 6:4–5; 2 Tim. 2:22–25; 3:1–9.
12. In the paragraphs that follow, I am drawing on my chapter "Christ, Scripture, and Spiritual Friendship," in *Two Views on Homosexuality, the Bible, and the Church*, by Preston Sprinkle, William Loader, Megan K. DeFranza, Wesley Hill, and Stephen R. Holmes (Zondervan, 2016), 124–47. Copyright © 2016 by Preston Sprinkle, William Loader, Megan K. DeFranza, Wesley Hill, Stephen R. Holmes. Used by permission of HarperCollins Christian Publishing. HarperCollinsChristian.com.
13. See Aristotle, *Nicomachean Ethics* 7.4.2; Plutarch, *On Moral Virtue* 447B.
14. Ovid, *Ars Amatoria* 1.505–24.

and "bed"—that Paul would have found in close proximity in the Greek text of Leviticus 18:22 and 20:13.[15] If that is the case, then we might look for the meaning of the words by returning to Leviticus and tracing the way it was understood in Jewish interpretations with which Paul would have been familiar. Given what we know of the blanket condemnation of same-sex sexual acts in the Judaism of Paul's day, traditionalists usually follow the NIV's rendering, which is explained further in a footnote to that translation: "The words *men who have sex with men* translate two Greek words that refer to the passive and active participants in homosexual acts." No matter whether the acts in question are consensual and egalitarian, traditionalists understand Paul to be ruling out any and all forms of same-sex sexual coupling.

Former archbishop of Canterbury and theologian Rowan Williams, writing from an affirming position, once criticized "an abstract fundamentalist deployment of a number of very ambiguous texts," referring to the way traditionalists appeal to texts like 1 Corinthians 6:9–10 to condemn the faithful loves of modern gay Christians.[16] It would be hard to disagree with such an assessment if 1 Corinthians 6:9–10 were all we had to go on in the attempt to think biblically about sexual ethics in our day. I have argued elsewhere, in part on the basis of its verbal ambiguities, that 1 Corinthians 6:9–10 should be considered a rather marginal text in the present discussion, while much more weight should be accorded to Romans 1:24–27 (and, beyond that, to Matt. 19:4–6 and Eph. 5:22–33).[17]

The passage in Romans 1 is no less negative in its judgment on same-sex sexual behavior, but unlike 1 Corinthians 6:9–10, it does not so clearly and directly speak to life in the church and whether excommunication and threat of eternal judgment is the appropriate response to professing believers who commit sexual sin. Indeed, Romans 1 does not feature any "rules" at all—it is a portrait of fallen human existence, with its own moral vision to contribute, but it is not a blueprint for how to negotiate dissension and dispute in the church.

Widening the Context (1): Paul's Pastoral Approach

Let's assume, however, for the sake of argument that we traditionalists are right that, in 1 Corinthians 6:9–10, Paul is condemning all forms of same-sex

---

15. Robin Scroggs, *The New Testament and Homosexuality: Contextual Background for Contemporary Debate* (Fortress, 1983), 83, 108.
16. Rowan D. Williams, "The Body's Grace," in *Theology and Sexuality: Classic and Contemporary Readings*, ed. Eugene F. Rogers Jr. (Blackwell, 2002), 309–21, at 320.
17. Hill, "Christ, Scripture, and Spiritual Friendship."

sexual coupling, even faithful, loving, and stable ones. Does it then follow that our approach to Christians today who affirm the goodness of same-sex sexual relationships should be one of warning and exclusion? Should we say to gay Christians, "You should not expect to enter the kingdom of God"?

Differences between Paul's Context and Ours

In order to answer that question, we need to zoom out and consider other texts alongside 1 Corinthians 6:9–10.[18] In the previous chapter, in which Paul explicitly discusses the excommunication of a person from the Corinthian church, he appears to take it for granted that the Corinthians will agree with him about the heinousness of the sin in question (5:1). He does not try to convince the Corinthians of his viewpoint, nor does he argue for the wrongness of same-sex sexual acts in 6:9–10; he presumably builds on his Jewish tradition, which we may assume he has passed on to the Corinthians (themselves not Jewish, or at least not predominantly so), and counts on the fact that they will accept his stance.

This means that any attempt to correlate Paul's situation with ours, as if the connection were straightforward, is inadequate. Churches today, at least those in Western societies, are confronting a situation that Paul in 1 Corinthians 5 never had to face: how to disciple people so that they are able to recognize as *sinful* a set of behaviors they're used to thinking of as *holy* (or capable of holy expression). Paul was able to assume a basic agreement about the immoral status of a man's sleeping with his stepmother (1 Cor. 5:2). We, on the other hand, inhabit cultures—including church cultures—in which same-sex sexual relationships, far from being considered immoral, are treated instead as life- and body-affirming, indeed as ways of enjoying the gift of God's love.

A priest in the Church of England once suggested to me that just as, for example, the church in the era of the Crusades was blind to its uncritical captivity to militarism, so now the church in the West is largely blind to its captivity to the values of the Sexual Revolution. He believes that Christians of later eras will look back on our generation as a time when we drifted along with the cultural flow. But in the meantime, we must take seriously the fact that those who give in to sexual sin today do not understand themselves to be sinning. On the contrary, they view their choices as faithful, even godly ones. So the matter is not as simple as being able to excommunicate "sinners" who

---

18. Much of this and the following section are adapted from my "Five Theses on Church Discipline," *The Living Church*, April 17, 2018, https://livingchurch.org/covenant/five-theses-on-church-discipline/.

are aware of themselves *as sinners*.[19] What this means, as New Testament scholar Richard Hays has put it, is that "the use of the New Testament in normative ethics requires *an integrative act of the imagination*, a discernment about how our lives, despite their historical dissimilarity to the lives narrated in the New Testament, might fitly answer to that narration and participate in the truth that it tells."[20]

Paul Affirms Identity in Christ

In addition to noting Paul's assumption that his hearers will agree with him on his definition of sexual sin, we should also see that within the rhetorical flow of 1 Corinthians 6 itself, Paul discourages the Corinthians from viewing themselves as among the "wrongdoers" whose same-sex sexual sin he identifies. Prior to 6:9–10, he has framed these ungodly persons as *outside* the Christian community. They are the ones who operate the secular law courts, unlike the Corinthian believers who, by virtue of their status as saints, will be the ones who will judge angels! Then, immediately following his list of ungodly persons in 6:9–10, he more overtly urges the Corinthians not to understand themselves as in danger of exclusion: "And that is what some of you were. But you were washed, you were sanctified, you were justified in the name of the Lord Jesus Christ and by the Spirit of our God" (6:11).

The point of listing the vices of the ungodly is not to make the Corinthians afraid of their own eschatological destiny but rather to reinforce their new, baptismal identity as those who are no longer part of the community of "wrongdoers." As Judith Gundry Volf puts it, "Paul wants to make the point that since the unrighteous have no share in the future kingdom, conduct typical of them should not characterize those *who will inherit the kingdom*."[21] Threatening the Corinthian believers with exclusion seems not to be the point. What Paul wants to emphasize is that the Corinthian Christians are different now, no longer defined before God by the past or shame of indulgence, and free to live in an entirely new, unencumbered way. The unrighteous will not inherit God's kingdom—but the point is that the Corinthians *are no longer* "unrighteous."

---

19. This paragraph paraphrases my colleague based on my best recollection of our conversation.
20. Richard B. Hays, *The Moral Vision of the New Testament: Community, Cross, New Creation; A Contemporary Introduction to New Testament Ethics* (HarperSanFrancisco, 1996), 300.
21. Judith M. Gundry Volf, *Paul and Perseverance: Staying In and Falling Away* (Westminster John Knox, 1990), 135. The whole discussion at 132–41 is instructive.

Paul Envisions Restorative Judgment, Not Punitive Judgment

Finally, we should note Paul's pastoral flexibility. He is certainly capable of urging the church to exclude a sinning member from itself: "When you are assembled and I am with you in spirit, and the power of our Lord Jesus is present, hand this man over to Satan for the destruction of the flesh" (5:4–5a). But even in that case, he hopes for the sinner's ultimate salvation: "so that his spirit may be saved on the day of the Lord" (5:5b). And elsewhere in 1 Corinthians, with regard to other habitual, impenitent sinners in the Corinthian churches, he tries to convince them of the error of their ways and warns them of the dire—even deathly—consequences of their sin (11:17–22). Yet he insists once again that these consequences are not God's final word: "When we are judged in this way by the Lord, we are being disciplined so that we will not be finally condemned with the world" (11:32). The sickness and dying that are the fruit of chauvinistic divisiveness among the Corinthians are not meant to be ultimately punitive but restorative. Not every persistent sin, it would seem, is the occasion for eucharistic exclusion; some simply merit fatherly correction.

All these contextual considerations should give us pause when seeking to apply 1 Corinthians 6:9–10 in the way that evangelicals today routinely do, often at a steep cost to LGBTQ believers.

Widening the Context (2): Contemporary Considerations

As we seek to apply the text in our varying contexts, we should also bear in mind the ways that our culture differs from Paul's and what implications those differences might have for our attempts to be faithful to Paul's instructions.

The Church Community Is at Fault Just as Much as the Individual Sinner

One of the relatively neglected aspects of 1 Corinthians 5 is how Paul not only counsels the Corinthian Christians to hand over the sexually immoral man in their midst to Satan (that is, to excommunicate him, in the hopes of his eventual restoration) but also stresses *their* collective failure in handling the situation in a godly way. Immediately after naming the presenting problem, Paul rounds on the church as a whole: "You are proud! Shouldn't you rather have gone into mourning? . . . Your boasting is not good" (5:2, 6). In context, Paul is accusing the Corinthians of hypocritical pride in their spiritual status when they cannot even muster the moral will to confront the flagrant immorality of one of their congregants. But his point may have a wider significance.

It highlights the fact that no individual sin is truly *individual*. We are all implicated in one another—or, to use Paul's organic metaphor, we are members of the same body (Rom. 12:5)—and one person's disobedience can affect the community, just as the community's disobedience can affect an individual.

What are the implications of this fact for thinking about church discipline in contemporary contexts? Primarily this: Any effort to discipline an erring church member must take into account the ways the church has helped make possible that member's sin. Church leaders who are traditionalists must face the fact of their own complicity in what they take to be the moral failings of those under their care. In the words of professor and author Alan Jacobs, commenting from his ecclesial location in the Episcopal Church:

> We all need to face up to the fact that almost no churches in the Anglican tradition, conservative as well as liberal, have taken catechesis seriously for a long time. To deny the sacraments to people the Church has failed to catechize is to make others suffer for the failings of the Church's leadership. . . . Almost everyone in our society—with the exception of monastics, the Amish, and a few fundamentalist Protestants—*has* been deeply and persistently catechized by the mass media into a very different model of sexuality than the Christian and biblical one. We should have the same compassion for them as we would for people who have been raised in a brainwashing cult.[22]

What does this mean for how traditionalists respond to affirming gay Christians? Jacobs reflects on that question in the following way, assuming that traditionalists have not changed their theological position:

> A great many conservative churches are effectively arguing that a person who has been catechized very thoroughly by the sexual mores of our culture, and has attended churches that either agree with those mores or at best fail to contest them, is obstinate if he or she doesn't immediately fall into line with whatever that conservative church affirms. I do not think this is a valid definition of obstinacy, and it places a far heavier burden on the individual to be compliant to one voice amid many than it does on the churches themselves to teach compellingly. There's just a fundamental lack of compassion for people who have been sold a thoroughly non-Christian account of sexuality all their lives—and, I believe, an equally fundamental failure to take their own apologetic and catechetical responsibilities seriously. At the end of the day I think it's, more than anything else, a failure of *patience*.[23]

---

22. Alan Jacobs, "The Sacraments and the Honey of Love: A Second Bleat," *The Homebound Symphony*, November 22, 2016, https://blog.ayjay.org/the-sacraments-and-the-honey-of-love-a-second-bleat/.

23. Alan Jacobs, personal correspondence with the author, December 5, 2017.

When we consider the question of whether to exercise church discipline in the case of same-sex sexual sin (that is, excluding an affirming Christian from the eucharistic assembly), in other words, we need a *communal* understanding of moral failure. We need to own up to the fact that gay sinners may suffer much more from *theological confusion* brought about by the *Church's* failure to teach and shepherd its members than they do from *willful rebellion*. Just as we would not lay the blame for the moral tragedy of abortion at the feet of a mother who chose to terminate her pregnancy without interrogating the culture and community—which left her with the perception she had no other choice—so we should not lay all or even most of the blame for what we understand to be sexual sin at the feet of all sexual sinners. Penitence should be the public posture and practice of any church that wishes to enjoin penitence on one of its erring members.

The Need for a Patient, Long View

Relatedly, if the church must own its failure to catechize its members in the matter of sexual ethics, then the church should also prepare for a long, slow process of redressing that failure and not expect an overnight change of heart, mind, and behavior from its members. The Catholic theologian Paul Griffiths once wrote, "In the America of our day, it is about as difficult (or as easy) to make what the Church teaches about marriage comprehensible and convincing (the latter more difficult than the former) to the educated locals as it is to make the doctrines of the Immaculate Conception or the Real Presence so."[24] Given that reality, any contemporary American Christian's acceptance of—let alone deep agreement with—Christian teaching on marriage is likely to take a very long time. In short, the complexity of our post–Sexual Revolution cultural moment should lead us to expect that many "conversions" to a traditional view of sex and marriage will be gradual and halting, and our pastoral care for those whom we believe to be in the wrong on these matters should be correspondingly gentle and patient.

On Not Pronouncing Damnation

Zooming out for an even wider angle of vision, I would like to build on the exegetical points above and move toward a theological conclusion through

---

24. From Paul Griffiths's blog, which is now defunct. I do not have a record of the date on which he made this remark.

a brief engagement with the work of the great contemporary ecumenical theologian Robert Jenson (1930–2017).

In the second volume of his *Systematic Theology*, Jenson addresses the matter of whether Christians should use the threat of exclusion from God's kingdom as a warning or a motivation to avoid sin and cultivate faith and virtue. In terms of evangelistic proclamation, Jenson is direct in disavowing "hellfire-and-brimstone" efforts to convert unbelievers: "Actual second-person threats of exclusion do not seem to have played a role in the apostolic kerygma to gentiles. . . . 'You individually are headed for eternal torment, believe lest you enter it' does not seem to have belonged to the apostolic missionary repertoire."[25]

But what about those who are already converted and continue to sin? If unbelievers should not be threatened with exclusion from the kingdom, what about believers who, despite knowing better, stubbornly refuse to repent from what the preacher believes is wrong? In a revealing passage worth quoting at length, Jenson responds to this separate question:

> If I am baptized, should I fear exclusion? Paul apparently thinks I should, and in the referenced passage [1 Corinthians 10:1–13] puts this fear into me ["if you think you are standing firm, be careful that you don't fall"]. And yet were this fear to determine any part of my believing life, all would be undone. For to hear and believe the gospel and simultaneously to fear exclusion from the Kingdom is impossible. . . . Such second-person threatening as Paul's to the Corinthians can therefore only be understood as addressed to believers insofar as they do not believe, insofar as the "old man" [Ephesians 4:22; Colossians 3:9] still lives. But it is addressed to them precisely to remind them that they no longer *are* this old man. . . . That is, the threat of exclusion is made precisely to turn us away from entertaining it. So again, if I am baptized, should I fear exclusion? Perhaps the confessor's proper answer is "Since you ask, No."[26]

Several features of this compressed statement are worth expanding on. In the first place, Jenson notes what we have already seen in this chapter: Paul

---

25. Robert W. Jenson, *Systematic Theology*, vol. 2 (Oxford University Press, 1999), 364. It is interesting to note Jenson's indebtedness here to the Swiss Reformed theologian Karl Barth's theology. When Barth went to hear Billy Graham preach in Basel, Switzerland, in August 1960, he was appalled by the way Graham motivated people to put their faith in Christ by threatening them with hell if they did not: "It was the gospel at gun-point. . . . He preached the law, not a message to make one happy. He wanted to terrify people. Threats—they always make an impression. People would much rather be terrified than be pleased. The more one heats up hell for them, the more they come running. . . . [But contra Graham, we] must leave the good God freedom to do his own work" (Eberhard Busch, *Karl Barth: His Life from Letters and Autobiographical Texts* [Fortress, 1976], 446).

26. Jenson, *Systematic Theology*, 2:362.

in 1 Corinthians declares that the ungodly will not inherit God's kingdom. This language is threatening and frightful and raises the question of what role it should play in a believer's life. Jenson's answer is that if a believer should internalize it and take it personally, such a believer would cease to have confidence in the good news of God's free acceptance in Christ—which is to say, the person would lapse back into unbelief. Perhaps in a paradoxical way, then, the right approach to such threatening texts is to see them as designed to usher their hearers away from thinking that they might exclude *them*. Jenson closes the paragraph by imagining someone coming to a priest or pastor in fear that they will not inherit God's kingdom. "Am I damned?" such a person asks the priest. And by the very fact that they are sitting there in the confessional, not wanting to be excluded but hoping to receive God's mercy, the priest has heard all they need to hear in order to quote the words of Jesus to the terrified sinner: "Whoever comes to me I will never drive away" (John 6:37).

One theologian influenced by Jenson's perspective, Eugene Rogers, has written about the threat of exclusion in terms of the three "persons" of grammar: Speaking in the first person, we should say, "If anyone is worthy of not inheriting God's kingdom, surely it is I, rather than my neighbor." Speaking in the second person, we should say, "You—whoever you are—believe the good news! God has taken away your sin and defeated your death through Jesus's life, death, and resurrection. Don't be afraid. Trust in God's mercy." And in the third person, we should say, "So-and-so may finally be excluded from God's kingdom, but as I have no way of speaking good news to this hypothetical person, I also have no way of knowing anything about her or his final destiny."[27]

Jenson expresses Rogers's third point like this: "The church must think that damnation is possible but is not to make it an article of faith, proclaim it, or threaten it except in such fashion as to obviate the threat. What sort of truth does 'Damnation is possible' then have? Perhaps God does not wish us to know."[28]

Conclusion

Where, then, does all this leave us? We have seen that 1 Corinthians 6:9–10 has enough ambiguities, and enough complicating contextual factors, that

---

27. Eugene F. Rogers Jr., *Elements of Christian Thought: A Basic Course in Christianese* (Fortress, 2021), 40.
28. Jenson, *Systematic Theology*, 2:365.

it ought not to be used to threaten affirming Christians with final exclusion from God's kingdom. Those contextual factors are not limited to those found within 1 Corinthians itself but also include factors of our own contemporary contexts: There is no neat, clean, straight line to be drawn from Paul's text to our current pastoral and cultural dilemmas.

But more importantly and urgently, to wield 1 Corinthians 6:9–10 as a threat of eternal destruction for affirming gay Christians today seems to miss the most important point of Paul's gospel: that assurance of the horrible fate of sexual sinners is not ours to have. Our job, rather, is to mention such threats only on the way to proclaiming their nullity. Christ is risen. He has borne all our judgment. He lives always to intercede for us. Trust him, and seek each day to surrender every facet of your being—including your sex life, as much as you understand what that means—to his lordship.

PART 2

Successfully Navigating Divides

6

Navigating Conflict in Community

Tim Otto

As theologian Stanley Hauerwas quips, Christians need to get good at conflict because we're not allowed to kill one another.[1] In this chapter, I'll explore essential ways to navigate conflict well so that we won't have to hide any bodies.

I know the difficulty of conflict firsthand. I've lived in an intentional Christian community for over thirty years, and while my community has been a source of life and joy (most of the time), times of conflict in our community have been some of the hardest in my life. I have felt discouraged and misunderstood when another leader in my community told me that I was an incompetent and misguided leader. In another conflict, I felt depressed and demoralized when I saw longtime friendships destroyed and beloved community members become bitter.

But I must also admit that times of conflict have been a crucible that have helped me face my imperfect self and mature in my discipleship. The people who identified my faults may have had some of the details wrong, but it's true that I'm a sinner who needs to grow up. Conflict can be a valuable opportunity

---

1. This is a paraphrase of an idea found in Stanley Hauerwas, *Disrupting Time: Sermons, Prayers, and Sundries* (Cascade Books, 2004), 195.

for transformation because most people become more willing to speak honestly during times of conflict.

In any disagreement, there are two dynamics: the issue we're arguing about and the relational dynamics between us. Suppose the disagreement is simply about biblical interpretation or sexual ethics. In that case, most communities can chart a course through it by doing things like listening to one another's experiences, exploring the relevant biblical witness, hearing from speakers on both sides, engaging in small-group or community-wide discussions, and then initiating a decision-making process to determine the community's stance going forward.

But when there are strained relational dynamics in a community, conflict can be more challenging to navigate. Disagreements about sexuality, for example, can exacerbate preexisting relational tensions and fissures. Because relational tensions tend to be the most challenging for communities, I will focus on relational dynamics during disagreements.

Develop a Vision concerning Conflict

One difficult aspect of conflict is that it can feel like a distraction from the primary mission of a community. Thus, there is tension from the conflict itself—along with conflict *about* the conflict. "Why are we wasting time on this when we have such important work to do?" some inevitably ask. There are three good responses to this question. The first relates to how we can *bear witness to the love of Christ*, the second to how we can *proclaim the good news of Christ's grace*, and the third to how we can embrace conflict as a pathway toward our own *transformation*.

Bear Witness to the Love of Christ

Conflict affects our witness, for Jesus says that if Christians don't live in love and unity, the world won't know that we're followers of Jesus or that the Messiah has come. One pastor describes John 13–17 as "Jesus's last huddle with the disciples before the most crucial play of the game."[2] In these final instructions before going to the cross, Jesus teaches his disciples, "By this everyone will know that you are my disciples, if you love one another" (John 13:35). In his prayer in John 17, Jesus asks God that the believers all "may be

---

2. Pastor Reed, "Nature and Purpose of the Church," Church of the Servant King, Gardena, CA, May 11, 1995, audio cassette.

one, Father, just as you are in me and I am in you. May they also be in us so that the world may believe that you have sent me" (v. 21).

Some Christians seem to think that we can live in love and unity because *real* Christians who are animated by the Holy Spirit will just agree on all the important stuff. This is like claiming that Christians can live joyfully because God never lets anything bad happen to them! Obviously, this just isn't true—nor is it true that "real Christians" always agree. Throughout the New Testament, it is clear that the disciples and first-century churches had explosive disputes. And a quick survey of church history reveals that God has not miraculously freed Christians from conflict.

But what *is* truly miraculous is when Christians face disagreements and *still* live in love and unity. Conflict is not a pesky distraction, but the test that reveals if we've understood the way of Jesus and are allowing the Spirit to weave us into a vital unity. It is worth devoting time and energy to navigating conflict because when we live through tension in love, we reveal to a conflict-riven world that there is hope in Christ as peacemaker, mender, and Savior.

Proclaim the Good News of Grace

Conflict also helps us make sure we're understanding the gospel and living in grace rather than trying to earn our salvation. In the Pulitzer Prize–winning book *The Denial of Death*, Ernest Becker makes a devastating indictment of most religions, offering the provocative metaphor that humans are gods who crap (he uses a different word). Though we have minds that can think about eternity like a god, we are constantly reminded when we defecate (and by all the ways we are deteriorating) that we are trapped in bodies that will die, stink, and rot.

Becker spends much of the book showing that humans are preoccupied with this dilemma and are constantly trying to find symbolic ways of showing that we deserve eternal life. One person might do this by carving his name into a newly poured concrete sidewalk, while another might pile up loads of money that will outlast her. One of the most common ways humans grasp at the eternal is to find ways of feeling superior to others. The subconscious logic asserts, "If I'm better than other people, then I deserve eternal life."

Becker sees religion as one of the ways that humans try to feel superior. We grasp onto a set of beliefs and think, "I've opened myself to the truth of this religion, and others haven't. I, therefore, deserve eternal life!" Yet Jesus offers us participation in God's eternal life entirely by grace—not because we are superior. The good news of Jesus proclaims, "Through no merit of your own, I give you eternal life as a gift. You are now free. You can relax. You can love others purely and do not need to keep playing sad superiority games."

Despite this, most of us do not fully grasp God's grace, so we keep playing superiority games. We insist that because we are "right" and others are "wrong," we're better than others. But those "wrong" people have just as much dignity, worth, and value in God's sight as we do. Ironically, when we think we are "right," we might be getting it wrong in God's eyes as we ruminate on our supposed superiority!

Whenever we're in a conflict, we can ask ourselves, "Am I living by grace?" In a moment when we are not feeling too triggered, we can ask,

- Am I remembering that the people I disagree with are every bit as loved by God as I am?
- Can I imagine that I might have similar views to those I disagree with if I had grown up with different life experiences?
- Is any of my energy for this conflict coming from my need to feel superior to others rather than from the issue at hand?

Gospel grace generally feels outrageous to human beings. God gives eternal life to the most undeserving people—like us! When we're experiencing conflict, let's remember that we are recipients of grace and not jump back into old merit-based, "I'm-better-than-others," self-righteous schemes of earning salvation. Conflict forces us to ask ourselves whether we've fallen into the human superiority game of trying to feel that we're better than others because we are "right."

A Pathway of Transformation

Finally, conflict can be a crucible for our own transformation. In Ephesians 4, Paul makes the astonishing claim that we can grow into the "fullness of Christ" (v. 13) by "speaking the truth in love" (v. 15). Paul models such truth-telling in the first four chapters of Ephesians by telling his readers that they are God's adopted children and are seated with Christ in the heavenly places (Eph. 1:5 and 2:6). Communities can often avoid conflict—or find their way through it with grace—by developing the practice of speaking positive truths to one another in love.

But sometimes we need to hear difficult truths about ourselves. During times of conflict, because the stakes are high, we often muster the courage to say difficult truths to one another. In conflict, we're usually obsessed with getting other people to change—but the only person we can control is ourselves.

Thus, we can weather times of conflict more gracefully when we begin to see conflict as a potential tool for *our own* change.

I was once in a conflict with a very perceptive and intelligent person who was extremely frustrated with me. At one point, we each made a list of concerns about each other. After this person read me his list, I realized that he had given me a gift that few friends had ever dared to offer. He had thought long and hard about my character defects and had handed me a map of my faults to which I was mostly blind. Now that I was aware of them, I had the chance to work on them and grow.

We are more likely to be able to hear difficult truths about ourselves when we invite others to speak into our lives. We can elicit such truths by asking people on the other side of the conflict questions such as, "How do you think I'm contributing to this conflict?" or "What do people say about me when I'm not in the room that it would be useful for me to hear?" We have to open ourselves to listen to the responses without being defensive. If this feels impossible, we can begin by asking the same questions to those on "our side" of the conflict.

Hearing difficult feedback is hard for most of us, so it can be very helpful to meet with a spiritual director or talk with a trusted friend who will be supportive but not shade the truth. When we are facing our shadows, we will need to have the support of loving friends and family around us.

As you reflect on the feedback you've received from others, offering a confession or apology where appropriate can change the tone of the conflict. Sometimes our confession might inspire someone on the other side also to confess. Of course, we can't offer an apology and assume that the other side will respond in kind. But when someone offers a confession or apology in humility, other confessions tend to follow.

In some situations, those on the other side may not admit to anything, or they may even use what we've confessed against us. Yet confession is good for our souls, helps us grow, and pleases God—even if it doesn't resolve the conflict.

At some point, after genuinely inviting feedback from the other side, it might be appropriate to speak the (difficult) truth in love to those with whom we disagree. If we are communicating *in love*, we cannot convey the slightest hint of superiority, condescension, or contempt. Instead, we need to express genuine care and appreciation for those on the other side of the conflict.

As the saying goes, "People will forget what you said, people will forget what you did, but people will never forget how you made them feel."[3] As we

---

3. This quote is often attributed to Maya Angelou, but apparently it originates with Carl W. Buehner. Rebecca Seales, "Let's Save Maya Angelou from Fake Quotes," *BBC*, November 12, 2017, https://www.bbc.com/news/41913640.

speak difficult truths in love, God may use those experiences to help everyone involved grow into the "fullness of Christ" (Eph. 4:13).

Listen for Emotions in Conflict

During a leadership conflict in my community, we called in a mediator. Early on, he had us listen to what another person said and then repeat it to that person's satisfaction. After paraphrasing the content, he told us to imagine what the other person was feeling—the emotion behind the words—and then describe it to the other person. While we hadn't practiced any of this before, it helped us listen carefully to each other and formulate our responses thoughtfully.

It also blasted holes in our chests and quickly got to our heart issues. The following is an example of such an exchange:

> *Abigail*: "I don't appreciate you constantly giving me feedback about the outreach project. One example is how you criticized me in Tuesday's planning meeting for not having flyers to pass out."
>
> *Bethany* (reflecting back the content): "I hear you saying that I give you a lot of unsolicited advice on the outreach project. For instance, the other day, I told you in the meeting that we should make up flyers to pass out."
>
> *Abigail*: "Yes, you got it. That is what I said."
>
> *Bethany* (reflecting back what might be the underlying feeling): "I wonder if you are feeling frustrated that I have so many opinions about a project that is yours."
>
> *Abigail*: "Hmm, not exactly. As I think about it, I realize I was feeling a little humiliated in front of everyone else that you had the idea about flyers and that I hadn't thought of it myself."

While this conversation doesn't solve the conflict, it is a solid beginning. Bethany doesn't need to identify the exact emotions that Abigail is feeling, but her effort to imagine what Abigail might be feeling communicates care.

Moreover, Bethany's attempt to imagine the feeling behind Abigail's words keeps Bethany from thinking, "Gosh, I try to be helpful by offering the most basic of suggestions, and Abigail gets so bent out of shape." As soon as Bethany tries to imagine plausible feelings behind Abigail's behavior, she develops empathy that may help her extend grace.

In the above exchange, even though Bethany didn't intuit Abigail's exact emotion, the conversation about the feeling behind her words gave Abigail a chance to reflect and locate the source of her irritation. Bethany's empathetic response gave Abigail space to think about her emotions so that she could be less defensive and get to the root of the tension.

We may think we want others to understand our thoughts, but most of us want others to understand our hearts—why we care so deeply about an issue and our sense that the other side doesn't get it. Yet when we are in a conflict, we sometimes get the message from others that our motivations and feelings are *bad*. If both sides can listen to the heart cares of each other and then try to interpret those concerns charitably and even communicate an appreciation for them, everyone will be much closer to resolving the conflict.

Our emotions tend to be at the heart of any conflict, and so we need to understand and empathize with the emotions of those on the other side to make progress in resolving the conflict. Yet it is important that we don't get swamped, coerced, or lost in others' emotions. To navigate emotions during conflict, we need to cultivate the skill of *differentiation*.

Differentiation

In Romans, as Paul addresses a controversy over what to eat and what special days to observe, he urges Christians to *care* if others are "distressed" by what they eat (14:15). In this instruction, he is encouraging followers of Christ to be empathetic about the emotions of others. In the same chapter, he writes, "One person considers one day more sacred than another; another considers every day alike. *Each* of them should be fully convinced in *their own* mind" (v. 5; emphasis added). Rather than ruling that "some" have it right while "others" have it wrong, he acknowledges that we will have differences—and exhorts us to respect one another's minds.

In the conflicts I've experienced in community, someone may feel deeply hurt by a conversation and insist that everyone else experience it the same way. Or someone may have compassion for a specific group and demand that everyone in the community feel the same way. Or one person might feel anxiety about the direction the community is taking and expect everyone else to feel the same. In each case, one person (or group of people) is trying to recruit others to share their emotions.

The key to staying afloat in these emotional storms is the skill of differentiation, which allows others to experience their emotions without letting them overtake us or the community. Differentiation requires a mature understanding that reality is complex, humans react differently, and there is not one "correct" emotion that everyone must feel.

One way to calm the storm is to help people name their emotions and tell the stories behind them. For instance, in an argument over the affirmation of gay marriage, one person may have a beloved aunt who was gay and faced discrimination for living with her partner, while another person may have a loving, gay uncle who sacrificially gave himself to celibacy to live his vision of a holy life. As we listen to and tell the stories behind our emotions, we develop empathy for one another and reveal the history of our strong feelings. This practice reveals that *my story* isn't *everyone's* story and gives us the freedom to acknowledge, with Paul, that we can *all* be fully convinced in *our own* minds without needing to convince someone else to *take on* our mind (Rom. 14:5).

When a community is engaged in a conflict, anxiety is one of the most pervasive and debilitating emotions. In John 13–17, Jesus tells his disciples to live in love and unity, but he doesn't give them much advice about how to do it. Yet as he faces his impending death, he says, "Peace I leave with you; my peace I give you. I do not give to you as the world gives. Do not let your hearts be troubled and do not be afraid" (14:27). When we experience conflict, the first thing we can do together is to invite the peace that Christ promises to pervade our hearts.

In *Failure of Nerve*, sociologist Edwin H. Friedman argues that anxiety in an organization makes for black-and-white thinking, scapegoating, reactivity, and an inability to imagine creative solutions.[4] If anxiety seems to be a chronic problem in your community, leaders need to take responsibility for setting the emotional tone as they seek to navigate any conflict. As Pastor R. Robert Creech observes, the best leader "is the least anxious person in the room."[5]

Our culture is increasingly a cauldron of anxiety, and anxiety is a pervasive characteristic of groups in conflict. As your community seeks to navigate conflict, it is important to assess your own anxiety level as well as the anxiety in the group. Before you engage the source of conflict, take time together to invite the peace of Christ to pervade your hearts and invite the Holy Spirit to help you have constructive conversations about the dynamics involved in the conflict. You might draw on books,[6] counselors, and mediators to help you address your collective anxiety.

---

4. Edwin H. Friedman, *A Failure of Nerve: Leadership in the Age of the Quick Fix* (Church Publishing, 2017), 136–39.

5. R. Robert Creech, *Family Systems and Congregational Life* (Baker Academic, 2019), 45.

6. I have found the following books to be helpful: R. Robert Creech, Jim Herrington, and Trisha Taylor, *The Leader's Journey: Accepting the Call to Personal and Congregational Transformation* (Baker Academic, 2020); and Peter Steinke, *Uproar: Calm Leadership in Anxious Times* (Rowman & Littlefield, 2019).

Discern If a Slope Is "Slippery"

While there are many potential causes of anxiety in the conversation about sexuality, one concern that often arises is regarding the "slippery slope" between sexual legalism and extreme permissiveness. First, communities need to acknowledge that there *is* a slope between extreme legalism and extreme permissiveness.

Some people might claim that their biblical interpretation offers a place of complete security and stability, a truly level ground, because they are reading "the plain sense" of what the Bible says and interpreting it literally. Yet, as a friend of mine says (thinking of Matt. 18:9, "And if your eye causes you to stumble, gouge it out and throw it away . . ."), "I haven't met any one-eyed literalists yet!" We're all standing somewhere on the "not everything is literal" interpretive slope, but figuring out where we stand on that slope will require the wisdom and guidance of the Holy Spirit.

After acknowledging that there is a slope rather than some safe place of permanent stability, the second question is to discern whether or not the slope we are standing on is slippery. Are we liable to careen downward to an unhealthy extreme, or can we move sure-footedly up and down the slope as we seek to respond to the stirring of the Spirit in truth and love? To discern whether or not a slope is slippery, we will need to look at the underlying logic animating the leadership and our community as a whole as we seek to respond to change.

To give an example, in a Christian community that is considering whether to become more affirming of gay relationships, those on the traditional side may be concerned that such a decision will begin a slide toward general sexual permissiveness. Given the values of modernity, this is a valid concern. A former pastor in my community, John Alexander, warned against an overemphasis on what he called FIRES, an acronym for Freedom, Individualism, Rights, Equality, and Self.

While these values are (at least in large part) gifts of the Judeo-Christian tradition, they can undermine Christian ethics when they become ultimate values (as they have in the West). If I'm *free* to do anything, if my highest call is to express my *individuality*, if I have the *right* to anything, if I'm *equal* to all others (not only in dignity but wisdom), and if my highest allegiance is to *myself*, then nothing is off limits.

Another potential concern is that of "queer theology," in the technical sense.[7] Queer theology has its roots in postmodern philosophy and revels

---

7. For a very brief, sympathetic definition of queer theology and recommendations for further reading, see "What Is Queer Theology?," *Open Table*, February 9, 2022, https://opentable.lgbt/our-blog/2022/2/9/what-is-queer-theology.

in being transgressive and deconstructive. It strives to overturn norms to de-stigmatize the marginalized. But it goes too far in subverting *all* norms. It is important to distinguish *queer* theology from an *affirming* theology that still values the Bible and Christian tradition in its conclusion that God blesses same-sex relationships.[8]

Thus, a crucial question we can ask as we seek to discern whether or not a slope is slippery is: *Are those advocating change arguing from abstract FIRES values or a version of queer theology? Or are their concerns rooted in Scripture and the Christian tradition?* If those advocating change are honestly wrestling with Scripture and Christian tradition, the slope they are standing on is not so slippery. But if their arguments focus on "universal" FIRES values or a lens such as queer theology, then there is reason to believe that the slope is slippery.

If a slope is perilously slippery, that doesn't mean you need to leave a community, but you will need to raise concerns about whether people are arguing from a primarily Christian or secular worldview. These overarching "meta" questions can be difficult to ask if you are on one side of the conflict, and so it can be important to ask a wise outsider, who can see the big-picture dynamics in the conflict, to help mediate.

Seek Outside Help

As with most potential emergencies, it is best to have a plan for navigating conflicts in your community *before* a crisis happens. Ideally, before a conflict unfolds, it would be wise to train one or more of your community members in conflict resolution and mediation practices. These trained members can intervene early to restore peace before a conflict turns into a conflagration.[9]

At one point, my community was in such a difficult conflict that we paid a trained mediator to help us listen to one another, differentiate our emotions, confront our collective anxiety, and make progress on the core issues. Our community survived because we made that crucial investment. No mediator is perfect, but a mediator can be the best chance of redeeming the pain of a conflict into something fruitful. When possible, it is best to have someone local who can work with you for as long as needed.[10]

---

8. For many, an affirming theology also means the blessing of gender transition for those with significant gender dysphoria.
9. Contact the Alban Institute at Duke Divinity School (https://alban.org) or the Restorative Church website for training resources (https://restorativechurch.org).
10. Contact your local Community Dispute Resolution Center for a list of local mediators and practitioners who work with faith communities.

Given the importance of having a vision for navigating conflict, we need to persevere with one another even though it is costly. As one pastor said, "The way we grow up is through making commitments and going through the difficulty of keeping them."[11] But at some point, we must ask, "Has this process become too toxic and damaging to those involved? Is it best for me to leave or (depending on the situation) to ask others to leave?" One sign of such toxicity is when community members are unwilling to cooperate in good faith with a mediator.

I've been at the center of several conflicts, and yet I am well aware that I don't know the whole story. Relational triangles, enneagram types, generational dynamics, power struggles, family-of-origin baggage, gender dynamics, and human sin sometimes swirl together and create destructive maelstroms that we can't calm or resolve. If you are trying to navigate a conflict in your community, you can be hopeful that the Holy Spirit will work among you to restore peace. But keep in mind, God doesn't always intervene to make everything work out in this life. Such an assumption reveals a superficial understanding of the gospel, so it is important to consider how to respond when things end poorly and fall apart.

Grieve and Forgive

When conflict ends poorly, the price can be shockingly high. An organization built by hard and faithful work over many years can quickly collapse. Networks of friends can unravel. Faith itself may seem impossible. Yet we can experience healing as we seek to grieve our losses rather than seeking self-preservation by blocking our emotions. While tears aren't mandatory in the grieving process, Marilyn Chandler McEntyre writes,

> Tears release me into honest sorrow. They release me from the strenuous business of finding words. They release me into a childlike place where I need to be held and find comfort in embrace—in the arms of others and in the arms of God. Tears release me from the treadmill of anxious thoughts, and even from fear. They release me from the strain of holding them back. Tears are a consent to what is. They wash away, at least for a time, denial and resistance. They allow me to relinquish the self-deceptive notion that I'm in control. Tears dilute resentment and wash away the flotsam left by waves of anger.[12]

---

11. Reed, "Nature and Purpose of the Church."
12. Marilyn Chandler McEntyre, *A Faithful Farewell: Living Your Last Chapter with Love* (Eerdmans, 2015), 78.

After experiencing soul-pummeling conflict, we need to find ways to grieve and recover by finding a wise friend or spiritual director with whom we can process. It can also be helpful to reflect on our hurts in a journal and then to read those entries out loud, inviting the presence of the Holy Spirit and making space to listen to God's response. Or you can write down injuries and then prayerfully burn them as a way of acknowledging and releasing your pain into the grace of Christ. In the aftermath of a significant conflict, reading books on grieving can also be helpful.[13]

Honest grieving can build a solid foundation for forgiveness. But in this process, it is important to distinguish between "reconciling forgiveness" and "unilateral forgiveness." Reconciling forgiveness aims to *restore* relationship with the people involved, whereas unilateral forgiveness *releases* those who have hurt us so we do not grow bitter.

One way to pursue reconciling forgiveness is for each person to listen empathetically to the other as they explain their version of events. As discussed above, in the course of listening and seeking to respond to how the other person might be feeling, the two sides engage in a dialogue that develops into a shared narrative. After listening and responding with empathy, each side can then apologize for any wrongdoing that they can honestly own, seeking to make amends and committing (if applicable) to develop safeguards together so that the hurtful behavior does not continue. Again, as noted above, bringing in an outside mediator can be helpful.

While pursuing reconciling forgiveness may seem daunting, the process recognizes the essential Christian confession that we are all sinners who need to repent and grow continually. Seeking reconciling forgiveness invites us onto the pathway of transformation and proclaims that we have hope for an ongoing relationship with those who have hurt us—and those whom we have hurt.

When someone leaves the process or cannot participate in the process of reconciling forgiveness, it is still possible to offer unilateral forgiveness for the sake of our own well-being. Unilateral forgiveness recognizes that ruminating on the wrong another has done to us will make us small and bitter. While unforgiveness might feel like a good way to punish the person who wronged us, it "is like drinking poison and hoping the other person dies."[14]

We can unilaterally forgive people whenever they come to mind by adapting the following prayer from the Twelve Steps: "God, please have mercy

---

13. For example, Jerry Sittser, *A Grace Disguised: How the Soul Grows through Loss* (Zondervan, 1996).

14. I've heard this from people who are working through the Twelve Steps of Alcoholics Anonymous.

on _____. May I extend the same understanding to _____ that I would cheerfully grant a sick friend. Please save me from anger and resentment."[15]

In unilateral forgiveness, our heart releases the other person, but our brain knows the damaging behavior may continue. Thus, it may be necessary to protect ourselves or others from that person's continued wrongdoing.

As Christians, we believe that God is continually at work, and we hope that we will see unexpected relational healing over the course of the long story of our lives. And even if reconciliation doesn't happen in our lifetime, we trust that we have all of eternity for God to restore and heal our relationships.

Conclusion

Conflicts resolve on a broad spectrum. At one end of the spectrum, we might imagine a community that fractures and breaks apart due to the conflict, with various factions still angry and unreconciled. At the other end, we can imagine a united community with a renewed sense of purpose and vision that the heat of conflict has forged. Many conflicts resolve somewhere in the middle, perhaps with some people leaving and the rest continuing to journey together.

Conflict is arduous, and many of us avoid facing it as much as possible. But fleeing the difficulty doesn't do anyone any good. If we are going to participate in God's reconciling rescue of the world, we've got to take up practices that work toward peace in the heat of conflict. If we are going to be peacemakers in our communities, we must recognize that we are undeserving recipients of God's grace and are not superior to others. We also need to be willing to hear helpful truths about ourselves from people who stand on the "other side" of an issue. And we need to care enough to listen to the deep feelings of others as we courageously advocate for our God-given convictions while also having the humility to ask for help. These postures will transform us into peacemakers.

Whether our attempts toward reconciliation are successful or not, they are always pleasing to Christ, who offered himself to the world as the way of peace. Whether we see the fruits of peace in our communities or not, we trust that the Holy Spirit will bear witness to the Peacemaker as we partner with Christ to seek the unity of the beloved community.

---

15. Adapted from Alcoholics Anonymous, *Alcoholics Anonymous Big Book* (BN, 2008), 67.

7

Speaking Truth in Love

Preparing the Heart to Engage

Tim Muehlhoff

At the last minute, you and your friends decide to attend a debate between two noted theologians being hosted by a local church. The odd thing is, in your rush you realize you don't know the exact topic. You've heard of the two participants, but what they'll be addressing is unknown. That being said, how would you want them to treat each other? In front of a full auditorium with the event being live-streamed to thousands, how do you want these two students of the Word to treat each other? Since it's a debate, you assume they'll have real disagreements and even interpret sections of Scripture from different points of view. But how should they interact with each other?

The apostle Paul seems to be clear that we should strive to speak truth in love (Eph. 4:15). Paul's admonition is a good reminder that all communication exists on two levels, not one. The *content level* relays our convictions, opinions, and biblical interpretations. Yet communication scholars argue that if the *relational level*—compassion, empathy, respect, and acknowledgment—is not first established, or if it's violated, our communication will be greatly hindered. As Christian communicators, we must be diligent to protect both the content and relational levels of our communication. Back to my original question: Not knowing the content of the debate between two Christian leaders, how do you want each to treat the other—particularly on the relational level?

Before I offer my opinion, let me situate myself. I'm a professor of communication at a conservative Christian university that has strong opinions about the topics covered in this book. When it comes to sexuality or traditional marriage, I sign a doctrinal statement every year that affirms what has been labeled in this volume as Side B (non-affirming). I sign the statement because it is what I believe. In addition, I'm the codirector of the Winsome Conviction Project (WCP) that seeks to introduce compassion, perspective-taking, and civility into disagreements between Christ followers.[1] For the past four years, I've met with churches and Christian organizations fracturing over issues of race, politics, COVID-19 protocols, and most relevant to this book, sexuality and gender. What we teach these groups is pertinent to the question posed at the start of this chapter: How do we want committed Christians to treat one another even when they disagree?

Welcome to the Argument Culture

Speaking truth in love has seemingly fallen on hard times. Nearly twenty-five years ago, Georgetown linguist Deborah Tannen coined the term *argument culture* to describe the pervasive, warlike stance we take toward one another as we disagree. "The argument culture urges us to approach the world—and the people in it—in an adversarial frame of mind."[2] The problem with approaching people in this type of mindset is that the relational level of communication is at best set aside, and at worst demeaned. This is especially true when there's an argument to be won. "When you're having an argument with someone, your goal is not to listen and understand. Instead, you use every tactic you can think of—including distorting what your opponent just said—in order to win the argument."[3] According to Tannen, the clearest expression of the argument culture is that we take complex arguments and simplify them in order to best dismantle them. "When there is a need to make others wrong, the temptation is great to oversimplify at best, and at worst to distort or even misrepresent others' positions, the better to refute them—to search for the most foolish statement in a generally reasonable treatise, seize upon the

---

1. For more information on the Winsome Conviction Project, see WinsomeConviction.com.
2. Deborah Tannen, *The Argument Culture: Moving from Debate to Dialogue* (Random House, 1998), 3.
3. Tannen, *Argument Culture*, 5.

weakest examples, ignore facts that support your opponent's views and focus only on those that support yours."[4]

The argument culture forces us into an adversarial stance; listening and understanding are eschewed in favor of winning a debate, and most importantly, complex views are purposely simplified in order to best attack them. As Christian communicators, do we want to model an alternative to today's argument culture? Don't be so quick to say, "Of course!" Since the creation of the Winsome Conviction Project, I've seen Christians in person and on social media take complex issues such as critical race theory, immigration policy, mask mandates, use of preferred gender pronouns, climate change, the viability of certain political candidates, and different ways to address the LGBTQ+ community and create wildly simplistic versions void of complexity or nuance. As we wrestle with the crucial issues in this book and the conversations that will surely follow, do we want to be a vibrant alternative to today's vitriol? If so, how? When the disagreements become deep and emotionally charged, how can we still speak truth in love? Where do we start?

After years of moderating conversations—some successfully, some not—the WCP has adopted what we call the *three-conversations approach*.[5] It's our conviction that any one conversation is actually three separate interactions.

Three-Conversations Approach

When having a difficult conversation with a person, we often focus solely on the actual talk at the moment. Right before we sit down with a person, we think about what we most want to say and the best way to do so. It makes sense, right? Words, once said, can't be taken back, and we need to think carefully about this interaction as it's happening. However, we mistakenly think the conversation we are about to have is the only one. In reality, every *one* conversation is actually *three*—the preconversation, the actual conversation, and the postconversation.

The *preconversation* is the one you have with yourself heading into the talk, which often surfaces fear, anger, bitterness, or hurt. All those emotions are carried into the conversation before a single word is uttered. These emotions can easily undermine any attempt at a positive encounter. The *actual conversation* is where you listen to understand, find points of agreement, do perspective-taking,

---

4. Tannen, *Argument Culture*, 265.
5. If interested in reading more about the three-conversations approach, see my book, cowritten with Sean McDowell, *End the Stalemate: Move Past Cancel Culture to Meaningful Conversations* (Tyndale, 2024).

evaluate a person's arguments, and use discernment to determine what needs to be said at this moment. The *postconversation* is the one you have with your friends where you process what was said. Any progress you may have achieved in the conversation may be quickly discounted, or counteracted, by your peer group. This insight into the multilayered nature of our interactions is not a cure-all, but it has shaped how I've come to think about engagement.

While each conversation warrants its own consideration, the focus of this chapter will be on the oft-neglected preconversation. In my experience moderating conversations, I've learned that if heart work is not done before the conversation, then emotions will often run rampant. "Fools show their annoyance at once," assert the ancient writers, "but the prudent overlook an insult" (Prov. 12:16). Primed by today's argument culture, overlooking a person's perceived or actual slight will take much prior work.

Understanding the Preconversation

When reading the Scriptures, it doesn't take long to discover the importance they place on our *heart*, with over five hundred references made concerning it. Why is the heart so important? One writer of the book of Proverbs boldly asserts that "everything [we] do flows from" the heart (Prov. 4:23), and just as water shows our reflections, our lives reflect our hearts (27:19). Keep in mind that when the Bible refers to our hearts, it's not just the seat of our emotions. Rather, it's equally our intellect, volition, and personality. In short, it's all of you! For us to have engaging, compassionate, and civil conversations, we'll have to make sure our hearts are ready even long before the conversation starts. Why? "For the mouth speaks what the heart is full of," asserts Jesus (Matt. 12:34).

Let Jesus's statement sink in for a moment. The attitude and emotions you have toward a person will bleed out into the conversation regardless of your attempts to hide them. If you feel contempt, anger, or disgust toward a person, then that person and anyone watching will pick up on it immediately. Adopting King David's approach, the following categories will prompt us to ask God to search our hearts and reveal to us anything that must be addressed at a soul level (Ps. 139:23–24). To facilitate soul-searching, each category will be accompanied by questions to ask in times of prayer and reflection in preparation to engage another.

Adopting a Gentle Approach

Today, Christians seem to think biblical gentleness is relative to how they are treated. *I'll be gentle so long as you are to me.* Thus, if a gentle approach is met with aggression, or we feel we are losing the debate, then it's easily abandoned. Yet, is gentleness relative? I'm not so sure. The codirector of the Winsome Conviction Project, Rick Langer, persuasively argues that biblical gentleness is a nonnegotiable. After pointing out that Jesus identifies himself as *gentle and lowly* when he asks us to take on his yoke (Matt. 11:28–30), Langer asserts that gentleness is a theme woven throughout the New Testament.

> Gentleness is a fruit of the Spirit (Gal. 5:25–26). Gentleness, and a host of other gentle-like virtues such as patience and kindness, are listed among the Holy Spirit's fruit in our lives. The proof that the *root* of the Holy Spirit has taken hold in our hearts is that we bear the *fruit* of the Holy Spirit in our lives—and that fruit includes gentleness. The list goes on and on. Gentleness is a necessary qualification for Christian leadership (1 Tim. 3:3). Gentleness is essential for our response to non-believers (1 Pet. 3:15). Gentleness is essential for restoration from sin and failure (Gal. 6:1). Perhaps most relevant for our times, Paul even suggests gentleness be applied to even the most extreme cases, cases where people have been snared by the devil and captured to do his will (2 Tim. 2:24–26).[6]

Yet, what if the position a theologian or someone in your church small group holds is one that you think leads to sin? Surely, gentleness wouldn't be the right approach to that type of view, would it? Such a view would need to be firmly called out and stringently rebutted. This seems to be the approach some Christians with significant platforms are taking toward those with whom they disagree. How would Paul advise in the situation where a believer is clearly in sin?

"Brothers and sisters, if someone is caught in a sin," asserts Paul, "you who live by the Spirit should restore that person gently" (Gal. 6:1). To be clear, this fellow believer is in sin, or leading others into sin. Paul is clear that this sin (content level) must be addressed, but equally clear is that it should be done gently (relational level). The word Paul uses for gentleness (*prautēs*) is a medical term and suggests careful mending of a broken bone.[7]

It's here that people often offer a valid objection: You appeal to Paul's gentle approach to followers in Galatia but leave out his far-from-gentle stance toward the Judaizers in his letter to Philippi. The Judaizers were a breakaway group of Jews who "endeavored to compel Gentile converts to submit to

---

6. Rick Langer, "Have We Become Moral Relativists about Gentleness?," *Christian Scholar's Review* (blog), May 26, 2022, https://christianscholars.com/guest-post-have-we-become-moral-relativists-about-gentleness/.

7. James Montgomery Boice, *Galatians*, Expositor's Bible Commentary, ed. Frank E. Gaebelein (Zondervan, 1976), 10:501.

circumcision and other Jewish practices in order to be saved."[8] In response, Paul holds nothing back and calls them dogs, evil men, and mutilators of the flesh (Phil. 3:2). It seems Paul takes a vastly different approach with groups who are not merely in sin but who want to fundamentally alter the gospel of Christ. Does the topic of this book fall into that category? For me, while this disagreement is paramount to the health of the church, I don't see it altering the gospel; rather, I see it affecting how we apply the gospel to differing individuals inside and outside the church.

> **Heart Assessment**
>
> - Do I view gentleness as being relative to how others treat me, or is it a biblical nonnegotiable?
> - What are ways people treat me that tempt me to abandon a gentle approach?
> - Does the disagreement over affirming and non-affirming rise to the level of altering the gospel?

Intellectual Humility

Modern philosophers have identified and focused on intellectual virtues—open-mindedness, courage, tenacity, fair-mindedness, curiosity, humility—that flow from a person's intellectual character, which can be defined as "the force of accumulated thinking habits that shape and color every decision we make."[9]

The ancient writers advocate the virtue of humility and give warning against its counterpart, pride. While the result of pride is destruction and disgrace, the humble person will experience honor, riches, and fullness of life (Prov. 11:2; 18:12; 22:4; 29:23). The defining trait of a humble person is that they "listen to advice" (12:15). Notice the writer did not say the advice would always be followed, but rather, it would be humbly considered. In commenting on this verse, Old Testament scholar Derek Kidner asserts that a prime way a wise communicator becomes aware of their own prejudices is to be open to the views of others.[10]

---

8. Homer A. Kent Jr., *Philippians*, Expositor's Bible Commentary, ed. Frank E. Gaebelein (Zondervan, 1978), 11:138.

9. Philip E. Dow, *Virtuous Minds: Intellectual Character Development* (IVP Academic, 2013), 22.

10. Derek Kidner, *Proverbs: An Introduction and Commentary*, Tyndale Old Testament Commentaries, ed. D. J. Wiseman (InterVarsity, 1964), 97.

My students once surprised me by asking, "When is the last time you changed your mind on a topic?" I must confess, the question gave me pause. One of the hazards of being an academic, or educator, is that we get paid to have learned opinions. And once those opinions are put in print, changing our minds becomes even more difficult and rare. Often when I listen to Christian academics discuss topics, I feel it more resembles dual monologues, rather than give-and-take dialogues. These monologues often show traits of *agenda anxiety*, which is defined as "the anxiety to get across all the points of whatever subject they are dealing with" in a debate.[11] With so much to say, listening and learning are sacrificed to get *all* points on record.

Accepting a humble approach to our Christian convictions means that we embrace the reality that all of us have blind spots, lack of information, and biases that keep us from seeing and knowing things clearly. As Paul states, "For now we see only a reflection as in a mirror; then we shall see face to face. Now I know in part; then I shall know fully, even as I am fully known" (1 Cor. 13:12). Assuming such a humble position—that in our human limitations, we know only in part—allows us to connect with individuals and groups who differ from us. Embracing our limitations allows us to enter such exchanges with the attitude that we can gain new information and learn from others.

Heart Assessment

- In approaching theological subjects, when is the last time I changed my mind?
- Do I feel the freedom to alter my position on theological concepts, or to embrace nuance?
- Do I approach others with the attitude that I might learn something?
- How much freedom to change my opinions does my community or institution allow?

Correcting Views of Others

In order to break a complex world up into more manageable, predictable pieces, we continually work through a three-stage process when encountering

---

11. Ruel Howe, *The Miracle of Dialogue* (Seabury, 1968), 87.

people: categorization, characterization, and correction.[12] When we first meet a person, we immediately place him or her into broad categories such as liberal or conservative, modern or postmodern, or in our case, affirming or non-affirming. Once we place them into a category, we assign specific characteristics to that person based on the category. In a recent class, I put the following categories, representing today's turbulent times, on the screen and asked students to respond with specific characteristics:

Black Lives Matter
Palestinians
Blue Lives Matter
MAGA
Israelis
Russians
Trans athletes
President Biden supporters

Students were fairly quick to offer their assessments of characteristics that came to mind. For some, it was easy to characterize certain groups as being *all* good or *all* bad. This tendency is what experts call *psychological splitting*, where we remove ambiguity about others by casting them in a completely negative or positive light. Thus, *my* group can do no wrong, while competing groups can do no right.

For our purposes, it would be helpful in the preconversation to ask, What characteristics do I attach to the categories of Side A (affirming) or Side B (non-affirming)? And, Am I in danger of falling prey to some form of splitting?

The correction stage—the *most* neglected—occurs only if we get to know individuals and address initial judgments. Splitting possibly becomes less pronounced as we see the strengths and weaknesses of each group. The problem is, our stringent categories often keep us from getting to know people on an individual basis. In his thought-provoking book *Talking across the Divide*, Justin Lee offers the following challenge: "In your life, look for opportunities to get outside your own bubble and listen to what other groups are saying."[13] Specifically, Lee suggests we diligently work to seek out diverse connections on social media to understand—not debate—other perspectives; when trying to

---

12. G. A. Quattrone, "On the Congruity between Internal States and Actions," *Psychological Bulletin* 98 (1985): 3–40.
13. Justin Lee, *Talking across the Divide: How to Communicate with People You Disagree with and Maybe Even Change the World* (TarcherPerigee, 2018), 93.

understand others, ask what books or social media sources inform their thinking; and particularly when an issue seems obvious, find bloggers or TED talks that present the other side. Be warned, such an approach comes with risks.

If we do begin to make changes to our categories that may be more favorable, our in-group often immediately counters our thinking: "I know you had a positive interaction with a person, but remember, that group is _____ [fill in the blank with a negative assessment]." In light of such peer pressure, do we keep our category changes, or do we conform to the position of our community?

> ### Heart Assessment
>
> - What characteristics do I hold for people in the category of Side A theologians? Are they mostly negative, or positive?
> - What characteristic do I hold for people in the category of Side B theologians? Are they mostly negative, or positive?
> - What personal contact do I have with theologians who hold differing views?
> - Does the history of my social media feed show diversity, or simply buttressing my own views?

Soft Start-Up

Relational expert John Gottman argues that the first thirty seconds to a minute sets the entire tone of a conversation. He even goes so far as to suggest you take a pause in a conversation if the start goes poorly or is harsh.[14] How we frame a conversation in our opening will determine if a person or audience will be able to receive what we are wanting to say. We see Paul modeling this in his decision on how to address idol worship.

While Paul was in Athens, we learn he was "greatly distressed to see that the city was full of idols" (Acts 17:16). The word for *distressed* can be translated as being sick to the stomach. In others words, these idols made him want to vomit. He is invited to share his thoughts with a group of Athenian leaders. Knowing how he feels, we assume how he'll respond: "Men of Athens, your worshiping of idols is an affront to God. And I'll have none of it!" Shockingly, that's not how he starts. Instead, Paul begins, "Men of Athens, I notice that you are very religious in every way" (Acts 17:22). What! Why not just start with idols making

---

14. John Gottman, *The Seven Principles for Making Marriage Work* (Crown, 1999), 26.

him sick? Because he wants to engage. Make no mistake, he eventually gives a masterful rebuttal of their false beliefs. Yet, he doesn't start there. He offers a concession and acknowledges that they are *very* religious and desire to worship. Their inclination is right, but their focus is skewed. Paul purposefully starts in a way that establishes the relational level of communication.

To be honest, this is the one that I struggle with most. In college, I was on a competitive speech team where I specialized in the persuasion category. Each competitor had ten minutes to present their argument. The relational level was set aside as you came out swinging, starting with your best evidence first. Ten minutes would fly by, and there wasn't time to start slow, cultivate common ground, or be nuanced—not with two judges following your argument and seemingly evaluating every word. The goal was to shut down the counter-perspective as quickly as possible to prevent them any momentum. Yet, *calling in* is the exact opposite approach: I offer my view in such a way as to allow the conversation to grow, and I take time to inquire about the other person's reasoning. If a person commits an error in interpretation, I don't jump on them, but rather, I ask questions to help them process. Competitive speech makes for a riveting sport, but it's disastrous for Christian unity.

> **Heart Assessment**
>
> - What can I say in the first minute of the conversation that doesn't foster defensiveness or seem like an attack?
> - What in the first minute can invite a person into the conversation, not shut them out?
> - What common ground can be cultivated before I marshal my best arguments?

Call In, Not Out

Rhetorical scholars agree with Gottman's assertion of the first minute setting the tone, and they have long studied what are called *discursive openings*. A speaker can start a dialogue in two key ways: either by *calling out* or by *calling in*. Calling someone out is "typically a public performance in which a person self-righteously demonstrates their superior knowledge, shaming an individual."[15] Theological discussions are particularly prone to this type of opening:

---

15. Jennifer Mahan, "Calling-In versus Calling-Out: 'Throwing Out My Activist Armchair,'" *If When How*, June 6, 2017, https://ifwhenhow.org/news/calling-in-versus-calling-out-throwing

"If anyone seriously studied the Bible, it would be impossible for them to hold this particular position."

"If we can make Paul unclear on this issue, then we can make him unclear on everything."

"In the original Greek, it's clear that the word isn't being used in the way you are suggesting."

"Church history is overwhelmingly on my side, not yours."

Such assertions, even if correct, can have a chilling effect on the conversation and audience. If the issue is so clear, why even have this discussion? Are the two participants in this conversation simply trying to one-up each other with knowledge of Greek or church history?

In contrast, *calling in* invites participants to explore common ground and experiences. "Calling in foregrounds, at a minimum, mutuality, patience, respect, and tolerance as a path forward when dealing with perspectives that we don't understand."[16] Central to calling in is a sense of humility, earnestness to understand, and allowing others to make mistakes without trying to shame them. Most importantly, the goal of calling in is to maintain the "possibility to further conversation among those with deeply held differences."[17]

Years ago, I did a debate on the historical resurrection with a noted atheist. In our pre-debate meeting, he confidently told me there are no good reasons to believe in the bodily resurrection of a dead man. Period. "Why then do the debate?" I asked. "To show you up in front of a packed auditorium," he responded, with a wry smile. Once the debate started, he quickly objected to any point he felt needed a rebuttal—often interrupting me. By eagerly calling me out, he left us no time to explore areas of common ground or interest in each other's intellectual or personal journey. It was, from the start, an intellectual chess match. Surely, when it comes to disagreeing over theological concepts, we want to do better.

Heart Assessment

- How might I call a person into the conversation?

-out-my-activist-armchair/#:~:text=Calling%2Din%20is%20a%20proposed,a%20spectacle%20out%20of%20it.

16. N. L. Tran, "Calling IN: A Less Disposable Way of Holding Each Other Accountable," in *The Solidarity Struggle*, ed. M. McKenzie and C. McDonald (BGD, 2016), 60.

17. Renee G. Heath and Jennifer L. Borda, "Reclaiming Civility: Towards a Discursive Opening in Dialogue and Deliberation," *Journal of Deliberative Democracy* 17, no. 1 (2001): 9–18.

> - When I'm passionate about an issue, do I tend to present my evidence or perspective as an open-and-shut case?
> - Am I heading into this conversation looking for the other person to make a mistake so I can exploit it?

Awareness That People Are Listening

Awareness that people are listening ought to prompt us to diligently search our motivations and attitudes heading into a potentially volatile conversation. The upcoming generation of young evangelicals are paying close attention to how we talk to one another. To be honest, they are not liking what they are hearing.

Scholars have identified what is commonly called a *communication stage* or talk stage. A stage is created when two people talking become aware that another person or party is watching and listening. No longer is the conversation merely between two people, but now others are listening in. In light of this reality, the speakers must assess how they are coming across to the third party and perhaps monitor *what* and *how* something is being said.

This sentiment seems to be what the psalmist is articulating in one of the most candid entries of the 150 recorded psalms. In raw emotional language, Asaph shares how he has nearly lost a foothold on his faith in Yahweh's goodness (Ps. 73:2). Why? He has "envied the arrogant" when seeing how their evil does not produce judgment but, rather, blessings upon blessings. "They have no struggles; their bodies are healthy and strong. They are free from common human burdens; they are not plagued by human ills" (vv. 4–5). Asaph's conclusion is that he's kept his heart pure in vain (v. 13). Yet, he refrains from giving full vent to his disillusionment for fear of how it would impact others—especially a younger audience: "If I had spoken out like that, I would have betrayed your children" (v. 15). Knowing he's on a talk stage provides him with much motivation to show restraint in venting. Christian communicators, when discussing potentially explosive issues, need to show the same restraint and embrace the reality that the faith of those listening may hang in the balance. Consider the following sobering statistics.

In 2018, the Pinetops Foundation estimated that roughly thirty-five million young people will leave the faith by 2050.[18] An equally disturbing study from Pew Research asserts that for every one person who commits to Christianity,

---

18. Pinetops Foundation, *The Great Opportunity: The American Church in 2050* (2018), 9, https://cdn2.hubspot.net/hubfs/4245467/The%20Great%20Opportunity.pdf.

four leave the faith.[19] When asked why they are leaving, these studies report that one salient reason is that respondents are fed up and discouraged with how people claiming to know Christ treat one another.

This sentiment was shared with me in an email after speaking at a church on the need to be kind to one another even in our disagreements. "We have struggled with church and committing to a church since Covid because of the ways we have seen members, and more importantly, leaders handle sensitive topics. We are discouraged and hurt by a lot that has been said." It's one thing to read an email by a stranger; another altogether when it's a friend. Mary, a person I've known and admired for years, sat across from me at a table at a local coffee shop and shared her heart: "I simply can't take it anymore how Christians talk about each other, especially on social media," she said with strong emotions surfacing. "I mean, to be brutally honest, if people are supposed to know we are Jesus followers by our love, we are failing miserably. I've hit a breaking point." Sadly, she's left the faith.

The pain etched on her face that day should be a powerful reminder to us that an entire generation of young evangelicals are watching the posture we take toward one another. Perhaps this is what the ancient writer suggests when they assert, "The tongue has the power of life and death" (Prov. 18:21). What I witnessed during our coffee conversation was a woman who had, over time, been beaten down from listening to Christian leaders and educators speak death to one another.

The data suggests that young believers are thinking about leaving the faith because of how we communicate with one another. Heading into a conversation with a person holding a differing theological or political position, will we solely focus on presenting content, or will we equally protect the relational?

Heart Assessment

- Do I view having to speak truth in love as a hindrance?
- Does the reality of a talk stage change how I speak?
- Will I accept the reality that how I talk may weaken the faith of others?
- How do I talk about others when off the talk stage?

---

19. "America's Changing Religious Landscape," Pew Research Center, May 15, 2015, https://www.pewresearch.org. If interested in hearing more about this exodus and how to respond to those contemplating leaving, see an excellent work by two colleagues: Sean McDowell and John Marriott, *Set Adrift: Deconstructing What You Believe without Sinking Your Faith* (Zondervan, 2023).

Attending to Emotions

I close our discussion of preconversation and heart preparation with the importance of understanding our emotional state before entering a conversation. This is key because our emotions will be passed on to the other person and vice versa. This transfer of emotions is called *emotional contagion*. "We catch feelings from one another as though they were some kind of virus," notes behavioral scientist Daniel Goleman.[20] How can this transfer of emotions happen so quickly? Behavioral experts explain that our complex brains have a low and high road when taking in information such as emotions.

The high road is the part of our brain that is keenly aware of facts and analyzes them accordingly. The low road is "circuitry that operates beneath our awareness, automatically and effortlessly, with immense speed." While the high road allows us to think about the data we are receiving, the low road lets us feel before we are even aware of it. When we "sense the sarcasm in a remark, we have the low road to thank."[21]

We cannot avoid emotional contagion and the transfer of our emotions because our low road is always subconsciously taking in information. This makes assessing our emotions before a difficult conversation crucial! Before every conversation, we must recognize and manage our emotions, knowing that they will, to some degree, be transferred to the other person and to the watching audience. If we are to engage one another over complex theological issues and maintain Paul's command to speak truth in love, then we'll have to surface and address our emotions beforehand.

Heart Assessment

- What emotions do I harbor toward the other side?
- Do I love those with whom I disagree as brothers and sisters in the faith, or do I view them as adversaries?
- Am I angry at them for holding their particular beliefs? How do I handle my anger?

---

20. Daniel Goleman, *Social Intelligence: The New Science of Human Relationships* (Random House, 2006), 115.
21. Goleman, *Social Intelligence*, 16.

Conclusion

I close with the insights of Supreme Court Justice Sonia Sotomayor. When newly appointed Justice Brett Kavanaugh was sworn in to our highest court, he came with much controversy and a highly publicized Senate Judiciary Committee hearing involving past claims of sexual assault. Additionally, his stated views deeply went against some of Justice Sotomayor's deepest convictions. How would she react? "When you're charged with working together for most of the remainder of your life, you have to create a relationship," she said. "The nine of us are now a family and we're a family with each of us our own burdens and our own obligations to others, but this is our work family, and it's just as important as our personal family."[22]

I recently attended a one-day seminar with Christian university presidents, administrators, and fellow educators. The moderator asked us to share: What did we see as the chief challenge facing Christian higher education? Issues of sexuality—how to affirm or not to affirm those within our universities who question their sexual identity—were mentioned by almost everyone. Thus, the issues of this book are not going away, nor are theologians holding differing views. When people inside and outside the church look to us educators, theologians, and thought leaders, what will they see? A *calling in* to this topic filled with gentleness and truth, or two entrenched camps? If we are to maintain truth and love—content and relational—then we must be committed to one another at the heart level. Not as a judicial family, but as the family of God. The work to make that happen must take place long before the conversation ever starts.[23]

---

22. Gina Martinez, "Justice Sotomayor on Kavanaugh Coming to the Supreme Court: 'The Nine of Us Are Now a Family,'" *Time*, November 17, 2018, https://time.com/5458068/supreme-court-sonia-sotomayor-kavanaugh-family/.

23. Parts of this chapter are explored in fuller detail in the following: Tim Muehlhoff and Rick Langer, *Winsome Conviction: Disagreeing without Dividing the Church* (InterVarsity, 2020); and Tim Muehlhoff and Sean McDowell, *End the Stalemate: Move Past Cancel Culture to Meaningful Conversations* (Tyndale, 2024).

8

Grace across the Divide
Tips for Christ-Honoring Dialogue

Justin Lee

When Christians have theological disagreements, we often begin by discussing and debating what the *right answers* are. That makes sense, because getting the answers right is important—for parents seeking to give good guidance to their children, for pastors seeking to give good guidance to their flocks, and for all of us seeking to honor and obey God. For some of us, the answers to the theological questions in this book are especially important because of how much they affect our daily lives. If God is telling us to do something or not to do something, we need to get that *right*.

But what if, after all our discussion and debate, we still disagree? When a disagreement is too important to ignore and not everyone can be right, how do we move forward together as siblings in Christ?

The secular world teaches us that these kinds of standoffs should be resolved with power and shows of force. But Jesus taught us that "the last will be first" (Matt. 20:16) and "the meek . . . will inherit the earth" (Matt. 5:5). Jesus demonstrated the power of humility and self-sacrifice in a world that sees those things as weakness. As Christians, our default approach to disagreement shouldn't be raising our voices to outshout the other side, but rather, demonstrating humility and grace toward our opponents, listening to and caring for them in a way that invites them to put down their weapons and open their hearts.

That's not usually our instinct, though. With major disagreements, our instinct is usually to argue and point fingers, accusing one another of being unwilling to admit the obvious truth. After all, if the right answers seem plainly obvious to *me*, how is it possible *you* could honestly not see what I see? With enough prayer and thoughtful study, shouldn't a group of sincere, devout followers of Jesus be able to agree on what the Bible teaches?

In theory, it certainly seems so. But as Yale student Benjamin Brewster observed in 1882, "In theory there is no difference between theory and practice, while in practice there is."[1] In *theory*, we would all come to this conversation humbly, with clear heads and open hearts, ready to be completely objective as we seek God's will together. In *practice*, though, it rarely works that way. As hard as we try to be objective—on LGBTQ issues and many others—none of us are truly objective. We're all influenced by our preexisting beliefs, personal experiences, and desire not to be wrong. We're all fallible humans with limited knowledge.

We can tell ourselves we're not influenced by any of that—that we're just being purely logical—but the reality is that human beings aren't purely logical creatures. In many ways, that's a good thing. God didn't build us as unfeeling machines; grace, empathy, and compassion are all gifts that help temper our logical sides and keep us from being cold and unkind. But our emotional sides can also be corrupted by our sin nature and lead to pride, defensiveness, and a tendency to see things only through the lens of what's most convenient for us. And this happens on an unconscious level: We can *feel* like we're being logical even when our perspective is skewed. However sincerely we seek to discern the will of God, we do so imperfectly and often without awareness of our own blind spots. We think *we're* the ones seeing things clearly and that the other side is unwilling to listen to reason, while they are equally convinced that the opposite is true.

Our best hope of arriving at the truth together, then, is to continually engage in prayerful, gracious *dialogue* with one another, challenging and sharpening one another, not as opponents, but as friends and siblings in Christ. This means sitting down with the people we disagree with and treating them the way we'd want to be treated—with kindness and compassion, even when they get things wrong. The point of this dialogue isn't just to talk endlessly; we do eventually want to be able to agree on the right answers, correcting our

---

1. Benjamin Brewster, "Portfolio: Theory and Practice," *Yale Literary Magazine* 47 (1882): 202.

mistakes along the way. But we can't wait until we're all in agreement before we start repairing the rifts our arguments have created. Through gracious dialogue, we can practice loving one another and working toward the truth at the same time.

I'm not proposing this as some naive idealist. I've spent the last twenty-five years of my life helping to organize practical, real-world dialogue between Christians who disagree on LGBTQ issues. If anyone knows how difficult it is, I do. I've made plenty of mistakes along the way and seen plenty of these attempts at dialogue go wrong. But I've also seen them succeed, time and time again, when no one thought there was a chance of success. I've seen what makes the difference between success and failure, and in this chapter, I'd like to offer seven key things you can do to find a productive way forward in these conversations—in your family, your congregation, or wherever else these issues threaten to divide us.

It's easiest to have these sorts of conversations one-on-one, in a quiet space without interruptions. But the following tips can be adapted for all sorts of settings and even for much larger groups, such as when a congregation is divided. I've used them to lead thoughtful, productive conversations among entire auditoriums full of people.

Tip 1: Start from Agreement

Before we talk about why we *disagree*, it's important to talk about all the ways we *agree*. At first, it can seem like there's very little overlap between the "traditional" and "affirming" sides of this conversation. But if we take a few steps back, we should have a lot of things in common that we can build on. (If we don't, we've got a much more fundamental problem we need to address!)

At the beginning of any in-depth discussion of LGBTQ disagreements with fellow Christians—whether one-on-one or in a large group—I like to start by establishing our love and respect for one another as siblings in Christ and our shared desire to seek the truth together. Then, I find it helpful for everyone to work together to establish a set of "givens"—points of common ground that both sides can agree on from the outset.

We might start with a short list of "things we agree on about God," such as

- We agree that there is a God who loves us and wants what's best for us.
- We agree that God has the right to give us boundaries.
- We agree that we're willing to do what God asks, even when it's difficult.

Then we might move into a short list of "things we agree on about the Bible," such as

- We agree that the Bible is morally authoritative.
- We agree that the Bible isn't always easy to interpret, and well-meaning Christians sometimes disagree on its interpretation.
- We agree that proper interpretation requires thoughtful consideration of translation and context and a holistic approach to the Scriptures.

Sometimes, by this point, you begin to realize that you're not on the same page about some of these fundamentals. If so, you may need to have a more basic conversation and decide whether you have enough common ground to even get into the LGBTQ disagreement at this time.

Assuming you do have enough common ground, the next step is to establish some givens on the specific issue you're discussing. If you're talking about your church's view on same-sex marriage, for instance, you might have a list of "things we agree on about marriage and sexuality," such as

- We agree that some people—including some Christians—experience attraction only to the same sex, they didn't choose to feel this way, and this may be a lifelong condition.
- We agree that such Christians are equally part of the body of Christ, equally loved by God, and equally in need of human connection and community.
- We agree that not all sexual desires are okay to act on.
- We agree that marriage is about much more than sex; it is also about companionship, love, family, etc.

You might notice that some of these givens are points commonly made on the traditional side, while others are points commonly made on the affirming side. That's intentional. We're not trying to "stack the deck" in favor of the answers we expect; we're trying to establish common ground. It's important for both sides to realize that, for instance, even affirming Christians can agree that obeying God requires self-sacrifice, and even traditional Christians can agree that people don't choose to be gay.

Whether we state them out loud or not, we all go into these conversations with our own personal sets of givens. Writing them out like this—and finding a set we can all agree on—serves three important purposes.

First, it reminds us of how much we have in common and that we're on the same team, not enemies trying to "beat" one another.

Second, it helps us avoid some of the ungracious accusations that might otherwise be thrown around in the midst of heated disagreement. Too often, when Christians disagree on how to interpret a passage, for instance, they accuse each other of not believing Scripture. If we've already established that both sides believe Scripture and are willing to abide by it, it allows us to focus on the real disagreement—on how to *interpret* and *apply* the passage.

And third, when we state our givens up front, we can discover major points of disagreement that we didn't know we had. If we don't all agree that Scripture is morally authoritative, for instance, that's important for us to know before we spend hours debating what Scripture tells us. There's not much point in an exhaustive analysis of Romans 1 if, at the end of it, one side is just going to say, "It doesn't matter anyway because that's only Paul's opinion."

If, in the course of naming your givens, it becomes clear that both sides don't agree on something important, don't despair! There's still hope for a productive discussion. It just means that you'll need to back the conversation up a bit and use the rest of the tips to learn more about why *that* disagreement exists before you can move forward to the more complicated disagreements.

Tip 2: Clearly Define Your Terms

As you're clarifying your agreed-upon givens, it's also helpful to clarify the definitions you're using for any key terms, even if you think those definitions should be obvious. For example, a few paragraphs ago, I wrote that both sides should be able to agree that "people don't choose to be gay." If, like me, you define *gay* as "generally attracted to the same sex and not attracted to the opposite sex," then you hopefully understood my meaning: We don't get to choose our *attractions*, though we can choose our *actions*.

But as I've worked with Christians across the country, I've found that some Christians use a very different definition of *gay*. To them, being *gay* means someone has chosen to take on a particular sociopolitical identity or to engage in a particular kind of sexual "lifestyle." If you define *gay* in one of these ways, the assertion that "people don't choose to be gay" might seem obviously false—*of course* taking on a chosen identity is a choice!

We're so used to our own definitions of these words that we don't usually think to stop and define them; we just assume that everyone else is using the same definitions we are. But a disagreement on even a simple term like *gay* can ultimately derail the entire dialogue. We might argue and argue about whether being gay is a choice without realizing we're using completely different definitions of *gay*. And if we don't agree on whether it's a choice, how can we have a meaningful conversation about what God expects a gay person to *do*?

This all makes it very important to define your terms up front. Are *gay* people those who experience unchosen attraction to the same sex, or those who take on a chosen cultural identity? Does being *bisexual* mean someone is currently sexually active with both men and women, or just that they're attracted to both? What does it mean to *lust*, and how is that different from unchosen feelings of sexual attraction?

Defining our terms is also helpful for people encountering words for the first time. One friend of mine spent a frustrating hour listening to a speaker talk about the importance of good biblical *hermeneutics*—a term my friend didn't know—without the speaker's ever explaining what a hermeneutic is. That talk may have had wonderful content in it, but all my friend could tell me about it afterward was how lost he felt the whole time. In the same way, those new to discussions of gender identity may be too embarrassed to ask what *cisgender* or *nonbinary* means.

It's easy for any of us to forget that people outside our circles may not be as familiar with certain terms as we are. By defining them up front, we can avoid confusion and embarrassment and make sure we all agree on what it is we're talking about.

Tip 3: Listen First, Listen Most

James 1:19 advises us to be "quick to listen, slow to speak and slow to become angry." Being slow to anger is obviously good advice to us all, but for those of us who are teachers and preachers, it can be particularly difficult to convince ourselves to *listen* in times when we feel most called to speak out.

For any Christian who wants to make an impact, though, the practice of listening is essential. Talking is easy. The world is filled with people who like to hear themselves talk. But as James understood, genuine human connection requires the difficult work of *listening*.

Modern social media platforms aren't built to encourage deep listening. They invite us to be *content creators*, spouting off our own thoughts and waiting to see what kind of responses we get, and *content consumers*, reacting to others' content to publicly express our agreement or disagreement. In theory, these platforms promise us greater connection with a wide variety of people. In practice, they tend to replace genuine connection and conversation with something far less relational: virtual soapboxes where we post our thoughts and others can choose to "like" or "comment" or "follow" or "subscribe." It all encourages us to make our *talking* primary and our *listening* secondary—or sometimes nonexistent.

This problem isn't limited to social media. Think how frustrating it can be when you call a customer-service line and can't make it through the maze of "friendly" computer menus to talk to a human being. Or when you do finally get to a person, but they seem more focused on reading from a script than listening to your specific problem. Sometimes you just want to talk to someone who will actually listen!

Modern life is filled with situations where people either don't listen or listen only in service of their own agenda. In such a world, one of the most powerful things a Christian leader can do is to demonstrate genuine, thoughtful, selfless listening. People are starved for it. When you listen to people, you show that you care. And when they feel heard and cared for, they're much more likely to care about what you have to say in turn.

This is an easy concept to understand in theory, but it can be difficult to put into regular practice. On important, controversial issues, it's challenging to stay quiet and listen to someone else express opinions that you know are wrong or ill-informed. But even if you're certain the other person knows less about a subject than you do, resist the urge to begin by preaching at them or trying to out-argue them. Instead, to demonstrate that you care, listen carefully to what they have to say, and ask thoughtful follow-up questions.

When you listen to someone, you build a connection with them. That's reason enough to do it. But listening is also a powerful tool for navigating disagreements. When you listen, you learn about the other person's motives, their fears, their aspirations, and their misconceptions—all things that are vital to know if you want to convince them to consider a different perspective. Meanwhile, the simple act of listening to them helps them see that you're not there to fight them. Being listened to tends to calm people down and help them relax. If they know you're genuinely interested in their perspective, they may feel freer to ask about your views as well.

The ideal situation is for both sides to be so fully committed to "listen first, listen most" that they're actually competing with each other to be the better listeners. But one of the great things about this is that you can fully put it into practice whether the other side does or not. If you want to make the most impact, be the best listener.

Tip 4: Ask for Stories, and Share Your Own

When you listen, ask good questions.

But don't ask questions designed to trap the other person or to open the door for a debate you want to have. In fact, don't start by asking them to defend their views at all. Instead, as much as possible, ask questions that they can answer with a story.

I used to advise people, "Don't just ask *what* someone believes; ask *why* they believe it." My point was that knowing the human side of the equation—the concerns or experiences motivating the other person's position—helps you to understand where they're coming from so that you can have a more productive conversation. But I've changed my advice. Today, I say, "Don't just ask *what* someone believes or *why* they believe it; instead, ask *how* they came to the conclusions they did." Ask them to tell you the story: When did they first become aware of this debate? Have their views shifted over time, and if so, why? What were the key moments in their life that shaped their understanding?

Here's why this matters.

Suppose Alice and Bob are arguing over the correct interpretation of 1 Corinthians 6:9. If we ask *what* their views are, Bob might say that this passage condemns all same-sex sexual behavior, while Alice might say that it has a much more limited scope. They could argue this back and forth for a long time without getting anywhere.

Suppose we go one step further and ask *why* they interpret the passage this way. Bob might respond by pointing to similarities between the Greek roots in this passage and the Greek translation of Leviticus 18:22, arguing that this shows a consistent position between Old and New Testaments. Alice, on the other hand, might argue that the same-sex relations of Paul's place and time bear little resemblance to marriages of same-sex couples today, and that a comment on the former doesn't tell us anything about the latter.

They've each given us a reason for their belief. But they could still argue this endlessly back and forth without getting anywhere, and we still don't know anything about how their personal experiences may have shaped their views. They're having an apparently logical argument, but real people aren't 100 percent logical all the time. There's more to this disagreement than these two rational arguments suggest.

So what if each of them were to ask the other for the *story* of what shaped their views?

Perhaps Bob would talk about how empathy had once led him to consider Alice's view. But when a church he loved reconsidered its position on same-sex marriage, it turned out to be the first step in a series of moves away from traditional Christian doctrine, ultimately leading it to become something he no longer recognized as Christian. For him, then, this isn't just a debate about one passage; it's a fight for the soul of the church—either to remain true to God's commandments or to water them down in the name of appeasing an increasingly godless culture.

Alice, for her part, might share how she had once held a position more like Bob's, but when her brother had come out many years ago, she had watched in horror as his family and church both rejected him. If he had had the option of a committed relationship, she thinks, he might have stayed in his faith and avoided spiraling into depression and self-destructive choices, things she blames on Christians' cold treatment of him.

Both of these stories, by the way, are based on actual stories I've heard from real-life "Alices" and "Bobs." And don't they immediately give you a greater sense of compassion and understanding toward these two people?

When we keep the discussion only on *what* we believe and the logical *whys* we can give to defend our beliefs, it's easy to see each other as opponents in a zero-sum game. One of us must win; the other must lose. But when we hear someone's *story* and start to understand how they came to care so much, it helps us build a relationship with them—a relationship we'll need if we're going to have real, productive dialogue.

In this case, Bob can grieve with Alice over the tragedy of how her brother was treated and agree with her that churches must do more to draw people to Jesus instead of pushing them away. Alice can agree with Bob about the importance of staying faithful to Scripture and the core principles of the faith. By recognizing why this conversation has such high stakes for each other, they can help reduce the emotional tension and find more common ground. Perhaps they'll even find things they want to add to their list of shared givens.

They will, of course, still need to deal with their very real disagreement over the interpretation of 1 Corinthians 6:9. Our personal experiences do not *replace* good Bible study. But having spent time with each other's stories, they can approach the passage with greater nuance and sensitivity to each other's concerns, keeping real people's faces in mind as they study, rather than approaching it as an abstract theological debate.

Tip 5: Keep It Practical

Even when we begin with stories, it's so easy for these discussions to turn into debates about abstract concepts and theoretical questions. But the issues we're facing as a church—and especially the issues LGBTQ Christians face—are practical, not merely theoretical, and our discussions need to reflect that.

When I was growing up, my approach to LGBTQ issues was mostly a theoretical one. I believed being LGBTQ was something people simply *chose* and could easily *change*. I knew (or thought I knew) everything the Bible said on the subject. And I sometimes lectured classmates on the sin of "homosexuality," unaware that there was more nuance to the subject than such a broad, abstract term suggested.

But when I began to realize *I* was attracted to the same sex, I suddenly had many, much more practical, concerns: *What if my feelings don't change? Should I marry a woman even if I have no feelings for her? If not, am I destined to be alone? What do I do about my loneliness and desire for companionship? Who will care for me as I get older if I have no family? How can I serve God in the church if my church holds me at arm's length for something I can't control?*

There's a big difference between having a position on "homosexuality" as an abstract concept and having answers to these sorts of practical, everyday concerns.

I now realize that abstract terms like *homosexuality*—or the newly popular *transgenderism*—are typically not helpful in these conversations. To illustrate why, I sometimes ask church audiences to consider this question: "Is heterosexuality before marriage a sin?" Once we get past the awkwardness of the phrase *heterosexuality before marriage*, we can quickly see what an unhelpful and ambiguous question it is. *Heterosexuality* can refer to many things, and yes, some of those things would be inappropriate before marriage. (Some would be wrong at any time!) But *heterosexuality* can also describe two people sharing a chaste first kiss or holding hands at the movies. It could refer to a teenage girl having a crush on one of her male classmates, or a boy recognizing for the first time that he is attracted to girls. All of these people are experiencing *heterosexuality* even if they're not sexually active.

We don't generally take positions on the abstract concept of *heterosexuality*; instead, we talk about practical guidelines for how heterosexual people ought to live, and we offer many kinds of institutions and supports for a wide variety of practical situations—couples' counseling, singles' mixers, guidelines for dating, divorce care, elaborate wedding ceremonies, support for abuse survivors, ministries to widows and widowers, and so on.

In a similar way, taking a position on *homosexuality* as a concept isn't particularly helpful. What one person means as a statement about sexual boundaries can come across to another person as condemning them for simply existing with feelings they never chose. LGBTQ people are not a monolith, and being LGBTQ is not the same as taking a position on an abstract "ism."

Instead, our conversations need to address the many *practical* issues facing LGBTQ people, offering a complete picture of what it looks like for someone who is gay or bi or trans to have an abundant life in Christ and actively participate in the life of the church.

Focusing on a practical way forward doesn't just apply to the future we envision for LGBTQ Christians; it also applies to what we ask of one another in these conversations. For instance, it's not helpful for affirming Christians to argue that non-affirming Christians should simply stop believing that the Bible says what they believe it says. Certainly, it's fair to make the best possible case for what you believe the Bible is saying, but if the other person doesn't find the argument convincing, we must ask practical questions about how we can continue to love one another and live together as siblings in Christ in spite of our disagreements. (We see Paul addressing a very similar situation in Romans 14; these are challenges that date back to the very beginning of Christian community.)

Whenever the conversation begins to get too abstract, it's helpful to have a gentle reminder that you're seeking a practical, godly way forward for all involved, not an abstract "yes" or "no" on the *concept* of being LGBTQ.

Tip 6: Continually Express Care

When I first began sharing my story online as a gay Christian more than twenty-five years ago, I received a thoughtful email from a fellow Christian named Ron. I soon learned Ron was very similar to me. He had grown up as a committed Christian, discovered he was attracted to the same sex, and spent years praying about and studying what the Bible had to say on the subject. But despite our similar stories, Ron and I had arrived at two very different conclusions: I had come to support same-sex marriage, while Ron would become a high-profile spokesman for celibacy as God's calling for gay people.

Over the years, Ron and I became close friends. We've given talks together many times on college campuses and at Christian conferences, not only to share our differing perspectives on Scripture but also to speak frankly on how we've maintained such a close friendship in the face of major disagreement. By now, Ron and I have discussed and debated our views on many, many occasions, both publicly and privately.

Those conversations haven't eliminated all our disagreements. They have, though, made both of us think carefully about our views, acknowledge our arguments' weaknesses, and work to correct our mistakes. We keep each other on our toes.

But as strong as our friendship is, there have been times when our debates have gotten heated and we've failed to handle things the way we should have. I remember one particular occasion, early in our friendship, when I suddenly lost my temper with Ron. We'd been having a friendly debate about the proper interpretation of a Bible passage, and we'd gone back and forth several times on whether his interpretation or my interpretation was the correct one. Suddenly, I found myself feeling very frustrated with the conversation, and I angrily (and unfairly) snapped at Ron.

Ron could have snapped back at me in response. He could have taken that opportunity to say that my anger proved that I knew he was right. But he didn't do either of those things. Instead, he quietly expressed concern and checked to see if I was okay. As I took a deep breath and thought about it, I realized that I *wasn't* actually feeling okay.

At the time, I had only recently come out to a number of friends and family members, most of whom hadn't taken the news well. I'd lost my closest friends and had been made to feel unwelcome in the church I'd grown up in. I was lonely and struggling with doubts about what kind of future I could possibly have. I felt like I was too Christian for the gay people I knew and too gay for the Christians I knew. I was grateful for Ron's friendship, and I'd appreciated the way our conversations challenged me to fully explore every theological question. But our endless debates had also touched a sore spot I hadn't realized I had: I was afraid, deep down, that my existence would *always* be the subject of debates and that I would never find acceptance and love anywhere. With all that swirling around in my brain, suddenly Ron's calm, efficient debate tactics had felt cold and cruel (though Ron is neither of those things). And without warning, all my loneliness and fears for the future had come bubbling up at once and had exploded in a burst of hurt and frustration.

Ron did exactly the right thing in that moment. He was kind and understanding. He apologized, though he hadn't said or done anything wrong. *I* was the one who needed to apologize, not him. But Ron's choice to express care for me in that moment strengthened our friendship immeasurably. I opened up to him about what I'd been going through, and I learned that I could trust him not to use my human weakness to score debate points.

That experience was a wake-up call for both of us. We realized that it's not always obvious what people are going through inside, even when they seem fine, and that these can be unexpectedly emotional discussions. People are worried about whether they or their loved ones will be accepted, about the future of the church they love, and about things that may not even seem directly related to the topic at hand.

People aren't machines; we're emotional beings, and we're all different. So rather than treat this as a logic puzzle to be debated without emotion, it's important for us to continually check in with each other, asking how the other person is doing and watching for signs that they may need a break to pray and process all that's been said. These conversations aren't "won" by pushing people to the breaking point. Instead, it's our kindness and care for each other that has the best chance of helping someone gradually open their heart to the possibility that they may have gotten something wrong.

Of course, no approach can guarantee agreement or force someone to change their mind. Even after all these years, Ron and I still have many points of disagreement. But our friendship has helped us better understand each other's views. It has increased our compassion and empathy. It has helped us avoid mistakes we might have otherwise made, such as settling for shallow answers peddled by others on our respective sides. And ultimately, if anyone on the other side were ever going to be able to change my mind, it would be Ron. That's the level of trust he's earned from me. I suspect that he, in turn, would say the same.

Tip 7: Tackle This Together

Even when we do everything else right, the fact remains that we have big disagreements on some important theological questions. What can it possibly mean for us to talk about being "one body" in Christ when we're so divided? We can't wait for full agreement before we practice unity. But we also can't ignore our disagreements in the name of unity; the issues at stake are far too important.

Instead, as Paul suggests in Romans 14, we can find unity in our gracious *approach* to our disagreements. Rather than approaching them as competitions with winners and losers, I suggest we approach them as shared challenges—like puzzles for us to tackle *together*.

My husband and I like to do crossword puzzles together on our mornings off. Sometimes, when we come to a tricky clue, we find that we both think we know the answer—but our answers don't agree. Perhaps one of us is sure the answer is *cords* and the other is just as certain it's *coils*. So what do we do? Do we declare both answers equally true? Of course not. Only one answer will help us solve the puzzle; any others will lead us astray. Do we, then, fight over which answer is right, each of us accusing the other of trying to sabotage the puzzle? Of course not! We know that we're both sincerely trying to solve the puzzle correctly. Rather than argue, then, we acknowledge the differing opinions but continue our quest to solve the puzzle *together* as two people who love each other and who, despite a disagreement, are on the same team with a shared goal of getting the answers right.

Eventually, as we work together to solve the other clues, we'll have to settle on one answer or another. But neither of us takes pleasure in "beating" the other or gloats when the other's answer is proven incorrect. We treat this as a *cooperative* endeavor, not a competitive one. We constantly support each other's attempts and encourage each other's efforts, and we both try to maintain a healthy dose of humility about our own ideas. That way, no one's ego is too bruised when he discovers his answer wasn't correct, and it's easier for both of us to concede when the evidence turns against our initial answer. Neither of us is always right, so we will sometimes disagree. But when we win, we win together.

The issues at stake here are a lot more important than a crossword puzzle, of course. This isn't a game. But like a crossword puzzle, we are on the same team, all trying to get the answers right.

I don't believe my friends on the traditional side are cruelly trying to exclude people, despite the accusations some have hurled at them. And I don't believe my friends on the affirming side are unwilling to heed the commands of God, despite the accusations some have hurled at them. On each side, we're trying to solve this puzzle correctly so that we can teach and practice what is true. And on each side, we have to have enough humility to admit that we could have made mistakes along the way.

A cooperative approach pushes us away from the arguments and debates that tend to result in both sides digging in their heels. It helps us instead to build relationships across lines of disagreement, recognizing that even though that other person may be wrong about something important, they want to solve this puzzle correctly just as much as we do. We can encourage that instinct, listen to their reasoning, and support their efforts to dig deeper even while disagreeing with their current conclusions.

As with any Christian endeavor, of course, we should pray continually through this process—both individually and together. We should listen to the wisdom of Christian tradition, make use of the best biblical scholarship, and trust God to guide the entire process. If we do, I have confidence that the Holy Spirit will lead us to the correct answers in time.

Meanwhile, by taking this cooperative mindset to seek that guidance—starting with common ground and clear terminology, listening to one another's stories, looking for practical next steps, and regularly expressing care for one another—we give ourselves the greatest possible chance of breaking through those emotional walls that so often prevent us from hearing the Spirit's correction.

In the end, of course, no dialogue tips can guarantee we'll wind up agreeing on everything, and each of us can be responsible only for our own behavior, not that of others. Not everyone will be willing to engage in this kind of dialogue. Even when they do, there may still be major points of disagreement, and that can be frustrating. But I have seen tremendous healing come from this approach. And in a world increasingly unable to communicate across lines of disagreement, our ability to love one another even when the stakes are high may be one of the most important ways we show the world who we are in Christ.

9

Loving through Difference
Navigating Side A/B Friendship

Steven Lympus and Taylor Telford

Jesus replied, 'The people of this age marry and are given in marriage. But those who are considered worthy of taking part in the age to come and in the resurrection from the dead will neither marry nor be given in marriage, and they can no longer die; for they are like the angels. They are God's children, since they are children of the resurrection'" (Luke 20:34–36).

These verses from Luke are not often quoted from the pulpits of North American churches. Even as the question of marriage for LGBTQ+ persons remains an inflammatory issue within the church, Jesus's relegation of marriage to *this age* and *not* the one to come rarely serves as a touchpoint. Instead, conservative churches tend to focus on a few biblical passages[1] to justify their prohibition of same-sex/gender marriage, or even to exclude LGBTQ+ people from the wider life of the church, while progressive churches provide an account of Scripture that is affirming of LGBTQ+ persons seeking same-sex/gender marriage.[2] But how does the fact that we worship a single, celibate

---

1. The passages commonly cited in the debate are Gen. 19:1–38; Lev. 18:22; 20:13; Rom. 1:24–27; 1 Cor. 6:9–11; 1 Tim 1:9–10; and Jude 6–7.

2. We intentionally include sex *and* gender throughout to honor the stories of all LGBTQ+ persons. Biological sex differs from gender in that sex is defined by one's sex organs/gonads and chromosomes (e.g., male, female, intersex). Gender is related to sex but is usually indicative

Savior who indicates that marriage is *not* an aspect of our resurrection life speak into questions of LGBTQ+ inclusion here and now? Even more importantly, how might this fact provide space for dialogue and connection between those who adhere to a conservative position and those who adhere to a progressive position?

In this chapter, we, Rev. Steven Lympus (he/him) and Rev. Dr. Taylor Telford (she/her)—two pastors, queer Christians, and friends—will lay out how we came to our differing Christian ethics of marriage; what is challenging about each of our positions, both within culture and within our friendship; and how we have learned from each other and grown together because of our differences.[3] To close, we'll argue that love doesn't necessitate agreement and that loving amid disagreement is a vital aspect of Christian witness here and now.

Our Stories

Because no theological issue can be separated from embodied lives, we begin by briefly sharing our stories, highlighting our experiences as queer Christians in the church and how we each came to our particular beliefs about marriage.

Steven's Story

I was born when the Jesus Movement was first hitting Montana, and my earliest memories are of hippies playing guitars and worshiping in our living room or on the rocky shores of Flathead Lake. Christianity was alive and vibrant, centered on Jesus, and deeply joyful. I wanted in on all of it. But I also knew from age seven or eight that something was different about me. I read Christian comic tracts that showed gay men holding hands and gay men protesting and gay men getting married, all with deeply pained expressions on their black-and-white faces. The faces of the "homosexual" men of Sodom were also depicted in agony as God blinded then burned them. The

---

of one's identity and expression in relation to one's body and cultural norms (e.g., masculine, feminine, nonbinary). See Mark Yarhouse, *Understanding Gender Dysphoria* (InterVarsity, 2015), 16–17. See also Megan DeFranza, *Sex Difference in Christian Theology: Male, Female, and Intersex in the Image of God* (Eerdmans, 2015), 29–30.

3. To be clear, this chapter will not be a debate! Nor will it be an in-depth look at the theological differences between Side A (affirming) and Side B (traditionalist) positions. There are plenty of resources out there for that kind of information. Instead, we offer our particular stories and how they inform our theologies, as well as our friendship, in order to provide a meaningful context for dialogue, love, and witness.

last frame showed a giant faceless God on the throne of judgment, sending a lonely little gay man into the burning agony of hell.

I believed that if people knew my secret, I would also be abandoned and cast out. Gay meant agony. So I tried to be as far from gay as I could, hiding at night in my closet (the symbolism is not lost on me now) and rage-crying for God to please make me straight.

He never did.

By my mid-twenties, I had come to terms with my orientation not changing, and though I had explored affirming theologies (Side A), I remained a traditionalist (Side B).[4] To be fair, at the time, I didn't know any evangelicals who were affirming, so it seemed like the two were mutually exclusive (they aren't). At the time, my traditionalist convictions stemmed almost exclusively from the few biblical verses mentioning same-sex relations, as well as an absence of any affirmation of same-sex marriages in Scripture.

Discerning a call and desire to be married and have a family, I felt stuck between the ex-gay movement's false promises of orientation change through conversion therapy and a life condemned to lonely celibacy. I know many couples living in mixed-orientation marriages now, as well as queer celibate friends living in kinship communities, chosen families, committed partnerships, covenant friendships, or other arrangements. But in the late 1990s and early 2000s, the evangelical church seemed to offer me only two choices: fake being straight or live life alone.

Laura and I met at the church that ordained me, and I came out to her on our second date. She put her arm around me and said, "We'll figure it out." And that's what we've been doing for the past twenty years, along with our four children, now teenagers. Though we have a robust community around us of celibate and married Side A and Side B queer Christians, we started out alone, thinking we were the only ones.[5]

When I reflect on my story, I wonder why it took so long to find a community that sees and understands me, and why I didn't find it in the church. Where were the gay Christian men who could have modeled for me what

---

4. *Side A* and *Side B* designations came out of the Bridges Across the Divide dialogues in the 1990s, and they are generally used by queer Christians to denote their theologies and ethics on marriage. *Side X* is a term referring to the "ex-gay" movement, specifically where it emphasizes orientation change. See Greg Johnson, *Still Time to Care: What We Can Learn from the Church's Failed Attempt to Cure Homosexuality* (Zondervan, 2021), 216–17. See also Justin Lee, *Torn: Rescuing the Gospel from the Gays-vs.-Christians Debate* (FaithWords, 2012).

5. Mentioning mixed-orientation marriages often carries remnants of the ex-gay movement, or somehow implies that the non-straight members of these covenants have been "healed" of their orientations. God can heal anyone of anything, but that is not my story. I am still gay, and I wouldn't want the story of our marriage weaponized or forced on anyone else.

discipleship can look like for us? Where were the mixed-orientation marriages and celibate partnerships and chosen families that could have given me hope for a future and not just fear of loneliness? Where were the Side A and Side B Christians showing me that it is possible to be honest about our theological differences and still love one another?

My traditionalist convictions around marriage remain the same today but have expanded beyond only a handful of prohibition passages to reflect a broader view of the biblical story: a marriage in the Genesis garden, the often-rough marriage between God and God's covenant people, and the final wedding feast in Revelation. Human marriage—a temporal "unity in distinction"[6] that God created between a woman and a man—points us to the divine, redeemed marriage between Christ and his Bride, the church, an eternal unity in difference on a cosmic scale. My understanding is that Jesus communicated this distinction by synthesizing Genesis 1 and 2 when confronted by the Pharisees with a divorce dispute (Matt. 19:4–12). But note that Jesus, a celibate man, also acknowledges here that marriage is not everyone's calling, and he does so by honoring sexual and gender minorities (eunuchs). Though I still hold the prohibition texts as important, I believe they reflect the Bible's deeper marriage story—so much so that if they were somehow not in our Scripture, I imagine I would still be a Side B traditionalist.

Taylor's Story

I grew up in Idaho in a politically conservative, evangelical setting where being queer was considered a sin and an abomination. No one was out in my schools or church growing up, and *gay* was used as a derogatory slur. This rhetoric was deeply embedded in my psyche, and I toed the party line, maintaining a narrow understanding of Christian faith. When I went to college, I experienced God challenging these constrictions: I met deeply faithful Christians who voted Democrat! I also noticed dissonance with my own sexual orientation.

Realizing I was attracted to women, I experienced deep pain because of the theological and cultural narratives I'd been given. Not only this, but because I was in an evangelical setting, I processed this almost entirely alone because of fear and shame. I prayed daily that God would change my desires (God didn't). I was a campus ministry leader and lived on edge, wondering if I'd be "found out" and judged.

---

6. I'm using language I first learned from Wesley Hill in a dialogue he did with Justin Lee at Biola University called "How Do We Love? A Thoughtful Dialogue on Sexual Differences" on October 7, 2014, moderated by David Nystrom, https://ghostarchive.org/varchive/x9sRFdckyeg.

Gradually, I was given the courage to start coming out to a few people, and through conversations with mentors I came to understand that my only option was foregoing partnership and being celibate for the rest of my life. I was met with empathy, but I was told, "This is your cross to bear." Around this time, those same mentors identified a call to ordained ministry in my life. So, as I sought to wrestle through my sexual identity, I was also discerning my vocation to ministry.

After serving as a youth intern for a year after college, I went to seminary and, again, had my understanding of God and of faith expanded as I encountered Christians who were queer or open and affirming *because of* how they read the Bible, not in spite of it. Though I still adhered to a Side B position, this gave me more interlocutors for dialogue and discernment. It was during this time that I had a transformative spiritual experience while serving as a hospital chaplain. There, I came out to my cohort (the first time I'd come out to a group of people, let alone strangers) and sensed the Holy Spirit inviting me to be open, to recognize that my commitment to celibacy was about *control* and not about faith—a simple invitation to trust, be curious, and be open to God in this aspect of my life.

Through that experience, alongside continued biblical and theological study, I came to believe that Scripture makes room for committed, covenantal partnerships—marriages—between people of any sex/gender. This change took place over years and was rooted in prayer and study. For me, the question and answer begin with the full revelation of God and humanity in Jesus Christ. Rather than starting with Genesis, it's important to read backwards from Christ, the new Adam (Rom. 5), who reveals the true character of humanity and its telos. In terms of sexuality and marriage, here is what that looks like: Jesus is single and celibate. This is an expression of the fulfillment of procreation, which, according to the second creation narrative, wasn't introduced until *after* the fall. The reason for this: procreation is God's gracious provision for continuing life after death.

In the Hebrew Bible, "eternal life" came through procreation (you live on after death through your lineage). Jesus is the fulfillment of the storied lineage of God's covenants through the Old Testament. In Christ, eternal life is now resurrection life—this is a new way of not only understanding life after death, but also *family*. This is why the New Testament church seemed so odd to so many people—the reorientation of family that comes with Jesus's resurrection and the coming of the Holy Spirit is expressed through their radical understanding that *all* believers are fellow siblings and members of the household of God.

We see throughout the Bible that marriage wasn't solely about procreation, but rather about a *kind* of kinship bond.[7] Procreation is secondary, not necessary to marriage. With this, Jesus tells us marriage is relegated to this temporal era; the new heaven and new earth will not involve marriage (Matt. 22; Luke 20). This is presumably because we will all experience whole, healthy, intimate, joy-filled relationships with one another in the resurrection. What then is the significance of sexual differentiation?

I contend that difference is not exclusive to a mere male-female account of sexual differentiation. We see in Scripture that there are those outside of the male-female binary—namely, eunuchs. Today, we would use the language of intersex.[8] In Genesis 1, we see a standard Hebrew poetic structure, called merism, where extremes are named *in order to imply all that comes in between*—night and day, land and sea, dawn and dusk, marsh and beach, and so on. Thus, knowing that the compilers and writers of the text would have been familiar with those outside of the male-female binary (eunuchs could be made so or born as such), it is not a stretch to read Genesis 1:27 as "male and female [and everything in between] he created them."

Relating this to the assertion that Jesus Christ is the true human, the one whose embodied particularity as the Jewish Messiah is what ensures the universality of his person and work, I believe this means that the more like Christ we become (in the *way* we relate to God and others), the more uniquely ourselves we are. Each of our embodied realities is the specific, God-given context for living out true human life in correspondence to Jesus. In this way, my understanding actually allows for *more* difference in a Christian understanding of marriage. Difference is not relegated to a male-female binary but is expanded to honor the radical difference and otherness of each person that is given by God in the diversity of human embodiments.

In short, while I acknowledge that the Bible does not explicitly affirm same-sex/gender relationships, I do believe it leaves room for same-sex/gender partnerships. "Biblical marriage" takes many forms (some more healthy than

---

7. Biblical scholar James V. Brownson's work is especially helpful on this topic. James V. Brownson, *The Bible, Gender, and Sexuality* (Eerdmans, 2013).

8. Megan DeFranza's work is an excellent resource for understanding the biblical concept of eunuch and the implications for today. See Megan K. DeFranza, *Sex Difference in Christian Theology: Male, Female, and Intersex in the Image of God* (Eerdmans, 2015). "Much like the term 'intersex,' 'eunuch' was an umbrella concept—a word used to cover a range of phenomena wherein humans did not measure up to the male ideal." She notes that barren women very well could have had an intersex condition and that Jewish commentaries and early Christian literature mention hermaphrodites or androgynes. "The ancients were quite familiar with variations of sex development and found ways to expand their binary model to include others" (DeFranza, *Sex Difference*, 68).

others, all contextually located). The underlying thread is covenant partnership that reflects God's relationship to God's people. By expanding the understanding of embodied difference based on the inclusion of those outside the male-female binary in Scripture (see Acts 8), my account allows for same-sex/gender marriage, makes space for questions of trans identity, and affirms that our unique, embodied particularity is theologically significant. In the resurrection, we neither marry nor are given in marriage. But we will all be *more* differentiated, *more* ourselves, because our God-given difference is the vehicle for relationship and intimacy.

Summary of Our Disagreement and Resonance

We disagree about marriage—specifically, whether sex difference is critical in a Christian understanding and practice of marriage. Our disagreement is important, but also temporary. Jesus made it clear that human marriage is not an eternal reality (Matt. 22:30; Mark 12:25; Luke 20:34–36). We both think it's sad that so much harm is done in Christian friendships and communities around a disagreement that one day, on the Last Day, won't matter anymore.[9]

We both see marriage as sacramental in that this temporal covenant relationship points us to the eternal covenant relationship between God and human beings.[10] Steven sees sex difference as critical in marriage because of the sacramental ways that a woman and man expressing unity in difference direct us to the unity in difference that human beings have with God. Taylor sees difference manifesting beyond a simple male-female binary: there is actually *greater* diversity and difference in the spectrum of sex (male, intersex, female) and gender, which can be expressed in covenantal marriage partnerships between people of any sex/gender.

We both affirm the dignity of all human beings as those in the image of God, and we hold these questions of sexuality and ethics as noncreedal

---

9. Addressing the complicated and sometimes loaded question "Will I be gay in heaven?" and the beauty humans experience as a result of the divine image in one another, Revoice founder Nate Collins writes, "This means that in one important sense, there will be no gay people in heaven, because there will also be no straight people. Instead, I suspect that everybody in heaven will be awestruck by the beauty of each image-bearer they encounter, because each will perfectly reflect the beauty of God." Nate Collins, *All But Invisible: Exploring Identity Questions at the Intersection of Faith, Gender & Sexuality* (Zondervan, 2017), 304.

10. Note: *sacramental* (generally pointing to grace), not *a sacrament* (particularly appointed vehicle of grace). We both adhere to the Protestant affirmation of two sacraments: baptism and the Lord's Supper. Christian dedication to a call to celibacy is equally, if not more, sacramental—pointing to an eschatological future we will all experience.

issues, which, though deeply important, are secondary to and informed by the primary aspects of Christian faith (God's love for the world in Jesus Christ).

The Challenges of Our Positions

While a Side A approach has gained traction within Western culture at large, it remains a minority in many Christian circles, particularly among older evangelicals. Even as someone who has dedicated myself (Taylor) to a life of theological study and service to the church, many Christians dismiss my gifts, calling, and personhood solely because of our disagreement on this one topic.[11] On all essential (creedal) questions, I am profoundly orthodox. And yet, because of my identity and understanding of marriage, I am excluded. This can also be a challenge in my Side B friendships—because we don't align ethically, there can be tension on whether they would invite me to lead in their congregations (even as my Side A position can make space for those who are Side B to lead in Side A congregations).

On the flip side, within affirming spaces and those looking to have the conversation about marriage and ordination as it pertains to LGBTQ+ persons, I am often typecast as the resident authority on sexuality and the church. While, yes, I've done a lot of work and study around this, that I am queer is not a dominant aspect of my personality. I'm glad to be able to leverage my story as a resource for Christian discernment, but, like many queer Christians, it can be tiring to be viewed solely through this lens, not to mention the oddity of having to talk about one's sexuality in ways straight people rarely do.

Lastly, within affirming spaces, I am often an apologist for my Side B friends. I recognize my privilege! As a Side A queer Christian, I'm accepted in the broader culture. However, my Side A theology makes room for and affirms the importance of Side B theology (more on this below), which means, contrary to common assumptions in church circles, I don't believe marriage is the telos of human existence! This can put me at odds with those in progressive circles who have not thought critically about the centrality of celibacy and singleness in biblical and historical approaches to Christian life. I'm deeply grateful for Steven and my other Side B friends from whom I've learned so much and who help me reflect meaningfully on these questions.

---

11. This is the experience of many queer Christians, regardless of their understanding of marriage. We constantly have to be ready to defend ourselves merely for existing.

The presenting cultural challenge about my (Steven's) position is that Side B does not see same-sex/gender marriage as faithful to the Bible's teaching in a Western cultural moment when many in and out of the church are affirming these marriages. Historically, traditionalists have enjoyed the privilege of society's blessing when it comes to marriage laws, cultural reinforcement, and general heteronormativity that helped keep this position the norm. In our North American context, this is shifting quickly, and traditionalists who haven't experienced challenges like this, or even what it's like to hold a minority opinion, are feeling new pressures that sometimes reveal a shallow and inconsistent theology of marriage and sexual ethics. Why, for instance, do many traditionalists support nonprocreative sex in marriage, including birth control or surgeries that alter sexual organs against their created purposes (vasectomy or tubal ligation), while claiming that procreation alone underlies God's original design for marriage?

But beneath the pressure that traditionalists may be feeling right now is an even deeper pain: the harm the church has done against queer people for generations. This is not the space to go into the dark history that LGBTQ+ people have experienced in the church, but it is important to recognize that a traditionalist theology has often been used to justify profound abuse and neglect of all queer Christians, regardless of ethics.[12] This dynamic often places a queer Side B Christian in a precarious place: I can be perceived as a threat by those who share my queer experience but have been harmed by my theology, as well as by Christians who share my theology but object to me identifying as queer.[13]

If we take Jesus seriously when he prays for us—*all of us*—in John 17, then we know how important it is to live in unity as his followers. Not in agreement, but in unity.[14] If we listen to Jesus praying, we know that the world, inside and outside of the church, is watching how we treat one another. What do outsiders see in the way that Jesus followers talk with and about one another when it comes to sexuality, orientation, and gender?

---

12. Significantly, the church's treatment of LGBTQ+ persons has also contributed to others leaving the church: "Nearly one-third of Millennials who left the faith they grow up with told Public Religion Research Institute that it was 'negative teachings' or 'negative treatment' related to gays and lesbians that played a significant role in them leaving organized religion." Jaweed Kaleem, "One-Third of Millennials Who Left Their Religion Did It Because of Anti-Gay Policies: Survey," *HuffPost*, February 26, 2014, http://www.huffingtonpost.com/2014/02/26/millennials-gay-unaffiliated-church-religion_n_4856094.html.

13. We would add here that there are wonderful exceptions now. See the work that Revoice, Posture Shift, and the Center for Faith, Sexuality & Gender and other Side B organizations are doing to care for queer people of faith and their communities.

14. John 17:23, *teteleiōmenoi eis hen*, literally "perfected finally into one."

I confess that the ways I (Steven) have often used two words in these conversations have sometimes diminished dialogue and hurt my relationships—namely, the words *clearly* and *orthodox*. When I've said that the Bible speaks "clearly" on this issue, I have implied that my Side A friends are *clearly misreading* Scripture, which feels arrogant to assume, or that they are *clearly disregarding* Scripture, which—let me assure you—one conversation with Taylor will persuade otherwise. Taylor and I arrive at different conclusions around sex differentiation in marriage; she is not misreading or disregarding Scripture. She holds a different interpretation about which she and I have healthy, strengthening conversations.

When I've said that I hold to an "orthodox" view of sexuality and gender, what I have implied is that my Side A friends are *unorthodox*, which subtly elevates important but secondary issues to a creedal level. Personally, I have concluded that these words, *clearly* and *orthodox*, are unnecessary for me to hold or communicate a robust Side B theology.[15]

The Gifts of Our Positions

Though I (Steven) remain a Side B traditionalist, my Side A friends have given me a depth of understanding and respect for Scripture's complex witness on sex and gender. Appreciation for Side A theology has deepened my love of Scripture and my Side A friends. For instance, I appreciate that Taylor's Side A theology finds a beautifully inclusive trajectory in Scripture from the beginning (God created them "male and female"—*and all those in between*) to the telos of Christ's new community in the New Testament. This trajectory includes every sexual and gender minority, especially some of the most marginalized and misunderstood like intersex and trans people. Her theology has a broader sense of difference in marriage covenants and is less in danger of gender essentialism or of forms of natural theology in which our specific bodies determine our personhood or justify our dignity.

Taylor's theology also has a rich history of honoring Scripture's witness to kinship and covenant relationships beyond different-gendered marriage, as well as Jesus's broadening of family beyond blood lines. Furthermore, in a time in our North American context when many queer Christians have left the church because of the ways traditionalists like me have mistreated queer

---

15. For a brief summary of the connection between insisting the Bible "clearly" speaks on homosexual identity and the fraught, and often Freudian, translations of Greek New Testament words, see Bridget Eileen Rivera, *Heavy Burdens: Seven Ways LGBTQ Christians Experience Harm in the Church* (Brazos, 2021), chaps. 3 and 7; esp. 47–49 and 90–97.

people, Taylor's theology offers hope for their return—or better yet, a future where queer people never have to leave in the first place.

Looking at life outside of the church in my cultural and geographic context, I owe a great debt to Side A Christians like Taylor who, along with other queer people and straight allies, have helped ensure certain rights and protections I enjoy in my social and political realities. For instance, in many cases, I can't be fired or lose access to housing, loans, insurance, health care, or any other services due to my orientation. Perhaps ironically, some of these things are only likely to happen to me if I'm working for certain traditionalist churches or Christian organizations.

As I've already noted, I (Taylor) believe Side B theology is crucial for helping the modern Western church think more robustly about marriage and Christian understandings of family. (Steven is an excellent example of this!) Whether progressive or conservative, most Christian circles assume marriage as a "natural" part of human life; they do not understand it vocationally, as something to be discerned as one calling among others. Church singles groups are for the purpose of meeting a spouse. Christian parents expect their children to grow up, get married, and have kids. Your family are those to whom you are biologically related. This understanding is part of the fabric of our cultural milieu. But it's not coherent with what Jesus and Paul have to say about marriage or family, and it departs from fifteen hundred years of Christian tradition that elevated celibacy as the higher Christian calling. Here, Side B theology holds up a much-needed mirror to Western Christianity's idolatry of marriage. It shows us that relationship with Jesus is what makes us whole, not marriage. Family in the Christian sense is determined by the bond of the Holy Spirit, not blood relation. It invites all Christians, regardless of identity or orientation, to give their whole selves over to God.

With this, Side B theology is a gift not only to the church but to the queer community—I've said to Steven, a gay man married to a straight woman, "You're the queerest person I know!"—and I stand by this! Steven, and other Side B Christians, whether in committed same-sex/gender (nonsexual) friendships, mixed-orientation marriages, or living lives of singleness and celibacy, show us that meaningful love and intimacy need not follow cultural scripts but can be expressed in truly queer (that is, other than culturally normative) ways.

Side B theology is invaluable for witnessing to the radical love of God that transcends sexual intimacy (and is the source of true, erotic love!), a love that invites us to lose our lives in order to gain them in a manner more full and beautiful than we can imagine on our own. And Steven's theology in particular lives out a radical faithfulness in orienting one's life and vocation around God's desires.

At the end of the day, even though we hold differing theologies of marriage, we are both held captive by the love command that Jesus gave us. We do well to remember that Jesus illustrates the "greater love" not with marriage or sex or any sort of theology, but with sacrifice: "to lay down one's life for one's friends" (John 15:13). We also do well to remember that our salvation in Christ is never dependent on being *right* in this or any nonessential theological disagreement. As Bridget Eileen Rivera summarizes, "*None* of us will ever be perfect in our understanding of God's law or in our submission to it. *All* of us will arrive at the judgment seat having gotten things wrong about gender and sexuality. That's the point of having a Savior."[16]

Side A / Side B Friendship as a Model for Christian Community

The reason why mutual appreciation for each other's theology is important—even if we disagree with each other—is that the opposite creates a hostile environment, *especially for queer Christians*.[17] Creating a reality where love and community for a queer person are dependent on their theological or ethical decisions is damaging for that person. This dynamic can force queer people, whether affirming or traditionalist, into adopting theological positions prematurely because they are doing so under the threat of losing love and acceptance in community, not the conviction of Scripture's witness to truth. Putting relationships at stake in theological disputes hurts everyone. Alternatively, A/B friendships model that relationships are not dependent upon a person's theology of marriage or sexuality.[18]

---

16. Rivera, *Heavy Burdens*, 175.

17. For an in-depth study of LGBTQ+ persons and communities of faith, see Andrew Marin, *Us versus Us: The Untold Story of Religion and the LGBT Community* (NavPress, 2016). Similar to our thesis, Marin highlights the need to develop a theology of commonality *alongside* a theology of difference. This means that, in a world predicated on the belief that love demands agreement, we need to advocate for the "lost art of loving in disagreement" (xiv).

18. As a young queer Christian, two things could have radically changed my (Taylor's) experience of coming to terms with my orientation: leaders providing clarity and modeling curiosity. Many congregations say "Everyone is welcome!" but fail to define precisely what they mean by this. LGBTQ+ persons will join only to later be denied full participation in leadership or marriage. In this way, clarity is kindness. Church leaders can honor LGBTQ+ persons not only by being clear about their own positions but by naming the fact that there are faithful siblings in Christ who believe differently *because of* how they read the Bible and their relationship with Jesus, not despite it! This invites a posture of loving openness. Curiosity is also kindness. Entrusting ourselves and one another to Christ means being alert

A/B friendships can also offer mutual understanding and encouragement across theological differences because we share so much experience. For instance, I (Steven) need my Side A friends who simply get me when I'm tired of people denying my existence as a gay Christian, correcting my language, or even feeling like yet another straight traditionalist's token gay friend. Taylor and I have different theologies in this area, but so much of our lived experience as queer Christians is common to us both.

The fact is, we don't need agreement in this area to be friends. Congregations probably need clarity when it comes to policies involving marriage or leadership; friendships don't need agreement on these policies, only love and good boundaries.

Switching issues can provide a test case: Christian friends often disagree about theological questions like baptism, the gifts of the Holy Spirit, women in ministry, eschatology, or a host of other things. Some of these disagreements are ethical, and even involve marriage and sexual practices like divorce and remarriage, nonprocreative intercourse, or non-intercourse procreation. It is common, at least in our North American context, for Christian friends to disagree about these and other important-but-nonessential matters. Why shouldn't we be able to disagree about sex differentiation in marriage? What makes this issue a friendship-breaker?

Though we don't need agreement to be friends, we do need friendship. Nate Collins, founder of Revoice, writes a chapter about friendship and desire that seems particularly relevant here. He concludes,

> The kinds of desires we experience tell us something about the kind of people we are. Desires for relationship tell us that we know we were never meant to be alone. Desires for friendship tell us that we know we need traveling companions on the journey of life. Passionate desire that attends to the goodness and virtue of others is an especially powerful force that can pull me out of myself as I am confronted by the beauty of another. And the inherent beauty we detect in others that draws us toward them reminds us that desiring friendship is a good thing.[19]

For both Steven and myself (Taylor), our friendship is important to us for many reasons, but at the core we simply enjoy having each other as fellow "traveling companions." We are friends not in spite of our theological differences but because of them: we met and became fast friends after Steven asked

---

to the ways that the Holy Spirit is alive and at work in fellow believers, especially those with whom we disagree.

19. Collins, *All But Invisible*, 128–29.

me to share the stage with him when the congregation he was pastoring held a "Loving LGBTQ+ Christians" event. Our friendship is not limited to queer topics; we also enjoy exploring new sushi places, tasting finer gins, and nerding out on Star Wars. The body of Christ is more complete and beautiful with each of us in it, and Christ's body would be weakened if either of us insisted on saying to the other, "I don't need you!" (1 Cor. 12:21).

We also share a deep concern for our other queer siblings, inside and outside of the church. Every statistic we find paints the picture of a group facing much higher rates of hate crime, abuse, rejection, self-harm, suicide contemplation or attempt, and a host of other threats because of the myriad ways society marginalizes us.[20] As Rivera writes of LGBTQ Christians in particular, "Unable to rid their existence of queerness, they are tempted to rid *themselves* of their *existence*."[21] Working for the church's care and inclusion of queer people, and insistence on our full human dignity and access to discipleship, are values and burdens we both share equally.

Recognizing that loving across difference is not an easy task, nor one to be embarked on alone, we offer the following points as a resource for those seeking to faithfully love amid disagreement, especially regarding questions of sexual differentiation in marriage.

Five Things That Can Help Make a Friendship Thrive across Theological Differences

1. *Inviting LGBTQ+ people (whose bodies are affected by the conversation) to lead the conversation if they so choose.* There is a difference between disagreeing with someone's thoughts or beliefs and disagreeing with someone's embodied life and identity. Note: Please understand that they may need to set clear boundaries if certain areas of a conversation feel harmful.
    a. If you don't understand what could be harmful, ask for clarity on boundaries.
    b. Take responsibility for your learning curve. Do your own work to research the stories and experiences of LGBTQ+ Christians. Don't expect them to do the work for you!

---

20. The Trevor Project provides an updated collection of data focused on youth: "Facts about Suicide among LGBTQ+ Young People," Trevor Project, December 15, 2021, https://www.thetrevorproject.org/resources/article/facts-about-lgbtq-youth-suicide/.
21. Rivera, *Heavy Burdens*, 62.

c. If this is a public conversation, honor their lifelong work and willingness to share by offering to pay them for their time and energy.
2. *Caring for each other.* Start by listening to each other's stories, especially to how the other has been hurt. Attend to shared experience and empathy first.
3. *Staying curious and asking honest, open-ended questions.* We Christians can disciple each other while disagreeing if we open ourselves up to being enriched by the other's story and theology without having to agree or persuade. Ask them: "How do you experience the Holy Spirit in your story?" Ask yourself: "How do I see the Holy Spirit in their life and story?"
4. *Honoring that we are all trying to understand Scripture, obey God, love Jesus, and live by the Spirit* in loving people the best we can, even as we come to some different conclusions on sex and marriage ethics.
5. *Holding space for honest dialogue* about theological differences and common ground.

Five Things That Can Threaten the Health of a Friendship across Theological Differences

1. *Sliding into issue-speak and forgetting this is personal,* affecting and often harming those of us who experience queerness in our bodies.
2. *Being suspicious of the other and imputing false motives.*
3. *Tying salvation or Christian orthodoxy to this single issue.* Assuming that a difference in theology or marriage/sexual ethics means the other is unbiblical or a bigot will harm the relationship.
4. *Insisting that Scripture is "clear" on this without acknowledging the complexity* of the Bible or biblical interpretations.
5. *Trying to change instead of understand the other's theology.* Dialogue is great; agendas kill.

Conclusion

We'd like to end where we began, remembering Jesus's words that marriage belongs to *this age* and not to the resurrection life to come. This doesn't mean that marriage doesn't matter in this life—indeed, marriage matters a great deal to us both—but rather that, one day, our disagreements about sex difference in marriage will no longer be relevant. We propose that this kind of friendship—this intentional curiosity, dialogue, gratitude, and love for the other—is desperately needed for the church today. In a society fueled by conflict, one-upmanship, and division, the practice of friendship with those with whom you disagree is a practical, personal, and profound way to witness to the character of God and the promise of the resurrection life to come.

We urge Christian friends who disagree on sex difference in marriage to frame their friendships in this sort of eschatological light, where healthy, boundaried disagreement can enrich rather than harm friendship. Thankfully, friendship outlives this disagreement. As David Bennett writes, "In the end, there will be no 'right side' of this issue to be on. There will be only one side, the kingdom of Jesus Christ, and the incredibly rich and diverse people who fill it."[22]

---

22. David Bennett, *A War of Loves: The Unexpected Story of a Gay Activist Discovering Jesus* (Zondervan, 2018), 184.

10

Is There Space at the Table in a Non-Affirming Church?

Brad Harper

In January 2015, I attended the conference of the Gay Christian Network (now Q Christian Fellowship) with my gay son, Drew. We were writing a book about our story at the time that would come out the next year—*Space at the Table: Conversations between an Evangelical Theologian and His Gay Son*.[1] At lunch I found myself sitting across the table from a gay man in his thirties who was sharing his journey with me. He was in a monogamous relationship with a man, and both were professing Jesus followers. I remember him telling me that they had attended one of the well-known "gay churches" for a while but eventually left and were currently attending a non-affirming church and just staying under the radar. I was puzzled. Why leave a church where gay relationships are not only accepted but also celebrated as part of God's good plan and go to a church where gay relationships were seen as sinful, a church where the only option for gay people was repentance and celibacy or heterosexual marriage? His answer was stunning. He said that he and his partner wanted to go to a church where the Bible was preached as the authoritative and infallible Word of God. The affirming church did not

---

1. Brad Harper and Drew Harper, *Space at the Table: Conversations between an Evangelical Theologian and His Gay Son* (Zeal Books, 2016; now self-published through Amazon in paperback and Kindle).

hold to that view, and as a result they rejected some key tenets of historic Christian orthodoxy that really mattered to them.[2]

This was the first time a gay Jesus follower had said this to me, but it would not be the last. More importantly, as I walked away from the conversation after that hour-long lunch, the impression I was left with was, "This guy really loves Jesus!" Everything he said to me painted a picture of a man who loved God with all his heart, soul, mind, and strength, and who wanted to love his neighbor as himself with the help of God's Spirit. He believed that the church, as a result of homophobia, had misread the Bible on sexuality and that God is fine with loving, monogamous gay marriages.

For days, months, and now years following, and after more encounters like this one, I found myself asking, "Lord, what am I supposed to do with someone like this?" What I was raised with in evangelical culture was that homosexuality was a choice and that gay people were doing nothing more than making perverted choices out of a heart of rebellion against God. But after hanging out with gay Jesus followers for a few years, not to mention having a gay son who grew up in the church, I eventually had to let go of that view, finding it to be misleading at best and just plain wrong in a number of ways.

For years, my speaking and writing on this issue have been, largely, in non-affirming evangelical churches, with the purpose of encouraging them to love their LGBTQ neighbors, to deconstruct their misleading and harmful stereotypes, and to learn to understand the experiences of people whom God loves. Over the last couple years, my work has moved further down the road, asking the question, Is there a place for LGBTQ Jesus followers in the non-affirming church, a place that goes beyond telling them they are welcome to attend but cannot really be involved in service and the life of the community?[3] I'm thinking about a church where the theology of the denomination or the local church holds that marriage in the Bible is meant to be between one man and one woman for a lifetime. And I'm thinking about a situation where a gay married couple wants to attend, serve, and be deeply involved in the life

---

2. As I write this in 2023, I realize that the landscape has changed and there are affirming churches that would be much more traditional in their view of Scripture, believing that it is the inspired and infallible Word of God. That was not generally the case at the time of my conversation with my new friend.

3. At this point, after examining the biblical arguments of those scholars who believe the church has misunderstood the Bible, and particularly Paul, on this issue, and who believe that Scripture does not prohibit same-sex monogamous marriage, I have not been convinced by the arguments. To be honest, as the father of a gay son who suffered much growing up gay in the evangelical church, I would be glad to be proven wrong on this issue. But so far, the arguments are not convincing to me. I also recognize that I could be wrong about this. See Preston Sprinkle, *People to Be Loved: Why Homosexuality Is Not Just an Issue* (Zondervan, 2015) for an excellent and gracious engagement by a non-affirming biblical scholar.

of the church. I'm imagining a situation where the approach is not, "Hey, let's just agree to disagree and not sweat the small stuff." I'm thinking about a church that believes sexuality is a significant issue in the Bible; God's plan for marriage is that it be heterosexual, monogamous, and permanent; and that God judges sexual sin and calls on the church to speak against it as well.

Let me set out my goals and my approach for this chapter. This chapter will not be an exegetical study. I am not an exegete by training; I am a theologian. Further, I have been asked to write a pastoral response rather than an academic one (though I realize these areas are deeply interconnected), and so much of what I write will be rooted more in my personal experiences and thoughts about the narrative of Scripture than in academic research. As to my pastoral background, I spent thirteen years as a pastor and church planter before spending the last twenty-four years as an academic theologian. I am also the father of a gay son, whom I love dearly and who has challenged me at many levels on this topic. Finally, both as a pastor and a professor, I have sat across the table from many dozens of people who shared with me their painful experiences of sexuality and gender, which they had kept secret from family and friends in the church for fear of rejection.

From a theological perspective I am going to look at biblical themes of God's engagement with his people on the issues of sexuality. I will argue that God, at times, makes accommodations for faithful followers who are living in a way that is at odds with God's plan for sex and marriage, examples where he does not affirm the rightness of their behavior, but where he also does not judge them.[4] Further, in some cases the narrative considers these characters faithful, godly people whom God uses to lead and to further his work in the world. I will also look at how sin needs to be understood as far more complicated than simply behavior or even thought-life, and that the condition of a sinner's heart impacts how God responds to that person. Finally, pastorally, I will ask if God's accommodating posture toward some of his followers might

---

4. It is important from the outset to explain what I mean by *judge* or *judgment* in this chapter. I mean that God does not speak judgment or condemnation to or about his followers in these situations about a behavior or practice that is a departure from God's ideal for marriage. Nor does he execute any clear punishing event. For example, when Achan steals valuables during the battle of Jericho, he knows that he is sinning, admits it, is condemned by God and Israel, and is executed. When I say that God does not judge some followers for marital practices that depart from God's standard, he does not respond to them in this kind of clear judgment or condemnation. On the other hand, Old Testament narratives sometimes infer judgment for wrong behavior without God directly responding to it at all. The judgment is seen in the problems that are created for the followers of God as a result of their actions or practices. For example, polygamy generally does not work out well for God's followers (see Abraham, Jacob, David, Solomon, etc.).

provide a possible approach for how to include faithful gay Jesus followers in the life of the church.[5]

The Patriarchs and God's Lack of Condemnation of Polygamy

In his discussion of the essential value of procreation in the Old Testament, Ron Pierce comments that one result of the Israelites' emphasis on procreation was the practice of polygamy, a practice that is not part of God's plan for marriage.[6] Nevertheless, God uses this "unsettling way" to bring about the arrival of the second Adam.[7] I agree with Pierce. My question is more about how God engages his people in the process. Why does God not judge polygamy among the patriarchs or in the Mosaic law? And further, he considers some polygamists (Abraham) to be faithful followers and blesses them.

As a theologian reading these laws and stories, I wonder about the judgment of God on all this, or lack of it. Polygamy is practiced both before and after the writing of the Mosaic law. And while polygamy may not be seen in the community of Israel as adultery, if a comprehensive biblical theology of marriage is about one man and one woman, polygamy is either adultery or fornication. Why does God so often not judge it, especially with his greatest leaders like Abraham and David?[8]

Divorce

In the case of divorce, we know from the teachings of Jesus that any man who divorces his wife apart from sexual infidelity and marries another woman is committing adultery. So my question is, What did the allowance of divorce by the law mean? Did it mean that the man who divorces his wife and then marries another is in perpetual adultery, but the community simply allows

---

5. When I get to the pastoral application section, I am going to deal with just one example—a case study of a gay/lesbian married couple in the church. The issue of gender dysphoria, in my view, is much more complicated in ways that I do not have space to address here. But it needs to be addressed as well.

6. As seen, for example, in Levirate marriage.

7. Ronald W. Pierce, "Sexual Ethics & Holiness in Genesis 1–3 and LGBTQ+ Christians," paper presented at the annual meeting of the Evangelical Theological Society, November 16, 2022.

8. While there are differences of opinion among scholars about whether polygamy is sanctioned in the Bible, I believe the preponderance of evangelical biblical scholars would hold that marriage is meant to be between one man and one woman, so that polygamy is not God's design for marriage.

that? Or are they married but the marriage is not legitimate? Or is it a legitimate marriage? If so, then it seems that the divorce and remarriage of two people would turn an illegitimate relationship into a legitimate one. Divorce is a departure from God's plan for sex and marriage. Yet divorce is allowed in the Hebrew Scriptures for reasons that sometimes are not very onerous (Deut. 24:1–4).

LGBTQ Similarities

Over the past several years, as I have thought about how God dealt with Old Testament followers who lived outside of God's ideal plan for marriage, I began to ask myself, Is it possible that gay marriage might fall into this same category—a departure from God's design for marriage, just like polygamy and adultery, but allowed without judgment in certain situations? If we view gay marriage under the complicated themes above, one might argue that monogamous gay marriage is another version of God allowing something that is outside his creation ideal for marriage, but that, through it, he regulates homosexuality, so that it is confined to a committed relationship, thereby reflecting exclusivity and permanence.

What I'm getting at here is something I will summarize more fully toward the end of the chapter. What do we do with the fact that in the biblical narratives, because of the fallen and difficult culture in which they live, God allows his people to live in ways that are sexually unethical according to his creation standards? What do we do with the fact that he still considers these people to be faithful followers and includes them, even as leaders, in the community of faith if their hearts are right toward him? And how do we apply those realities in the church today?

Sin and the Heart vs. Behavior

These Old Testament narratives should cause us to think carefully about our theology of sin and judgment. Traditionally American evangelicals have tended to think about sin largely in terms of behaviors. Our fundamentalist roots, which many of us grew up with, produced lists of good behaviors and sinful behaviors (the list of sins being much longer). The twelfth-century theologian and philosopher Peter Abelard argued that a proper theology of sin must go beyond the act itself. Abelard focused more on the motive, specifically talking about sin in terms of contempt for God. When one knowingly consents to sin, he has contempt for God. Conversely, where there is no contempt, it follows, there is no sin. Further, consent to a sinful act is only contempt for God when we *know* that it is sin.[9] Abelard writes, "Indeed, God alone, who considers not so much what is done in mind as in what mind it may be done, truly considers the guilt in our intention and examines the fault in a true trial. . . . For he particularly sees where no man sees, because in punishing sin he considers not the deed but the mind, just as conversely, we consider not the mind which we do not see but the deed which we know."[10]

Here Abelard adds two things to behavior, which are sometimes more important in determining sin and in bringing about God's judgment. First, there is motive. It is clear in Scripture that certain acts that seem on the surface to be obviously sins and worthy of God's judgment do not bring God's judgment because of the situations in which they were done and the motives for doing them (e.g., David feeding the bread of the presence to his hungry soldiers, which Jesus says in Matt. 12 was an act of mercy). Then there are deeds that seem good on the surface but, because of the motive, are judged by God (e.g., Simon Magus asking for the power to heal, which Peter condemns because Simon's heart is not right before God).

Second, there is how much a person knows. Abelard says that consent to an improper act is only sin when we know that the intent to do it shows contempt for God, which is then confirmed by the act itself. I don't necessarily agree with Abelard on this, but what seems clear is that God does not always judge the same unethical act in the same way when done by different people. For those with lesser understanding, he sometimes restricts his judgment, or may not even judge at all. And it seems Jesus concurs with this when he tells the Pharisees that in the day of judgment, they will incur a stricter judgment than common (perhaps unaware) people, because they know better. But this goes beyond mere ignorance. Paul, in Romans 14, argues that if a person believes that a certain food is unclean, even though objectively it is not, for him it is unclean and therefore for him to eat it would be a sin, if for no other reason than because he is violating his conscience. This, perhaps, is not an issue of lack of awareness so much as an issue of disagreement between two Jesus followers as to the moral propriety of an action. So, regarding sin and particularly judgment for sin, the level of knowledge is important because

---

9. Though Abelard does not refer to it, perhaps he has in mind the "unintentional sin" in Num. 15. It carries a lesser consequence than intentional ones.

10. Peter Abelard, *Ethics* 41, quoted in Thomas Bushnell, BSG, "Sin, Punishment, and the Judgment of God," https://tb.becket.net/writ-abelard.html.

only if someone knows that an act is a sin against God can they have a heart of rebellion toward God when they commit it.[11]

The bottom line for Abelard is that sin and God's judgment of sin are rooted primarily in the motive of the one doing the sinful action. And motive depends on knowledge. If an individual does not know or believe that an act is sin, then the act cannot be done out of a heart of disobedience and, therefore, it does not display contempt for God. This approach is not universally applied and clean. Uzzah's motive for reaching out to steady the ark seems pretty good. But he is judged anyway (1 Chron. 13). But the fact is that God allows, and sometimes even commands, acts that violate his moral ideal and then does not judge those who commit these acts.[12] Did Abraham know that polygamy was wrong? No way. He did not have Torah, and polygamy was part of the air his culture breathed. Also, in certain cases, it could be helpful to women in difficult circumstances. So, when we look back at the patriarchs, do we admire and want to emulate their hearts of obedience to and reverence for God? Sure, at least in the moments when their hearts were right. Do we admire and want to emulate their polygamy? No, because we believe it violates God's ideal.

Similarly, God allows divorce, a practice that does not conform with God's creation plan for marriage. The rabbis said divorce was not a sin as long as you gave your wife a proper certificate of dismissal. So perhaps even here, men believed that what they were doing was okay since the religious leaders affirmed it, the law allowed it, and it was confirmed by the social structure. In any case, God allows the practice but puts limits on how it is done so it will not cause so much damage and, in some cases, so it will protect the vulnerable, usually women, by commanding that the husband let his wife go (Exod. 21; Deut. 21). So, does divorce create a good and right situation, or is it just that the way God required them to divorce their wives was good and right because it was less harmful to the women than simply being kicked out?

In both cases, God allows, and sometimes even commands, his people to do things that violate his creation structures for marriage. And when they do these things with honest and submissive hearts, God does not judge them.

---

11. I am careful about the idea of ignorance here. As Karen Keen, one of the editors, remarked when I told her about my approach in this chapter, the idea that affirming scholars or gay readers of Scripture are ignorant can be understood as degrading—a point well taken. So, when I refer to lack of awareness, I may not be referring to someone who has simply not done the appropriate amount of study or who does not have all the information; rather, I may be referring to someone who has done all the work but arrives at a conclusion that others consider to be incorrect. In this case, whichever person is incorrect "does not know" that they are incorrect, for they truly believe they have arrived at the right interpretation of Scripture.

12. When I say that God commanded acts that violate his moral ideal, I am referring specifically to God's command for Levirate marriage, which in most cases likely resulted in polygamy.

Application to LGBTQ Jesus Followers in the Church

Might this be a foundation for an approach of Christlike acceptance without affirmation regarding monogamously married gay Christians? I am not asking this because I am currently committed to this position but because I am trying to understand how these narratives inform us about God's treatment of his people regarding sexual ethics and apply that to the issues the church faces today. Bottom line, according to God's creation model for marriage, polygamy and divorce are not what God designed. But as God engages his people, revealing himself to them in a fallen world, he sometimes accommodates himself to their ways of understanding themselves in this world and to the difficulties and suffering this causes. Sometimes, with consideration for that, rather than judging his people for polygamy or divorce, God regulates the practices so that they are closer to his ideal. And those who obey him in these less-than-ideal situations are not judged.

Is it possible that God might respond in similar ways today to those in the church who believe with sincere hearts that we have misunderstood the Bible's teaching on homosexuality, believing that God is okay with loving, monogamous gay marriages—that God might allow a practice that goes against his creation values in light of the difficulties of a fallen world and the enormous suffering that gay Christians experience in faith communities defined by heterosexuality? Might God see gay Christians' practice as a departure from his design for marriage, but because they are living it out with love, exclusivity, and permanence, which are central to God's design for marriage, decide not to judge them?

Of course, one of the legitimate objections here would be, "If we can allow that, is there any sexual/marital practice or model that we could never accept?" Well, in 1 Corinthians 5, Paul does not seem to allow any acceptance for a man having sex with his father's wife. So the question is, How do we know which sexual/marital practices God will accept, yet without affirmation, and which ones he will not accept under any circumstances? How do we know which sexual behaviors fit into which category?

Surely some will say, "Look, whatever confusing questions we are presented with by Torah, Romans 1 is clear: God rejects all forms of homosexuality and condemns those who practice it, full stop. So we should not allow gay couples to participate in the church." I get that position. But after years of hanging out with the queer community, I have encountered many people who are clearly devoted Jesus followers and want to live lives that honor him but believe we have misunderstood the text on sexuality and marriage. I disagree with them, but I cannot and will not just conclude, like many do, that they really know what they are doing is wrong and are simply making a perverted, sinful choice—that their hearts are rebellious. The sinners in Romans 1 seem to me to be basically giving God the finger, saying, "I know this is wrong, that I am disobeying you and that I will be judged for it, but I don't care, and I'm going to do it anyway." The gay Jesus followers I have known do not present like the people in Romans 1 at all.

So where do we go with all of this in the church? If God's willingness to make accommodations for his followers at times, when they are living outside of his plan for marriage, could include Jesus followers who in good conscience believe that the Bible and God are fine with monogamous gay marriage, what would that look like? How could these Jesus followers fit into a church that teaches that marriage is only meant for one man and one woman? How would it look for a local church like this to go beyond welcoming to a place of integrating a gay or lesbian couple into service in the church? Should there be boundaries in the church for participation, service, or leadership for married gay or lesbian members?

An important place to begin is the Eucharist, asking, according to this model, Should married gay people be allowed to participate in the Eucharist? While "low church" American evangelicals have not placed an incredibly high value on the Eucharist or made it a key element of church participation or church discipline, the overwhelming majority of the historic church has. Early church liturgies show that confession of sin precedes the Eucharist. Believers are to search their lives and recognize and confess sin before coming to the altar of the Eucharist. Further, as part of the system of penance, not only were members who committed serious sin required to confess and repent; they were also often kept from the Eucharist for a period of time so that they recognized the seriousness of their sin, and so that the church could make clear that sin has consequences.

This practice has a biblical basis in the way that Paul calls on the church, in 1 Corinthians 5, to deal with a man who is having sex with his father's wife. He tells the church not to eat with such a person. Growing up as an evangelical, I was taught that this passage meant, for example, that believers should not go to lunch with an unrepentant sinner. Besides the fact that meeting with a sinning fellow believer for lunch actually might be one of the best venues for calling them back to repentance and restoration, I believe this interpretation limits the passage too much, considering Paul's teaching in the rest of the book and the early church's understanding of sin and the Eucharist noted above.

Even if this passage governs social practices of eating, it would certainly also include eating with unrepentant sinners at the Lord's table. As we move further through 1 Corinthians, we see just how central the eucharistic meal, including the "agape feast," was for Paul. It is the Eucharist that is the one loaf and one cup of our ecclesial unity. It is the meal that brings together rich and poor and all other social groups at odds with one another in the world. And it is so serious, so powerful, that apparently some members have become sick, even died, because they have taken the Eucharist with sinful hearts. Thus, keeping unrepentant sinners from the Eucharist is not only a punishment but a protection, perhaps from the judgment of God.

So, does Paul's admonition for the church to prohibit the man sleeping with his stepmother apply to gay or lesbian married church members? I don't think so. And the issue for me goes back to God's view of the heart in judging sin and/or making accommodations for his people. In the ancient world where the church was growing, everyone would have known that this man's action was sinful. Like Absalom having sex with his father's concubines on the roof of the palace, this would have been a personal assault on his father. The entire community would have been in an uproar about this, sensing the shame the father was having to endure publicly. Moreover, the son knew it was wrong. There would have been no thoughtful discussion about how more recent study of Scripture was indicating that the church had misunderstood the Bible on this point and that sex with one's stepmother was okay with God. Bottom line, this man was clearly in a situation of heart rebellion against God. He knew what he was doing was sinful and offensive and decided to do it anyway.

On the contrary, many gay and lesbian Jesus followers are convinced that the Bible has been misunderstood and that God is okay with loving monogamous gay or lesbian marriage. I may disagree with them, and the church may disagree with them, like most of us would disagree that God was okay with Abraham's or David's polygamy. But God made accommodations for them and did not condemn them, because their actions were not an issue of heart rebellion. They were doing what they believed to be right and what the law at that time allowed them to do. If such a scenario applies to married gay or lesbian Jesus followers, then the church would accommodate their participation in the Eucharist. The pastoral staff might meet with a couple like this and let them know that particular church's convictions about marriage but indicate that they are welcome to participate in the Eucharist and that they, like all believers, will stand or fall on this issue before their master, Christ (Rom. 14:4).

The Eucharist is not for sinless believers. It is for sinners who bring all their *known* sin before Christ for forgiveness. What unknown or unacknowledged inappropriate behavior is there in my own life each week as I partake? In my own experience, numerous messed up (sinful) ways that I have related to people or treated people, even my loved ones, only became clear to me later in life, often in therapy. Before that, I thought my approaches were just fine, even right. But they were not. Yet I participated in the life of the church, in the Eucharist, even in leadership with a clear conscience. As an example of this, consider the fact that there were Christian slaveholders at the Eucharist in the early church. Paul makes it very clear to Philemon that, in the church, there should not be slaves—that Onesimus is Philemon's equal in Christ. But nowhere does he demand that Philemon release Onesimus from slavery in the public sphere. And Philemon clearly would have had no sense that slavery was a sin. Further, Paul does not indicate any threat of church discipline for Philemon, nor that Philemon should refrain from the Eucharist until he releases Onesimus.

In 1844, a further expansion of the Philemon themes took place among Methodists in America. James Osgood Andrew was a Methodist bishop in the South who, it was argued by Northern pastors, should not be a bishop because he owned a slave. Andrew was probably a slaveholder in all good conscience, given the biblical arguments from Southern Christians that God was fine with slave ownership. There is no evidence that he believed he was sinning by owning a slave. But the Northern bishops ruled unanimously that he was sinning and must surrender his office. The result was the wholesale departure of southern Methodism to form the Southern Methodist Church. Interestingly, with slavery, we are dealing with an issue of no small biblical discussion where God accommodated the fallen culture of his people, allowing them to own slaves as long as they treated them better than the pagans did.[13]

So, if the non-affirming church allows a married gay or lesbian couple to participate in the life of the church, to share in the Eucharist and to serve, would that mean they are eligible to serve in all positions of leadership? Not necessarily. In Paul's stipulations for eligibility for eldership in 1 Timothy 3, he requires male elders to be "one-woman men." What does Paul mean by this? It is unlikely he means that elders must be married, since that would eliminate Jesus, and perhaps Paul as well. Nor would he be referring to a man who remarried after his wife died, since there are no biblical or cultural prohibitions of that. To be a one-woman man is to be monogamous. Perhaps polygamy is, then, the first thing that comes to mind. Some Jewish people practiced polygamy even into the first century AD, but it was not allowed in the Roman Empire for citizens. But clearly a Roman man of means could have a wife and also a slave whom he slept with. Whatever the issue, Paul is clearly

---

13. My own understanding of biblical anthropology is that slavery, the owning of another human being with complete control over them, is antithetical to human dignity and flourishing rooted in the creation story. Thus, slavery is a departure from God's plan for humanity.

referring to a practice that is outside of God's ideal for sex and marriage. Whatever that practice might be, it is prohibited for elders.

Interestingly, Paul's reference implies that there were men in the church who were not one-woman men. If not, what would be the point of this prohibition? What Paul does not do is prohibit such men from being participants in church life. He just prevents them from being elders. If so, what we have is men who in all good conscience are living in a way that is not according to God's plan for marriage. They are not judged for it, but there is a limit to the kind of leadership they can be eligible for in the church.

What would this look like in the church? Married gay and lesbian couples who believe we have misunderstood the Bible on marriage and who, in all other aspects, demonstrate lives of love for Christ and service to the church could be serving participants in the life of the church. But elders and perhaps pastors, if they are married, would be required to be heterosexually monogamous.

My friend Preston Sprinkle has said to me regarding my approach, "Brad, pastorally that would be a nightmare. How would you determine the difference between people who know what they are doing is wrong and those who, in all good conscience, believe it is right?" It is a fair question. But what are the alternatives, pastorally, for non-affirming churches? Basically, there are two other alternatives: tell gay couples they are sinning and need to either repent or leave, or tell them they are welcome to attend the church but can have no significant participation. For most gay Christians, understandably, neither of these two options are acceptable.[14]

Throughout this chapter, I have argued that God accommodated people who, with good hearts and clear consciences, were living outside of his ideal for sex and marriage. At the same time, I recognize how this approach will be less than satisfying to many of my gay and lesbian friends, who understandably want more than simply accommodation. They want to be welcomed and celebrated. I get that. But in this chapter, I am dealing with their participation in a non-affirming church where the celebration of their sexual and marriage practice may not be possible. Further, the people God accommodated were far from on the sidelines of God's community and work. God accomplished significant elements of his good plan through those who, in good conscience,

---

14. I recognize that even my broader approach, because it prohibits gay couples from the highest levels of church leadership, is still unacceptable to many LGBTQ Christians. But the only other option for non-affirming churches is to take the position that our disagreements over biblical morality in marriage and sexuality are the kinds of issues where we need to just agree to disagree and move on, in which case they are no longer a non-affirming church, but maybe just a silent church. Most non-affirming Christians simply do not believe that is how Scripture addresses this topic.

were living in ways that were outside of God's ideal. Through Abraham, God blessed all the families of the world. Through Jacob and his two wives and two concubines, he created the twelve tribes of Judah. Through David, he wrote psalms.

Throughout my career as a pastor and theologian, I have urged my parishioners and students to "live in the tension" that is always created by the engagement of an infinite and holy God with finite and fallen humans. Sometimes this means carving out a mediating position on issues of importance to both theology and community life. I have also told my students that living in the tension often means being "shot at from both sides," something I'm confident will happen to several of my cocontributors to this book after it is published. My friends who are more conservative on this issue will likely argue that my approach is unworkable, at best, and unbiblical, at worst. My more progressive friends will likely respond that my paradigm still treats LGBTQ persons as second-class citizens in the church. I understand both responses. But sometimes mediating positions are the only places I can stand in good conscience in the already-but-not-yet kingdom of God.

PART 3

Ministry with LGBTQ People, Families, and Friends

11

A Shared Pilgrimage

Eve Tushnet

I spent part of my forty-fifth birthday doing chores in the house that I'll soon be sharing with my partner, listening to a podcast called *Dear Alana*. This podcast tells the story of the life and death by suicide of a young Catholic woman who had experienced anti-gay "conversion therapy" and counseling from priests, ministries, and her Catholic therapist. But it isn't just her story. The podcast's narrator, Simon Kent Fung, got to know Alana Chen's family because her story resonated so deeply with his own experiences—for example, whereas Alana had tried to become straight, in part because she thought she might be called to be a nun, Simon had sought conversion therapy so he could pursue a possible vocation as a priest.

As I listened, while I washed dishes or shelved books, I began to hear echoes of many more stories. Alana had expressed her spiritual journey through music—her inner conflict, her self-doubt, her struggle to discern the difference between obedience and self-erasure. Similarly, my partner has shared with me the song lyrics she had written in her own closeted days, when she was desperate to love God and it felt like the only way to love him was to annihilate some of the deepest parts of herself.

Simon, Alana, and my partner all took different paths. My partner and I are practicing Catholics; we are planning to enter a covenant of kinship, modeled on the promises of Ruth to Naomi, which will unite us for life and call us to care for each other, become kin to each other, make a life together, and follow God in unity of heart and soul. Alana rejected her formerly fervent faith, which had been so powerful that she dreamed of spending her life as a religious sister. When her hometown paper ran a story on a new state ban on conversion therapy for minors, Alana said, "I think the church's counsel is what led me to be hospitalized. . . . I've now basically completely lost my faith. I don't know what I believe about God, but I think if there is a God, he doesn't need me talking to him anymore."

When I asked Simon about his relationship with the Catholic Church today, he said that he'd had to reject the "inerrant apologetic of certainty" that he was given early on in his life of faith. "In many ways [that narrative] was set up to fail," he reflects. "There was simply no way it could withstand the complexity of living and maturing. I'm now returning to a simpler version of faith—one that's a lot more honest." He is "rebuilding" his relationship with the Catholic Church on that basis.

The more I thought about it, the more it seemed that for any hurt a gay person might receive in Christian churches—from seemingly mundane slights to shocking cruelty and spiritual abuse—I could think of people who ended up with very different relationships to their faith in the wake of that pain. Bullying in Christian schools, fear that God hated us, rejection from parents, losing ministry jobs when we came out or were outed, being so miserable and confused and exhausted that our bodies broke down under the stress, being told that our longings for love were the result of demonic activity: I can think of people who have experienced all of these forms of pain who stayed Christian or who left the faith or who became a different kind of Christian. Some people who experienced these things still believe (as I do) that sexual activity is reserved for marriage between one man and one woman, and others report that leaving that belief behind was the best thing they ever did for their mental health. Trauma is not a Play-Doh Fun Factory that squeezes survivors out into uniform and predictable shapes.

A Community Forged and Divided by Our Hardest Experiences

The fact that LGBTQ Christians can experience similar harms and yet end up in very different places offers a lot of hope for bridge-building and ministry. But it also helps explain why ministry in our communities can be so challenging. In this chapter, I'll speak about one aspect of the challenge, and I'll explore a few of the gifts queer Christians can offer one another and the church. What follows is based on about twenty years in various communities of LGBTQ/same-sex-attracted Christian believers, as well as dozens of formal interviews and hundreds of informal conversations exploring others' experiences. In other words, it's based on anecdote. I think my observations comport well with what other, more professionally qualified observers have described. Specifically, the clinical psychologist Alan Downs's *The Velvet Rage: Overcoming the Pain of Growing Up Gay in a Straight Man's World* has helped shape my thinking about the challenges queer people face when we seek community with one another. But I know that what I say here is limited by my own experiences, communities, and perspective.

No matter where a queer Christian currently stands in their walk with Jesus, that position is hard-won. I've participated in several groups for LGBTQ and same-sex-attracted Christians that hope to welcome people regardless of their relationship to "the historical sexual ethic." None of them have found this kind of ministry to be easy. So maybe this is one thing I've learned: The pain many queer Christians have experienced in our churches can lead us to see—and treat—one another as threats.

When I was involved with an LGBTQ ministry in my hometown, one person I spoke with said that he couldn't attend our meetings because the place where we met held a lot of bad memories for him. He'd been there a lot during a time in his life that he now looked back on with regret. That ministry attempted to meet people wherever they were. That was part of the group's strength—it was a place where we could pray for and encourage one another, no matter what our relationship to Catholic teaching. For those who found the group to be helpful, it was what Brian Arao and Kristi Clemens have dubbed a "brave space": not a safe space, but a space where conflicts are handled with deep respect.[1] This ministry served people well when we learned to set aside our judgments and expectations and to see the beauty in one another's lives.

But over the course of the group's life, people left it because it was too progressive or too conservative. These are inadequate terms for what were often painful and personal decisions. One member left after our archdiocese required its priests to read out a letter opposing gay marriage; another left because he didn't feel that we were a good support for his decision to live chastely. These people were both acting to defend the ways of love that they had found. They didn't feel that they could live out those paths with integrity within our group. I'm sorry about that. I'm grateful to the people who stayed despite differences, and yet at the same time, I know it's not my place to tell the people who left that there was nothing threatening in our group.

---

1. Brian Arao and Kristi Clemens, "From Safe Spaces to Brave Spaces: A New Way to Frame Dialogue around Diversity and Social Justice," in *The Art of Effective Facilitation: Reflections from Social Justice Educators*, ed. Lisa M. Landreman (Stylus, 2013).

These acts of self-protection aren't mine to judge. What I think I can judge are the ways in which our churches sometimes pressure queer people to view or treat one another as threats; and I can judge the ways in which I have treated other queer Christians as threats. In earlier years, I sometimes articulated my own beliefs through uncharitable misinterpretations of others' beliefs. I used other people's hard-won convictions the way a cat uses a scratching post. I spent many years in political activism opposing legal gay marriage, naively refusing to hear what other people were telling me about the homophobia that activism fueled in their churches and communities. Without getting into a debate about the best possible legal structures for recognizing the care and commitment of gay couples, I think it's fair to say that I spent my time badly. I should have been advocating for queer young people. Instead of battling the political enemy of gay marriage, I should have been fighting the terrible spiritual enemies—namely, despair and self-hatred.

Even during that time, I genuinely did try to stand within queer communities rather than separating myself from them. I had been involved in queer communities before I became Catholic, and I had seen people in these communities cherish one another, create beautiful or sublime art, and show great courage. I feel very lucky that I was not taught, growing up, to view queer communities as enemies of my faith or seething dens of sexual sin. I didn't think that I had to separate myself from gay people in order to be a Christian. When straight pastors and mentors urge the people in their care to identify as "same-sex attracted" rather than "gay" or similar terms, one of the effects, whether intentionally or not, is to separate the person from the majority of gay people. That's one reason I call myself gay today. I still have responsibilities to gay communities. Having enjoyed the benefits of solidarity, I want to pay my dues (and paying my dues means serving and supporting other gay people).

And yet some people flee gay communities and a "gay identity" because these are sites where they were harmed. For some people, retreating from gay communities or from identifying with gay people is a strategy for recovery from sexual addiction or sexual trauma. I am not personally convinced that this is a good place to remain indefinitely, but it is a part of many people's stories, and I'm not sure it's my place to question them. They are often defending a hard-won peace.

That "hard-won" aspect of people's defensive stance is really the main point I'm making here. Anyone who identifies as LGBTQ or same-sex attracted and Christian has traveled a complex, confusing, and often painful journey to get there. The harder you've had to fight for something—especially something as precious as faith, recovery, or self-acceptance—the more fiercely you're likely to defend it against anything that seems like a threat. Add to that the fact that human nature is such that we often perceive even people just living a different way as if they are implicitly judging us. Add to *that* the fact that even when they swear they aren't judging us, sometimes they really are! (And even when we swear we aren't judging them, sometimes we really are, and we don't even know it.)

In arguing that there are reasons, rooted in painful personal experience, that LGBTQ and same-sex-attracted Christians may struggle to welcome one another across divides of belief (especially belief about the boundaries of Christian sexual discipline), I am *not* arguing that our challenges are greater than those of our straight brethren. The most strident rejections of the possibility of ministry across divides of belief often come from people with no apparent skin in the game, whether they are acting out of misguided allyship or boring old homophobia.

There are forces in our churches and communities, and the broader culture, that make it easier for us to treat one another as threats. There are people in "traditional" churches who will try to shame you away from spending time in queer spaces or being a friend to queer people. There are people with more "progressive" beliefs who will feed your anger at your church or your upbringing in ways which keep you stuck, or even foster your self-pity, instead of helping you articulate the reasons for your anger, acknowledge the grief which often fuels it, and ask the Holy Spirit for whatever you need in order to begin the long journey of forgiveness.

And yet I have been surprised, even awed, by how often queer Christians are willing to do the hard and painful work of moving through our fears, judgments, shame, or anger in order to listen to one another and live in solidarity. There are so many reasons for queer Christians to mistrust one another that it is amazing to me how often we are, somehow, able to remember that we *are* one another. To God be the glory!

We are divided not by trivialities but by deep differences in our understanding of church membership, obedience, authority, scriptural interpretation, and, of course, sexual morality—an area that even the ancient world recognized that the Christian churches focused on with a strange intensity. Our divisions will not be wholly overcome until we have received the unity we pray for: "that all of them may be one" (John 17:21). And yet there are still ways to proclaim that we all seek to live as members of the body of Christ—and joys we can only experience if we recognize and support this aspiration in one another. The rest of this essay will explore some of those ways and joys.

Living as If We're One Community

One way to view one another as fellow pilgrims on the way of Jesus, in spite of differences over something as personal as our sexual ethic, is to remember how often people change their beliefs about that ethic. This change occurs in both directions—and in complex ways that can't quite be described as moving in one direction or another! Some people begin their Christian journey certain that sex is reserved for marriage between one man and one woman, but then come to believe that Christian marriage can include unions of two people of the same sex. Some people start out believing that gay marriage is what God is calling them to, and later come to believe that Christian discipleship requires a "traditional" approach. Some people start out traditional, go through a period of questioning, become progressive for a while, and then return to "tradhood," having discovered a new way of being traditional. Some go prog-trad-prog.

Some decide that they are personally called to celibacy but that the overall question of a Christian sexual ethic is not for them to discern—you might call them agnostic about it. Tim Otto writes eloquently about his decision to take a vow of celibacy in obedience to the intentional community where he lives, even though he does not share what was then their belief that gay marriage is wrong.[2] Some people basically say that they're not sure, and so they are just trying to muddle through, act with love, and trust in God's mercy. Some people are kind of flighty and believe one thing on a rainy Tuesday, and another on a sunny Saturday! All of us are fools for love.

So many of us have held a different belief from the one we hold now. The gay person who is on one side of the ethical divide today may be on the other side tomorrow, or may already occupy a position more complex than we realize. If we are only able to nurture the faith of people who agree with us about sexual ethics, we will have to abandon anyone whose ethic changes. In *Dear Alana*, Alana Chen describes how betrayed she felt when her Catholic friends and mentors stopped reaching out to her or responding to her own attempts to maintain relationships after she stopped practicing her faith. I think she felt used as well as abandoned: like she had always been just a moral project for them, not a friend.

Learning to cherish and shelter one another across divides of belief can also nourish our own souls. Reconciling with the "other" gay Christian may be a way of reconciling with, forgiving, or honoring what was best in our

---

2. Tim Otto, *Oriented to Faith: Transforming the Conflict over Gay Relationships* (Cascade Books, 2014).

own past selves—at least, it can be that if we avoid simply projecting our own experiences onto other people.

When we view each other as fellow disciples first, and adherents of theological positions second, what can we offer one another? Well, first of all, we can offer one another prayer. Perhaps the best thing about the LGBTQ ministry in my hometown was that we prayed for one another. Celibate people prayed for people in gay marriages; people who no longer considered themselves Catholic prayed for priests.

And this shared prayer was the purest distillation of something else we offered one another: an acknowledgment of the fullness of one another's lives. Most of us in that icon-adorned room (or on that picnic blanket, etc.) knew what it felt like to be viewed merely as a category: a priest, a homosexual, a PFLAG parent, or a lapsed Catholic. In learning enough about one another to offer specific prayers, we learned to see beyond the label—or, maybe a better way of putting it, to see what the label meant to the person who bore it. We learned how the labels had shaped one another's lives, and where the labels had proved inadequate. We were able to glimpse some of what priesthood means to some specific priests, and what transition means to some specific transgender people. We were able to glimpse some of what it means to be Catholic, by seeing what it meant for these specific people to come to the Catholic Church for fellowship.

When we share our life with others, we receive opportunities to serve them—in the spiritual works of mercy, which include all the forms of mercy that are easiest to make obnoxious, but also in the corporal works of mercy, which are less malleable by our pride. I've attended same-sex weddings, and because I was there for the couples in those celebrations, they have allowed me to be there for them in harder times. I've been helped and encouraged by queer people with "progressive" beliefs, and I have tried to repay their kindness. I've known people who hold "traditional" beliefs, but nonetheless have offered real comfort and encouragement to "nontraditional" same-sex couples dealing with mental-health struggles; they've offered material, practical help, including mutual aid and help finding a job. Christians with a "traditional" belief might fruitfully ask ourselves where we've talked ourselves out of opportunities for *service* because we feared that others might interpret our actions as offering moral approval of same-sex marriages or sexual relationships.

The Deeper Gifts

I hope that we can offer one another examples of same-sex love. Many of us trads have needed the witness of more "progressive" queer people, who showed us that our desires did involve love: that we, too, could hold love and responsibility in one hand. When I asked what my longing for women meant, I'm grateful that I got answers other than, "It means that you're sexually perverse and incapable of self-control." And the first places where I received a hopeful interpretation of my desires were gay communities. Queer Christians who do not find any hopeful interpretations of their desires often struggle with self-hatred, despair, self-harm (including through sex), and rage against God.

This much may seem obvious to more-progressive Christians. What may be less obvious are the ways in which more-traditional queer Christians, especially those living celibately, can also offer examples and models to those who hold a different sexual ethic.

There are a lot of reasons someone might end up seeking ways to live well without sex. You may not have found a partner; you may find the hunt for a partner depleting and demoralizing. You may perceive an inward call to celibacy, whether within one of the various Christian traditions of celibate life or in some more complex or unstructured way. You may be in a same-sex marriage or partnership in which sex has receded, or where the diminishment of sexual desire for your partner has started to cause problems, and you're struggling with how to express your love without the urgent, undeniable *fact* of sexual union.

These are situations of intense stress, which can cause shame, self-hatred, and depression; envy and resentment, the twin tempter-demons of the "incel"; conflict within a loving relationship; and unwise decisions and compromises with one's faith, such as "opening the marriage" or acting out sexually. (I'm not here to tell you what your sexual ethic within marriage should be; I'm just saying that for many queer Christians, same-sex marriage comes with an expectation of sexual exclusivity, for all the usual biblical and emotional reasons.)

Having models of loving, fruitful celibacy—in partnership, in community, and in ordinary lay life—may offer comfort as well as guidance. And many "trad" queer Christians can offer our experiences, our imperfect lives, as sources of this comfort and guidance. I'm not saying celibate queer people can solve the normal queer problems of normal queer people. We are weird! Many of us would say that our way of life would not be possible if we were not convinced that this is the life Christ has called us to. Jesus, not celibacy, is the source of our strength. But our experience with celibacy has given us some practical wisdom—and maybe even some insight into the meaning of some people's same-sex desires.

Let me lay it on you bluntly: I don't think it can be true that the sole purpose or fulfillment of gay desire is same-sex marriage. To make marriage or sexual relationship the sole arena of adult love, the sole marker of adulthood, and the one true expression of our eros is to replicate within gay communities the idolatry of marriage that our straight brethren already commit. It is to leave many, many queer people feeling like failures. It is to make a life shaped by love something you can miss out on, and something you can lose.

"Trad" queer Christians have been forced to explore, often with little responsible shepherding, more unexpected ways of living out our longings. When I first became Catholic, I sought to live out my desire to love and serve women, and to participate in "women's community" (this permeable, lightly held ideal is perhaps my most '70s dyke-culture desire), by volunteering at a crisis pregnancy center. That was maybe a weird idea, and it won't work for many people for many reasons. But for me it became an anchor of my spiritual life, a chance to encounter the deep realities of thousands of women and open my heart to them, a cure for self-pity (heterosexual people also experience pain in navigating their sexuality), and a reminder of God's power. Later, as I learned more about the history and spirituality of Christian friendship, I sought to live out the love that is at the heart of my lesbianism by deepening my friendships and my willingness to sacrifice for my friends.

Now, I am living out that love primarily in my partnership, learning to cherish, honor, and be kin to one particular woman within celibacy. I have had to confront new-to-me questions of shame, boundaries, and our mammalian need for physical connection, and I've had new encounters with the sacredness and beauty of the body. I'm learning to explore unexpected paths of life-giving love. Through my relationship with my partner, God is opening my heart: making me less self-righteous and more compassionate. Our partnership is shaping my prayer life and offering me new ways to trust in God.

Covenant friendship, celibate partnership, and other forms of committed nonsexual love are, in their own ways, affirmations of the reality of same-sex love. They are living reminders that God calls some people to share a life with someone of the same sex. They stand in a tradition of biblical heroes and foremothers, celibate saints who found soulmates, and hermit pairs (yes, you can be a hermit with a friend; I know it sounds perverse).

But they are not the only good expressions of gay desire. Only a tiny minority of even "trad" queer people are living celibacy in partnership. And when we begin to place "partnership" in the niche our church cultures give to marriage (and our secular culture gives to romantic relationships and sex) we once again create a church of winners and losers, haves and have-nots. More than that, we ignore and perhaps miss out on the many other paths of love to which the Lord calls us. Maybe the deepest expression of your eros will be in art—I don't know what Tomie dePaola's sexual ethic was, but I know he gave us so much beauty from the gifts God poured into his gay, Catholic heart.

Maybe you will find safe haven for your deep longings in an unexpected friendship, like Fr. Henri Nouwen's friendship with Adam Arnett, the developmentally disabled man who inspired Nouwen's book *Adam: God's Beloved*. Maybe your desire will bear fruit in mystical prayer, where your soul, who wandered the walls of the city for so long and was beaten by the watchmen, can at last tryst with the divine Lover, and you can know yourself beloved.

I think, and this is more speculative than the preceding paragraphs, that all our loves are in some way a foretaste of and preparation for the life to come. And we know from Jesus's own words in Matthew 22:30 that in the resurrection there is no longer marrying nor giving in marriage. "Trad" queer Christians living celibately have had to wrestle with this teaching more than most, and we have discovered some beauties in it, which you also, regardless of your orientation or sexual ethic, may need someday—and perhaps today.

And we can offer one other gift, or rather, the two "sides" can offer a gift to each other, in the work we have done to understand the Christian virtue of obedience. If there is one thing gay Christians know (and I'm not sure there *is* one thing we all know!), it's that obedience can be weaponized against us. No matter what her sexual ethic, the queer Christian has had to acknowledge the ways obedience can become self-hatred and self-harm, and the ways it can become complicity in others' abuse of power.

And yet there is more to be said about obedience, I think, than simply its potential for abuse. Jesus links love and obedience: "You are my friends if you do what I command" (John 15:14). Obedience is one language for talking about acts and attitudes that can also be described with words like *trust*, *humility*, and *discipleship*. These words, too, can be and have frequently been used as weapons of oppression and abuse. But so has *love*; so has *faith*. I would argue that queer Christians need models of what obedience looks like when it is *not* destructive, when it is not self-censorship or complicity. I am not sure we can have models of queer Christian life without some rescuing of obedience. And as a Catholic, I'll add that it seems to me that the shocking individuality of the saints—the weirdness of the saints!—suggests that obedience need not diminish individuality, and can even heighten it. Perhaps God has given us our strange souls because he wants the strangeness of our particular obedience.

The Catholic concept of "development of doctrine" marries obedience and questioning. All queer Christians, whether "trad" or "prog" at any given moment, have had to work out how we unite these aspects of the life of faith in our own souls. Some trads may emphasize questioning—there's a cottage industry of trad Christians deploying queer theory in service of the traditional

A Shared Pilgrimage

teaching, in ways that are sometimes disingenuous but often fun and sometimes even illuminating. And some progs may emphasize obedience—it isn't true that adopting a progressive sexual ethic means you become a relativist or even a partisan of the individual interpretation of Scripture. But I think it is fair to say that many trads have framed our problem as one of developing an obedience that won't destroy us, and many progs have framed their problem as one of learning to question in a way that is still responsive and responsible to Scripture. In both our theology and our practical daily discipleship, we have much to learn from each other.

These are only a few suggestions, from the most practical to the most theological, of what we can gain as churches and as individual Christians when we are able to see all queer Christians as members of the body of Christ. We often fear or resent or anger or even harm one another; we may need to make amends or work toward forgiveness. We may struggle to see one another as individuals, rather than as avatars of ways of life that have harmed us deeply. But these are not the only truths about our relationships to one another. We are one another. We have been one another when we have been able to see all queer Christians as pilgrims together. We belong, not to the "trad" or the "prog" side, but to one another and to Christ above all!

As I listened to *Dear Alana* and filled the bookshelves in what will soon be my home, the shelf I filled first is the queer Christian shelf. It includes works that have shaped my own queer Christian life. So, there's St. Bernard of Clairvaux's sermons on the Song of Songs, and Peter Brown's masterful study of sexual asceticism in the early church, *The Body and Society*. There are works by dissenting Catholics, like Andrew Sullivan's *Love Undetectable*, and works by trad Protestants, like Wesley Hill's *Spiritual Friendship: Finding Love in the Church as a Celibate Gay Christian*, and works by people whose positions can't be so quickly summarized, like Tim Otto's *Oriented to Love* and Bridget Eileen Rivera's *Heavy Burdens*. There are works by people who lived before the invention of "sexual orientation," works by people who lived at its dawn, and works by people who might reject those identity terms if they were offered. There's Dunstan Thompson's poetry, with its movement from anguished promiscuity to grateful devotion. There's a literal princess diary kept by a pioneering novelist of lesbian love, who was buried in her Dominican habit. There are depictions of tender monastic friendships and modern gay men discovering love in the face of AIDS.

I have needed all of it. I hope I'm learning to be responsible to all of them.

12

Courage Is Ministry

Sally Gary

Following Jesus requires courage. Courage to risk status and reputation. Courage to stand up for and associate with people that your community wants you to avoid. Courage to risk comfort and security—even life itself. That's what endears me the most to Jesus—his unwavering desire to associate closely with those who were seen as undeserving of the religious elite's time and attention, people whom the law said were unclean.

Courage to See and Acknowledge a Person

The Gospel of Luke tells us the story of the woman who washed Jesus's feet with her tears and dried them with her hair, anointing them with perfume (7:36–50). The religious leaders reacted, accusingly asking Jesus if he knew what kind of woman was touching him. It took courage for Jesus to *see* her and defend her. It would've been lesson enough if he simply didn't stop her or reluctantly sent her away, but Jesus went a step further by publicly acknowledging her. He knew what they were thinking, doubting him as a prophet for associating with this sinful woman.

In the same way, it took courage for Jesus to see Zacchaeus up in that tree and call out to him. Even more courageous to risk going to Zacchaeus's home to spend time with him. There was a whole crowd of people standing around, and they knew exactly who Zacchaeus was. They had every reason to not associate with him, knowing that tax collectors were unscrupulous traitors, betraying their own people by working with the Roman government and taking an extra cut off the top for themselves. But Jesus does the unthinkable. He looks up and *sees* the man that no one else sees and says, "Zacchaeus, hurry and come down, for I must stay at your house today" (Luke 19:1–10, NRSVue).

It took courage for Jesus to withstand his faith community's relentless questioning about his associations: Why does he eat with sinners? (Matt. 9:11). Even Jesus's own friends, the disciples, didn't understand the choices he made regarding the company he kept. They had been raised in the same system of monitoring who is in and who is out, asking at one point if they should call down fire and brimstone on the Samaritans (Luke 9:54–55).

When Jesus sat alone talking with a Samaritan woman at the well, the disciples were shocked (John 4:27). Jesus went completely against tradition by engaging this woman who had a questionable relationship history. The mere fact that she came to the well in the middle of the day by herself, and not accompanied by the other women from the village, tells us she's an outcast. Yet Jesus knows all the details of her life, that she's been married five times and even now was cohabitating with another man. He *sees* something when he looks at her that others don't.

In the parable of the religious leader and tax collector, Jesus sees what others miss (Luke 18:9–14; see also Matt. 23:27–28). To everyone else, the righteous one seemed to be the devout faith leader, but it was the tax collector who was open to God, despite all outward appearances. It took courage for Jesus to see and name what others did not.

When it comes to LGBTQ people, what do you see? Would you risk your reputation to befriend a gay or transgender person?

Courage and Pastoral Wisdom

"I can't sign that," my pastor friend, Peter, told the leadership of his church after they placed a freshly drafted policy statement regarding marriage on his desk in front of him.[1] He would later tell me that the day went down as one of the saddest days of his life, if not *the* saddest.

It's one thing to be a preacher; it's another thing altogether to be a pastor. My friend Peter was a true pastor, who would meet you for coffee to listen

---

1. "Peter" is not his real name. Some names and details in this chapter have been changed to protect confidentiality.

while you poured your heart out or visit you when you were sick. For decades, Peter served as lead pastor of a large conservative church in the South. The first time I watched him do a baby blessing on a Sunday morning, I was so moved by the way he held the infant in his arms that I snapped a picture with my phone. It was evident that this man had held many a baby, and the child, along with her parents and grandparents gathered around her, was completely at ease with Peter.

So, years later, when I learned that Peter had been forced to step down from that church, I was horrified.

Looking back, it all started when Peter invited me to spend time with his congregation and meet with LGBTQ individuals and their families who were members of the church. During this season, I was presenting workshops to around twenty-five churches a year to help congregations have pastoral conversations about faith and sexuality. Peter's church was wrestling with questions and concerns similar to those I had faced in other congregations. The workshop started with a Saturday gathering that brought together an intergenerational group of grandparents, parents, and high school students. It was a delightful time of roundtable discussion, with people sharing a range of beliefs about sexuality. The following morning Peter interviewed me during both Sunday services. At the end of each service, my cell phone number was projected onto the screen above us in the sanctuary, and people were invited to text me to set up private meetings over the next three days. By the time I went to bed Sunday night, every hour was filled, from 8 a.m. to 9 p.m., Monday through Wednesday.

Over the next few days, I listened to LGBTQ people in this church who weren't out to anyone. I met with parents and grandparents of LGBTQ children who were not sure how to respond, as well as with other parishioners who had a lot of questions. After decades serving this church and listening to their hearts, Peter knew the members of his congregation needed someone to talk to who understood firsthand the needs of LGBTQ people and their families. As the parents of a gay teenager, Peter and his wife, Valerie, needed it too.

Over the next few years, other leaders in the church became increasingly concerned with Peter's and Valerie's own processing, particularly in regard to their views on same-sex marriage. As a result, the leadership came up with a policy—a statement of faith regarding marriage—that they required all staff members at the church to sign.

But Peter was hesitant. He respected the fact that he worked at a traditionalist church, and he explained to the leadership that he had no intention of using the pulpit to teach a view contrary to the policy. But he also shared that, by signing the policy, it felt like a betrayal to his gay child and his own personal evolving views on sexuality. He assured them he would not go against the policy in his pastoral role at the church, but he needed to support his family. Peter explained, "What will this do to my relationship with my child, especially when my role is both father and pastor?"

When Peter refused to sign the piece of paper that day, the church would no longer allow him to remain on staff. He lost everything he had worked for during all those years of service. He lost the vocation he loved and the stability of a job. All of it, gone. Stripped of the identity he had lived and breathed for much of his adult life, Peter was forced to start all over.

Most of all, Peter and his family lost relationships they had invested in over many years, a whole network of friends, a community, a place of belonging. The incessant questions and second-guessing, if not outright judgment, from people they had thought were friends "closer than a brother," were incredibly painful. Peter and his family felt instant exclusion. And we haven't even talked about the impact the leadership's actions had on Peter and Valerie's gay child—especially the impact on their teenager's faith in God and faith in the church.

If only their church's leadership had shown courage to walk through the messiness of theological conviction with pastoral wisdom. After all, Peter had committed to respecting the traditionalist stance of the church. But their fear of being associated with a pastor who supported his gay child led them to pressure a father to choose between his family and his church. Peter's and Valerie's courage cost them more than they could have anticipated, but they were committed to living with integrity, to standing by LGBTQ people, as faith leaders and as parents.

Courage to Follow Jesus Publicly

"No one could perform the signs you are doing if God were not with him" (John 3:2). Those were the first words out of Nicodemus's mouth when he came to visit Jesus "at night." A religious leader, Nicodemus made his confession in secrecy, lest any of his colleagues discover his curiosity and deep desire to know more from Jesus. John's Gospel mentions Nicodemus three times: the visit under cover of night (John 3:1–12), his admonition to the religious leaders that the law requires Jesus to be given a hearing before judgment (John 7:45–52), and Nicodemus's purchase of a hundred pounds of spices to prepare Jesus's body for burial (John 19:38–42).

We might surmise from these brief moments that Nicodemus sincerely cared for Jesus. And yet Nicodemus was afraid to publicly acknowledge his belief in Jesus as sent from God.

I've always thought of this story from Nicodemus's perspective, understanding how risky it would have been for him to come right out and openly support Jesus. At the very least, as an elite member of the Sanhedrin, he would have lost status, income, reputation, and community, putting his own well-being at risk, along with his family's. He was obviously a man of great reputation among his people and, undoubtedly, wealthy to have purchased a hundred pounds of spices. He was a man of influence, and yet Scripture reveals his reluctance to use that influence to publicly affirm Jesus, at least initially.

Perhaps he sincerely believed he could do greater good for Jesus as an insider among the religious leaders, bringing them along. Maybe he reasoned that if he stayed and withheld his true beliefs, he could have more influence on those who didn't see Jesus for who he was. Perhaps he truly believed he was helping Jesus by keeping quiet and staying put.

And maybe he did have opportunities to say things as an insider, as someone who was respected among his fellow leaders, that no one else could have said. But I also wonder how Nicodemus's secrecy felt to Jesus. How did it feel knowing that Nicodemus had, at least on one occasion, come to him, recognizing God in him and wanting to know more from him, and yet did not want anyone else to know he was associating with Jesus? I wonder how Jesus might have felt looking into Nicodemus's eyes, if Nicodemus was able to make eye contact with him at all. I can't help wondering if Jesus wished Nicodemus would stand up for him.

Jesus, if only in his humanity, must have wished that someone in a position of influence would acknowledge him, as he faced harassment and death threats. In fact, Jesus longed for his own people to come along. "How often I have longed to gather your children together, as a hen gathers her chicks," he mourned over Jerusalem (Matt. 23:37).

Over the years I've talked to countless pastors who lead non-affirming churches, yet they themselves want to do more to support LGBTQ people. They stand to lose everything if they reveal their true beliefs and feelings. Many believe they can have more influence by staying and continuing to pastor from within; undoubtedly, the conversations they are able to have as "insiders" have an impact. In this way, they are able to help others come to understand another perspective on LGBTQ people. That might not otherwise happen, and that's a potentially positive outcome.

But my heart longs for the Nicodemuses to stand openly by me, not just to visit me by night with private reassurances, when the lack of public acknowledgment has real consequences for me and other LGBTQ people. Eventually, Nicodemus managed to work up the courage to say Jesus deserved to have a hearing with the council, but when the other leaders challenged Nicodemus, "Are you from Galilee, too?" the biblical record indicates only his silence (John 7:51–52). Nicodemus couldn't quite bring himself to publicly declare his support for Jesus.

When I first came out, and for several years afterward, I was content, grateful even, to be allowed simply to attend any church, because for much of my lifetime, openly LGBTQ people would have been barred from membership. I was happy to receive the crumbs. But after a while, the small scraps that fall from the table fail to nourish.

The Ministry of Courage

It takes boldness to associate with people whose friendship might impact our own social standing or opportunities in a negative way. Most of us mean well, and so more often than not, the way we disassociate with others is subtle. My experience has been mostly of folks who are somewhere in between—not wanting to completely abandon connection, but not willing to go out of their way to give a public shout-out.

Shortly before I came out publicly, a friend admitted to me that she had wrestled with whether she could be associated with me. She expressed concern that if people saw us socializing, others would automatically make the assumption that she, too, was gay. But after further thought, she decided to take the risk because my friendship was important to her. That conversation has made other friendships—ones in which no deliberation was required, in which there was never a question about whether we could be seen together in a restaurant or sitting on the same pew at church—all the more precious to me.

Some of my friends prefer to fly under the radar; they haven't walked away, but they are less likely to engage with me publicly. These friends avoid "liking" or commenting directly on my social media posts, even though I see them interacting regularly with our mutual friends. Some will, instead, send me a private text in direct response to a post. Recently, I attended a conference and ran into old friends, and we all happily took photos together. But I found myself asking if it was okay to post the pictures. Were all of these friends willing to be publicly associated with me?

One of the most hurtful experiences I've had was being denied admission to an annual Christian retreat. I'd been to the retreat center twice before with the same group of friends, but after getting married to a woman, I was no longer welcome. Of all the Christian retreats I've experienced over the years, this one was by far the most encouraging and uplifting. I'd felt a deep sense of belonging with this group. So, when the retreat center announced the next annual gathering, I delightedly submitted my application to attend. But within a few days, the director contacted me by phone and apologetically began to explain why I would not be allowed to participate. All the retreat center leaders were privately supportive of me, she said, if not fully affirming. But they were concerned about the cost of publicly associating with me. It stung to hear they decided to exclude me from an event that had been such an inspiration to me.

Last year, I reached out to an evangelical leadership support network that I thought could meet my need for self-care amid a busy ministry life. I longed to be encouraged and refreshed by sharing my heart with peers. The organization putting on the year-long group advertised it as a spiritually nurturing opportunity for leaders. But when I wrote to inquire about participating, the facilitator told me he would have to ask the other group members if they were comfortable having a gay married woman in the group. Demoralized, I didn't have the heart to follow up.

I long for others to say, "I know this woman, and I know her heart for Jesus, and even if you disagree with her, we can still welcome her into this space."

I long for people to treat me like Jesus, who publicly stood up for "that kind of woman" by challenging her accuser, "Do you see this woman? . . . You did not give me a kiss, but this woman, from the time I entered, has not stopped kissing my feet" (Luke 7:44–45). I long to see people publicly announce to everyone that they are going to Zacchaeus's house to eat a meal together. I long for those who will sit at the well with a Samaritan woman, knowing friends will be shocked when they find out.

What would happen if we had the courage to say, "Everyone has a place at the table. I want to sit down and eat with this person." Yes, it will cost something. We might be discredited, become the subject of gossip, or lose a job. After all, it cost Jesus something to make room for the social and religious outcasts of his day. In fact, they ended up killing him for it. But that didn't stop him from saying, "Do you see this woman?"

Courageous Priorities in Ministry

Would you interrupt time with a leader who could open doors for you to, instead, give your attention to someone else whose affiliation with you could ruin your reputation?[2]

---

2. This section about the unclean, bleeding woman is partly excerpted from a sermon I gave at Restore Austin Church on April 28, 2024.

Jesus prioritized an unclean woman over an influential leader. When we first read the narrative in Mark 5:21–43, it seems the story is going to be about Jairus, a leader in the local synagogue. Jairus was an important man with an important request. A family member was dying and needed help. Jairus fell at Jesus's feet and begged him to come and heal his twelve-year-old daughter. At first Jesus responds to the request and heads toward Jairus's house, with a crowd of people following along to watch.

But in the middle of this throng of people, Jesus stops. He stops because he feels power go out of him, and he wants to know who touched him. The disciples roll their eyes, believing it's obvious—the whole crowd is pressing against Jesus. Of course somebody touched him. But they're probably also thinking, "Come on, we've got to get to Jairus's house. He's the leader; he's the priority right now. If you take care of this important request to save his daughter, this leader could open doors for you. His influence could get powerful critics off your back." And, certainly, Jairus is beside himself, saying, "Come on, come on, come on!"

But Jesus doesn't budge. He stops and asks, "Who touched me?" Then he turns and sees the unclean woman, trembling at his feet. He had every legitimate reason not to see her, to just keep going and do the good work he was about, saving a life. But he stops. And he listens to this woman tell her whole story.

The unclean woman has been bleeding for twelve years. According to Jewish law, her bleeding makes her unclean. She had consulted doctors, spending all she had, to no avail. It stands to reason that she is anemic, with all the physical distress that brings with it. And when you don't feel good for twelve years, you can get pretty depressed, especially when you live in an age and culture that believes you're suffering because you did something morally wrong. The shame and humiliation she must have surely felt! Not to mention the isolation.

Socially, she is alienated. Her clothing is unclean. Her bed is unclean. Everything she sits on and anyone who touches her, or touches her clothing while she is bleeding, is considered unclean. After twelve years, she may have been abandoned by a husband, if she had ever been able to marry in the first place. She would have been left alone much of her life, apart from a few family members—too unclean to be touched. Yet she pushes through crowds and touches Jesus.

And Jesus stops. Jesus prioritizes the unclean woman's request over the powerful community leader's request. He sees her. When Jesus encounters a person, whose touch could make him unclean, he violates social expectations to choose the unclean person. Jesus's public association elevates the woman, sending a message to the crowd that she is just as worthy of his time as Jairus.

Jesus prioritizes the one everyone else thinks is not the priority. In the end, Jesus takes care of both the woman and Jairus. But he doesn't care for Jairus at the expense of the woman.

Today, I see the opposite happening over and over—the needs of the "unclean" LGBTQ people are being demoted to prioritize the needs of "safer, more respectable" people in the church. When LGBTQ people knock on the doors of the church and ask for belonging, ministry leaders are prioritizing everyone else. "It would be too risky to prioritize LGBTQ people," they say. "Better that sexual and gender minorities go somewhere else than cause a church to lose members who aren't ready to incorporate the unclean." It takes courage to interrupt care for the ninety-nine to tend to one (Matt. 18:12–14).

Courage Doesn't Come Easily, but It's Worth It

I know firsthand that courage is hard to practice. I know what it's like to be a rare voice speaking about sexuality and gender in my church denomination. I know how it feels to walk into rooms with audiences looking back at me with somber faces, unsure of how to respond to me, uncomfortable with the topic, and yet to whisper a prayer under my breath and take the risk to pour my heart out to them. I know what it's like for my insides to shake like Jell-O as an angry man jabs his finger accusingly in my face, "You're nothing but a practicing homosexual!" I know what it feels like to have a woman scream at me in the middle of a sanctuary after hearing my story, berating me for talking about such things in church.

When I first realized that my feelings for a girl in college went far deeper than friendship, I had every intention of taking that secret to my grave. Every day I prayed for God to take those feelings away. I was filled with shame. I had no idea how this had happened, nor did I have any idea how to make it stop. But God gave me courage to tell someone, at a time when it was strictly taboo for anyone to say they were gay.

I was in the middle of the Bible belt, in a conservative church, where such things were considered unspeakable. I knew people who had been outed and shunned by their families. It took courage for me to tell my mama and risk the most important relationship in my life. And for every friend I came out to personally over the next few years, it took tremendous strength. Every time I told someone, I was petrified of losing their friendship.

When I was invited to return to my alma mater, Abilene Christian University, to teach in the communication department, God placed a dream in my heart for what became CenterPeace, a ministry to provide support for LGBTQ people and parents with LGBTQ loved ones, as well as to equip churches to have constructive conversations on faith and sexuality.[3] This was back in 2001, and, at the time, I had only come out to a few people in my inner circle. But God gave me courage to approach the university administration about where the Spirit was leading me.

I asked the president of the university if I could share my story in the daily chapel assembly. And risking the backlash, he said yes. He faced criticism from people who asked, "Why do you have somebody like her on the faculty?" But he stood by me, and soon I was looking out into a sea of five thousand faces in chapel, sharing something deeply personal with the entire campus, knowing that I would be viewed differently after that. But I knew God was calling me to stand with others like me and invite them to do the same—to associate with those we had all been told to shun.

I wasn't the only one who was brave. It took courage for my parents to go to family counseling with me and to choose to stand by me. It took courage for friends and colleagues to continue associating with me after I publicly came out and began speaking on this controversial topic. It took courage for a university president to say yes. Their courage to walk alongside me has made all the difference.

I asked university colleagues and church friends to help me put the new CenterPeace ministry together. They risked venturing with me into unknown territory. At the time, there were few resources out there to help us know we weren't alone. Certainly, there were no Christian resources in our Churches of Christ world to reassure us that LGBTQ people can reconcile their faith and their sexuality or that a parent doesn't have to choose between their church and their child.

In 2013, seven years after CenterPeace became a nonprofit, a pastor of a large church in Dallas reached out to me. In an email he wrote, "I can't get you or CenterPeace out of my mind. Call me." I did. And the following year, I moved from Abilene to Dallas at Pat's invitation. He wanted to be supportive of CenterPeace, realizing it was a ministry his own church (and others) needed. His congregation alone had five families (that he knew of) with LGBTQ children. Pat offered me office space at his church, along with administrative support and a place to call home. I asked him every hard question, making sure he understood what people would ultimately say about him and his church for hosting this ministry. He didn't flinch.

---

3. To learn more about CenterPeace, see our website, CenterPeace.net.

The church lost members for bringing me there, even though I wasn't teaching about the theological debate—just providing space for LGBTQ people and their families to come out and receive support and friendship. It took courage for this pastor, the rest of the staff, and the church as a whole to have their names associated with CenterPeace, to provide financial support, and to allow me to use their facilities for every event, whether meetings with other pastors or fundraising dinners or national conferences. And I am forever grateful for their bravery.

When I face challenges—and I do continue to face opposition and rejection—I remember all that God has already done. Lately, memories of the Spirit's work over the past two decades have given me hope during hard times. When I announced in 2020 that CenterPeace would become openly affirming and that I planned to marry a woman after years of serving in ministry as a single person, I faced the repercussions. Churches and conferences that had welcomed me in previous years stopped inviting me, donors ceased giving, old friends went silent.

Before I announced my upcoming marriage, I was terrified once again of losing my entire world, a faith community full of rich spiritual heritage and history. It was the world my mother passed down to me and raised me to love. I spoke the language and knew my way around this denominational community as only a true insider could. In coming out as fully affirming and marrying a woman, I risked losing all of that.

But I knew firsthand what my silence would do to the very people for whom I was attempting to provide care. I couldn't allow yet another generation's faith to be lost to disillusionment with the church. God again gave me the courage to take the next step. And I've had enough positive experiences to reassure me that my whole world isn't going to crumble. For every friend I've lost, God has provided new ones.

Helping to create space for constructive conversation in churches, building Christian community for LGBTQ people, and fostering reconciliation within families has brought me such joy over the last twenty years—joy that far surpasses the enormous fear I first felt in coming out and embracing my calling to this holy work. I can't imagine doing anything else. And none of it would've been possible without the brave friends and colleagues who have walked alongside me.

What about you? What courageous action is God calling you to when it comes to supporting LGBTQ people? Whatever it looks like, I believe God will give you boldness to persist, knowing you're not alone. In the pursuit of whatever God calls you to, even in the darkest days, when you face the possibility of losing everything you hold dear, you can find great joy. I surely have.

13

What We Learned from Listening to Sexual and Gender Minorities

Mark A. Yarhouse, Stephen P. Stratton, and Janet B. Dean

When it comes to ministry, we can learn from listening to Christians who are personally navigating faith and sexual or gender identity. Listening allows us to better appreciate and respond to challenges that sexual and gender minorities face, including those related to self-acceptance and identity formation. We hope this chapter will contribute to helping ministry leaders promote the health and well-being of those navigating these concerns.

As research collaborators, we have studied the experiences of sexual and gender minorities at Christian college campuses for over fifteen years. This research is reflected in our book, *Listening to Sexual Minorities* (2018), a recent article, "Listening to Transgender and Gender Diverse Students at Christian Colleges" (2021), and a current project comparing sexual and gender minorities at Christian colleges with straight and cisgender students at those same institutions and at public/state universities. In this chapter, we draw on this research to share what we have learned by listening to Christian sexual and gender minorities.[1]

---

1. The conversation on sexual identity and faith has a longer history in Christian circles than the conversation on gender identity and faith. As a result, our research is more expansive

Sexual-Identity Development Process

Sexual-identity achievement is a developmental process. That is, sexual identity, or the act of labeling oneself based on one's sexual attractions, is a process of formation with various notable milestone events that end in an achieved identity, which is sometimes referred to as "sexual-identity synthesis."

Common Milestones

What are the common milestone events in the developmental process? Common milestone events in identity synthesis for sexual minorities include

- first awareness of one's same-sex sexuality;
- initial attributions about what those attractions mean;
- disclosure of one's sexual attractions to someone (i.e., "coming out");
- first same-sex sexual behavior;
- private identity (how you think of yourself);
- public identity (how you choose to be known by others);
- forming a same-sex relationship.

Not every person who is a sexual-minority experiences each of these milestones. A percentage of Christians will report not using sexual-identity labels, such as *gay* or *queer*. Likewise, a percentage of Christians will elect not to engage in same-sex behavior or form a same-sex relationship. But these are common milestones that many sexual minorities report as significant.

Additional milestone events are wrestling with different ethical conclusions, as well as with religiously motivated expectations to change one's sexual orientation. In one study of celibate gay Christians, many reported wrestling with theological positions on same-sex relationships or expectations to change their sexual orientation.[2] Some choose to remain celibate even with the assumption that their orientation is not going to change. We suspect that something similar occurs among those who move to a revisionist position—that is, they wrestle with expectations to change their orientation, remain celibate, or enter a mixed-orientation marriage prior to adopting a position that affirms same-sex relationships.

---

for describing sexual-identity development than it is gender-identity development. Also, the experience of sexual minorities and gender minorities are unique; although there are some commonalities, there are also many differences.

2. Mark Yarhouse and Olya Zaporozhets, *Costly Obedience: What We Can Learn from the Celibate Gay Christian Community* (Zondervan, 2019).

Psychological Distress

When it comes to psychological distress in the development process, those without a viable strategy for holding together both faith and sexuality are the most vulnerable. Healthy development at the intersection of religious/spiritual identity and sexual identity involves moving from a minimal strategy for managing the complexities of faith and sexuality to a more conscious and intentional strategy. Indeed, the capacity to integrate faith and sexuality requires the development of both emotional and cognitive complexity. Individuals early in the process or with delayed development tend to experience more psychological distress than those who have grown into a reliable strategy for holding these two vital aspects of human personhood.

There are two important things to note regarding psychological distress. First, development at this intersection tends to cycle from unsettled to settled across time.[3] It is not a linear process from a premature to a mature strategy. Longitudinally, there is a back-and-forth movement from less complex to more complex internal structure. Second, this recurring cycle of settled to unsettled and back again may be interpreted as an ongoing developmental process of negotiation and renegotiation with culture, broadly speaking, and social relationships, more specifically. It might be said that the process of learning to hold both faith and sexuality is the struggle for a secure contextualized self. The growth of that secure self appears to be intimately related to how one relates to God and others, which in turn seems to be related most directly to how psychological distress is managed.[4]

Sexual minorities, especially in their college years, initially connect their developmental experience to a sense of settledness or unsettledness. An appropriate image might be that of riding a wave in the ocean. Individuals learning to navigate sexual-identity development are, at times, settled on the crest of the wave and, at other times, unsettled in the trough. The length of time surfing on the crest or in the trough can be extended or brief, and the movement "up or down" on the wave can be related to internal prompts, external experiences, or some combination of the two. For example, one student reported that he was very settled in friendships that had grown during his years at a Christian college. We might say he was riding the crest of the wave until he began to

---

3. Janet B. Dean, Stephen P. Stratton, and Mark A. Yarhouse, "Holding Faith and Sexual Identity Together: Sexual Minority Students' Patterns of Holding and Their Related Self-Perceptions, Mental Health, and College Experiences," paper presented at Christian Association for Psychological Studies International Convention, Dallas, TX, March 30, 2019.

4. Janet B. Dean, Stephen P. Stratton, Mark A. Yarhouse, "The Mediating Role of Self-Acceptance in the Psychological Distress of Sexual Minority Students on Christian College Campuses," *Spirituality in Clinical Practice* 8 (2021): 132–48, https://doi.org/10.1037/scp0000253.

contemplate graduation. The grief and potential loss of his social support structure began a period of unsettledness—a trough that lasted until secure relationships were established or reconfirmed.

From our research on self-acceptance, we believe that individuals who are able to hold themselves securely across time do not experience settledness or unsettledness to define their "wave surfing" experience. It is not one or the other, especially for those who shared with us how they negotiated their faith and sexual development across time. Instead, we saw in these students an apparent movement away from dependence on the immediate experience of settledness and unsettledness as the primary indicator of distress.

Those students appeared to grow across time to be able to acknowledge both settledness and unsettledness, while seeming to develop a more dispositional way of holding these experiences. Indeed, it looked as if we were seeing some students acknowledge a more complex means of holding their experiences both cognitively and emotionally. We suspected that these students had grown into a way of holding themselves that did not depend on resolving every question or having every inconsistency in their lives put right. To be clear, this was not seen in all students in our research, but it did appear to be a developmental trajectory that needed further thought and continued research.

Before our research with these students, we tended to see settledness and unsettledness as thesis and antithesis, respectively. We hoped to find clues in their narratives as to how they mitigated unsettledness and moved forward in their development. Or one might say that we hoped to eliminate the antithesis to enhance growth and development for both faith and sexuality without distress. As we listened to the voices of students, however, what we found was more complex. With greater understanding, sexual-identity synthesis, initially viewed as only settledness, began to be perceived as a potential advance in self-development that transcended the settled and unsettled split.

The ability to hold moments of both settledness and unsettledness seemed related to a new quality of relating to themselves that was related to increased self-acceptance. Some in faith-based settings might call it grace. With greater self-acceptance came a more mature way of managing psychological distress. We will talk more about self-acceptance and grace in sections below.

Gender-Identity Development Process

While Christian sexual identity has been broadly studied, Christian gender identity is less explored. Students navigating gender identity and faith report Christian institutions are lagging behind in this conversation compared to the conversation on sexual identity. Even our own research on sexual-identity development, which began in the mid-2000s, may appear to have greater breadth and depth simply because we have not been studying the unique experience of gender minorities for as long. In many ways, Yarhouse's 2015 book, *Understanding Gender Dysphoria*, helped to launch this gender identity discussion for Christians in the West, and it prompted our research team to begin listening in earnest to Christian students who brought this developmental experience to their colleges and universities.

When we started listening to gender minorities, we found them to be acutely aware of the lack of long-standing theological reflection when it came to gender issues, beyond the inclusion of women as ministry leaders. They also confronted general ignorance of this growing cultural discussion among peers as well as faculty and staff. It seemed that the conversation regarding sexual identity on campus had little perceived impact on the awareness of gender-diverse experiences. In fact, we were often informed that gender minorities either felt ignored or faced assumptions that their needs were the same as those who were navigating their sexual-identity development. As a result, gender-minority students openly regretted the absence of well-informed people with whom they could share honestly and openly, making their identity development more arduous.

Gender identity is not studied with reference to milestone events in the way that sexual identity is studied. Rather, gender identity generally develops between ages two and four in terms of when a child knows that they are a boy or a girl, or experiences a different gender identity than that. Recent research has documented a rise in cases in which gender identity is discordant for the first time in adolescence rather than in childhood. This is often framed as "early" or "late" onset and is usually noted with reference to gender dysphoria or the experience of distress that can accompany discordant gender identities. Studies, such as the U.S. Transgender Survey, that do not look at gender dysphoria per se report that as many as 60 percent of transgender adults report experiencing their gender identity in childhood (prior to age eleven) and 40 percent at the onset of puberty or later (age eleven and older).[5]

Until more recently, with the 2020s political culture in the United States, the discussion of and research in the experience of gender diversity in Christian higher education has been notable for its silence and ignorance more than anything else. We wonder if the paucity of opportunities for gender minorities to process their gender-identity development might explain findings that

---

5. S. E. James et al., *Report of the 2015 U. S. Transgender Survey* (National Center for Transgender Equality, 2016).

these students showed signs of increased psychological distress but seemed to have little awareness of this part of their experience.

The Importance of Social Embeddedness

To begin listening to people who are navigating gender-identity development, we started in 2019 by interviewing Christian gender minorities over a two-year period. Specifically, we took a narrative approach, asking gender minorities to organize their lives into different chapters, as though they were books.[6] They were given the opportunity to share how they had negotiated gender identity and faith through these different developmental chapters. The chapters were generally associated with different developmental life periods: childhood, middle school, high school, and college years. In listening to this small sample of gender-minority students, we heard that the experience of gender-identity development across all chapters is directly related to the quality of social embeddedness.

Whether or not a life chapter was recalled as satisfactory related to the security of attached relationships to family and friends. Moreover, the current situation for this sample of college and university students, which was surprisingly hopeful, seemed to be related to an achieved relational context in which they felt known and valued. We realize that the description of this sample of gender minorities from Christian colleges and universities is not generalizable to all others, but we found the report of secure self-in-context to be strikingly similar to the narratives of sexual minorities with secure social embeddedness. All of our studies pointed to the value of safe and secure relationships for identity development, whether it was gender- or sexual-identity development.

Positive Effects of Participating in Social Activism

When it comes to creating safe and secure contexts for gender-identity development, the current political culture has an obvious impact on perceptions. Whether or not someone is trying to navigate traditional faith and gender, most people in these formative, college-age years are experiencing a sense of cultural insecurity that impacts them personally.[7] Moreover, students

---

6. M. Hardyman et al., "Self-Reflections from a Sample of Christian Gender Minorities at Faith-Based Colleges about Their Developmental 'Life Chapters,'" paper presented at Christian Association for Psychological Studies National Conference, Louisville, KY, March 30, 2023.

7. Similarly, see Lindsay Y. Dhanani and Rebecca R. Totton, "Have You Heard the News? The Effects of Exposure to News about Recent Transgender Legislation on Transgender Youth and Young Adults," *Sexuality Research and Social Policy* 20 (2023): 1345–59, https://doi.org/10.1007/s13178-023-00810-6.

tend to be cautious about letting others into their developmental process, leaving them alone or with reduced social support networks. But research has noted the positive psychological and social benefits of activism. Dawn Szymanski, James Goates, and Charlotte Strauss-Swanson reported that activistic strategies could be a "potential collective coping response" that fosters post-traumatic growth and positive community connection.[8]

In our interviews with gender-minority students, as they moved into later college years and looked to the future, they were surprisingly aware of the gender experience of others. There was a discernible theme showing how they wanted to take their "growing up" experiences and use them for the good of others who are navigating gender-identity development. This theme stood out because of the contrast with previous developmental periods, when their experience was, not surprisingly, more self-focused. They talked about advocating for those who were following in their footsteps in colleges and universities.

From our interviews, we hypothesize that activism could indeed be related to positive outcomes for those who are undergoing identity development in these culturally precarious years. But we wonder whether the relational connections that are formed in their collective advocacy might be a mediating variable. In this case, activism and advocacy provide avenues through which persons find safe and secure communities and potentially even greater self-acceptance and grace to self. This research remains to be done.

Understanding the Mental Health of Sexual and Gender Minorities

The conversation around mental health and well-being of sexual and gender minorities often leans one-sided, toward concerns about minority stress. When religion is brought into the discussion about mental health, it is frequently cited as a source of minority stress and an obstacle to mental health and well-being. We do see minority stress as an important part of a larger conversation about mental health and well-being. But our findings paint a more complex picture, particularly among sexual and gender minorities of faith. Religion is not unilaterally "bad" for the mental health and well-being of sexual and gender minorities, nor is it unilaterally "good." No simple narrative can explain the various experiences of these individuals.

---

8. Dawn M. Szymanski, James D. Goates, and Charlotte Strauss-Swanson, "LGBQ Activism and Positive Psychological Functioning: The Roles of Meaning, Community Connection, and Coping," *Psychology of Sexual Orientation and Gender Diversity* 10 (2023): 70–79, https://doi.org/10.1037/sgd0000499.

Benefits of Faith

Many are quick to assume that faith, when not affirming of sexuality, *must* cause psychological difficulties in sexual minorities, particularly among those who live in the intersectionality of sexual identity and religious campuses. In our Christian college sample, nearly half of the sexual-minority students were just like other psychologically healthy college students, experiencing little to no distress in their daily lives.[9] That said, about 40 percent of students were experiencing moderate psychological distress, and about 10 percent reported severe distress.

What we have seen, especially among sexual minorities of faith, is a complex dynamic in which one's relationships with God, with others, and with oneself are important elements to mental health and well-being. In particular, strength in each of these relationships seems to contribute to better mental health, while disruptions in these relationships seem to lead to psychological distress.

Intrinsic religiosity is the degree to which people experience the presence of God in their lives and allow their faith to shape how they live. Sexual minorities on Christian campuses with high levels of intrinsic religiosity tend to have significantly less psychological distress and greater well-being than those with less intrinsic religiosity. In other words, if these individuals have a high degree of internalized faith, they seem to navigate the tensions between sexuality and religiosity more effectively, resulting in better mental health.

Sexual-minority individuals with lower levels of internalized faith tend to have poorer mental health, which we propose may be due to a sense of a double marginalization in that they fail to fit their campus community in terms of both sexuality and religion.

Contrary to our expectations, we repeatedly heard from Christian sexual-minority students, particularly those with strongly internalized faith, that they believed God loved them.[10] Their struggle was not with God; rather, it was in their relationship with the church. Support from others—including the church, family, faculty and staff, and friends—does seem to play a role in the psychological health of sexual minorities. In fact, the most beneficial relationships seem to be those with straight, cisgender friends.

---

9. Dean et al., "Mediating Role," 132–48.

10. Mark A. Yarhouse et al., *Listening to Sexual Minorities: A Study of Faith and Sexual Identity on Christian College Campuses* (IVP Academic, 2018).

Self-Acceptance

What is it about internalized faith and friends that helps sexual-minority students to flourish? While we know that both faith and social support tend to be beneficial for many people, we found that both of these contribute to greater self-acceptance in sexual minorities. It's this self-acceptance that seems to lead to better psychological health.[11]

Often when people think about self-acceptance for sexual minorities, they assume this means accepting one's sexuality *and* affirming same-sex relationships. Our research, though, suggests that self-acceptance may be the acceptance of one's sexuality regardless of one's moral position about sexuality. It seems that sexual minorities with more traditionally orthodox views of sexuality can find self-acceptance just as those who affirm same-sex relationships, although the process may take a bit longer in the case of the former.

Social support, particularly from straight, cisgender friends, together with a relationship with God seem to help Christian sexual minorities grow in their self-acceptance by giving them a safe space to find a way of holding together their sexual and faith identities. Given that most Christian sexual minorities want to be able to do this, they likely would benefit from more assistance in learning how to more effectively navigate tensions between these identities without the outcome being prescribed by others.[12]

Grace to Self

We have noted how faith and self-acceptance are important for the mental health and well-being of sexual minorities in particular. Similarly, we are beginning to look at this with gender-diverse Christians. Recently, we introduced and applied the concept of "grace to self."[13] Grace to self is a little different than self-acceptance, but it may be related. Rodger Bufford, Timothy Sisemore, and Amanda Blackburn conceptualized "grace to self" as a trait that reflects the way people make space for grace in relation to their own self-experience.[14] It is grace applied to the ways people manage themselves, as an intrapersonal, acceptance-based process within oneself.

---

11. Dean et al., "Mediating Role," 132–48.

12. Steven Meanley et al., "Psychological Well-Being among Religious and Spiritual-Identified Young Gay and Bisexual Men," *Sexuality Research and Social Policy* 13 (2016): 35–45, http://doi.org/f77zbr; Yarhouse et al., *Listening to Sexual Minorities*.

13. Mark A. Yarhouse et al., "Stewarding Diverse Sexual and Gender Identities," in *Stewarding Our Bodies: A Vision for Christian Student Development*, ed. Perry L. Glanzer and Austin Smith (Abilene Christian University Press, 2023), 201–18.

14. Rodger K. Bufford et al., "Dimensions of Grace: Factor Analysis of Three Grace Scales," *Psychology of Religion and Spirituality* 9 (2016), http://dx.doi.org/10.1037/rel0000064.

In our recent work, we reported the potential relationship between self-acceptance and grace to self for sexual and gender minorities.[15] Namely, Christians' mature acceptance of themselves is experienced through the virtue of grace. Self-acceptance and related grace-filled approaches to oneself mediate how effectively sexual and gender minorities manage difficult and distressing circumstances.

Grace to self may be a catalyst for the reflective movement toward a more integrated and cohesive self in identity development among sexual and gender minorities. It may actually promote an intentional process of development that leads to the integration of two aspects of personhood that are most complex for sexual and gender minorities—religion/spirituality and sexuality/gender. We believe grace facilitates a particular way of holding self that resists self-division and shame and may actually facilitate healthy relationships with God and others.[16]

We are only at the beginning of a line of research looking at the concept of grace to self as it applies to Christian sexual and gender minorities. We see it as potentially significant research that may open additional pathways toward healing for many who have felt estranged from themselves in light of their same-sex sexuality or discordant gender identity.

Importance of a "Holding Environment" for Sexual and Gender Minorities

A final lesson learned in our work studying sexual and gender minorities of faith is the importance of one's environment. We strongly believe that the impact of one's environment on emotional and spiritual well-being cannot be overstated. In our line of research on Christian college students, that environment is a faith-based campus of higher education. Although we are usually studying undergraduates, we have given considerable thought to how to extrapolate from findings in Christian colleges and universities to other developmental eras.

When it comes to personal well-being in faith-based institutions, one's environment is seldom neutral. It is often viewed as either supportive or not for the individuals navigating development as a sexual or gender minority. We have found that, above all else, "supportive" means that these students are not hindered from developing socially secure and fundamentally safe

---

15. Yarhouse et al., "Stewarding Diverse Sexual and Gender Identities," 201–18.
16. Yarhouse et al., "Stewarding Diverse Sexual and Gender Identities," 211.

relationships. When we listen to students, we find that they notice how they are being "held" by the embedding communal structure they are in.

As an example, mature students understood that administrators were part of the "macro" level of the institution, whose focus tends to be as much on external stakeholders, such as boards and donors, as on the internal communal environment. Communications in the form of news releases, ethos statements, and policy mandates were seen as being written and delivered with this macro level clearly in mind, but with the relational "micro" level receiving less strategic consideration. And whether students agreed or disagreed with the macro-level pronouncements (often concerning theology or traditional sexual/gender ethics), they tended to speak with passion about the impact on the micro level.

Many of the participants we interviewed talked about negotiating the macro conversation that happened "above their heads," including when they disagreed with some aspect of the content or the tone. They heard those macro messages as crafted and delivered for others—that is, external stakeholders. How those messages were held by the micro community made a difference in well-being. Those who disagreed with the macro-level institutional structure appeared less impaired developmentally when the micro-level "holding environment" was civil and compassionate. As long as the communal environment did not hinder the development of relationally safe and secure connections, students tended to report that they could develop toward their self-determined goal of holding together their faith and sexuality/gender. That formative process of learning to hold their own experience seems to grow best in an environment that offers them safety and security during their development.

Increasing Microaffirmations and Limiting Microaggressions

One of the hallmarks of formative holding environments is related to the presence of microaffirmations versus microaggressions. Microaggressions are the "everyday verbal, nonverbal, and environmental slights, snubs, or insults, whether intentional or unintentional, which communicate hostile, derogatory, or negative messages to target persons based solely upon their marginalized group membership."[17] Microaggressions may be seen as small and even inconsequential relational events, but they can have a significant impact on perceived safety and security for sexual and gender minorities. We have seen these microaggressions hinder the experience of being held by friends and

---

17. Derald Wing Sue, "Microaggressions: More Than Just Race," *Psychology Today*, November 17, 2010, https://www.psychologytoday.com/us/blog/microaggressions-in-everyday-life/201011/microaggressions-more-just-race.

other members of the community. But elimination of microaggressions alone may fall short of a formative "holding environment" if microaffirmations are not considered as well.

Our research suggests that increasing microaffirmations is associated with perception of the community as a viable place for development at the intersection of faith, sexuality, and gender.[18] Microaffirmations are "apparently small acts, which are often ephemeral and hard-to-see, events that are public and private, often unconscious but very effective, which occur wherever people wish to help others to succeed."[19] These small acts may frequently be recognized in retrospect, but they can still be powerful environmental influences that may mitigate the effects of microaggressions.

We have learned from students that microaffirmations fall into the categories of support and nonjudgmental relating.[20] In relation to the way people experience being held, microaffirmations are building blocks for a sense of safety, stability, and comfort. One more thing about microaffirmations: they tend to be diverse and highly individualized. When it comes to dependable acts of "holding" a Christian who is a sexual or gender minority, they cannot be general affirmations. The affirmations must be relationally tailored to the unique individual.

Offering Apologies

As we strive for communities that are actively aware of limiting microaggressions and increasing microaffirmations, we realize that formative holding, either within a broader community or in individual relationships, does not necessarily depend on perfect performance. Although our intent is participation in safe and secure relationships, mistakes can inadvertently occur in messy human encounters with the best of intentions. From experience, we have found that taking responsibility for errors in a nondefensive manner can provide opportunity for relational growth.[21]

Effective holding environments flow with apologies that lead to nondefensive learning and deepening trust. If managed openly and without avoidance,

---

18. Stephen P. Stratton et al., "The Impact of Micro-Affirmations on a Sample of Sexual Minority Students in Faith-Based Higher Education," paper presented at Kentucky Counseling Association Conference, Louisville, KY, November 2019.

19. Mary Rowe, "Micro-Affirmations and Micro-Inequities," *Journal of the International Ombudsman Association* 1 (2008): 46.

20. Stratton et al., "Impact of Micro-Affirmations."

21. For more discussion, see Heather Stringer, "Psychologists Are Teaching Health Care Teams to Identify and Address Microaggressions," *Monitor on Psychology* 54 (2023), https://www.apa.org/monitor/2023/07/psychology-addressing-microaggressions.

even mistakes can create the opportunity for sexual and gender minorities to learn how to hold their own developmental experience in safe and secure relational space. Self-acceptance and grace to self can be caught as well as taught when relationships are intentionally formational. All who are part of the community can learn and grow. In churches we often connect this goal to discipleship.

Holding All the Boxes

Healthy holding environments are places where sexual and gender minorities learn to hold their identity boxes without shame or fear. We thought early on in our research that we'd find students resolving the complex developmental process at the intersection of faith, sexuality, and gender by "dropping one of those boxes." In this metaphor, students might move onto campus with all of their "identity boxes" but drop one of them as the least complicated way to live on campus.[22] That is, it might be easier to try to forget about religious or spiritual development, or it might be simpler to set aside sexual- or gender-identity development. That's what is meant by "dropping a box." We did not believe it was necessarily the healthiest option theologically or developmentally, but we thought that students might move toward what seemed like a less complicated path.

What we found as we listened to Christian sexual and gender minorities is that we were wrong. Complicated or not, most did not want to drop any boxes. They were not interested in listening to secular voices telling them they should drop the faith box. Nor were they willing to listen to faith-based voices suggesting they drop the boxes related to sexual or gender identity. The largest group of students did not want to lose their grip on any of these self-related containers. They wanted a new and stable way to hold all the boxes. Most hoped that Christian colleges and universities would be places where they could learn to hold their identity boxes without shame or fear.

Healthy holding environments appear to promote this kind of self-development. The majority of sexual-minority students in our research were actively working to "integrate" faith and sexuality, although there was not one uniform way for that to happen. Most were in the midst of developing a hold that fit them and their values and beliefs. Interestingly, the group that appeared to be faring the worst in their development were those who had not settled on a hold that worked for them. Those individuals had the most distress and

---

22. Yarhouse et al., *Listening to Sexual Minorities*.

the least self-acceptance.[23] Those who had found a method of holding these aspects of self, even tentatively, seemed to have a way of managing distress with faith and acceptance. They had settled on a cognitive structure that seemed to bring intrapersonal safety and security.

It's important to remember that this development of a mature internal structure is likely not finished in the college years. As we described above, development continued to show unsettled moments, alternating with more settled periods, as internal and external events brought questions or conflicts to consider. This seemingly normal process appeared to advance for some into the formation of greater cognitive and emotional complexity in the method of holding faith, sexuality, and gender. The result for these students was a relationship to self that was more accepting, despite fluctuations in experience that might be associated with distress.

We also saw that a faith-based community can play a major role in the development of a secure contextualized self. Using our box metaphor again, it's achieved by creating intentional communal space for the unpacking and repacking of "identity box" contents. We like to say that students learn to hold themselves by experiencing the safe and secure hold of the community, while they are packing and unpacking their self-related containers.

Conclusion

We have been studying the experiences of Christian sexual and gender minorities for many years. In this chapter, we have offered reflections on what we have learned from this important line of research, particularly what we have learned from listening to Christians navigating faith and sexual or gender identity. These reflections also lend themselves to recommendations of sorts—namely, to consider the developmental process for sexual and gender identity formation; to appreciate the mental-health challenges that Christian sexual and gender minorities face, including those related to self-acceptance; and to recognize the importance of environment in aiding or undermining how one learns to hold aspects of one's identity. Each of the things we have learned offers direction that we hope can contribute to the overall promotion of health and well-being for people of faith navigating sexual or gender identity and faith.

---

23. Stephen P. Stratton et al., "Updating 'Holding Patterns': The Intersection of Sexual Identity and Religious/Spiritual Identity," paper presented at Kentucky Counseling Association Conference, Louisville, KY, November 2019.

14

Evangelism and the LGBTQ Community

Elizabeth Delgado Black

Evangelism and missions have always been an important aspect of my Christian faith. As a child, I loved to share my faith with friends and family who showed interest in my stories of God's love. Growing up in the Southern Baptist Church, which prioritized evangelism and traditional methods of conversion (sharing the Romans Road, weekly altar calls, and leading people through the Sinner's Prayer), only encouraged and solidified that calling in my life. After graduating from Bible college, I entered vocational missions doing Jewish evangelism. Unexpectedly, it was during my time as a missionary in the Jewish community that I began to meet LGBTQ people who were curious about the Christian faith, many of whom did not know any other Christians and had no one to go to with their questions.

It was clear that those I encountered coexisted with Christians, but very few had authentic relationships with people of faith who demonstrated and offered the gospel tangibly. It deeply troubled me that Queer[1] people were living without any Christian witness, and I was compelled to discover ways

---

1. The term *queer* was originally used as a homophobic or transphobic slur. However, more recently it has been reclaimed by the LGBTQ community to describe an individual or corporate identity within the gender or sexual minority experience. I will be using *Queer* interchangeably with the abbreviation *LGBTQ* when addressing this community, reflecting the ways in which

to reach out to this people group that, seemingly, had not been missionally engaged. In my efforts to develop an LGBTQ evangelistic framework, I began to understand how deeply the church had failed in understanding and administering gospel proclamation within the LGBTQ context.

An Inaccessible Faith

A Christian friend asked if I would meet with a young Jewish woman named Linsey,[2] who had been asking questions about God, the Bible, and Jesus. We began meeting over coffee to discuss her questions about Scripture and Jesus. I listened to her perspectives and shared mine, watching her interest grow beyond her intellect to her heart. At one of our meetings, Linsey sat down with enthusiasm and resoluteness I hadn't encountered in her before. She shared that she was convinced Jesus is Lord. She had been praying, asking God to guide her, and she knew that he was the one for whom her soul longed. However, her elation was short-lived when she remembered there was one thing standing in her way of adopting the Christian faith.

I waited for her to tell me what it was and watched her shuffle in her chair, struggling to find the words. Then, with a prematurely rejected expression, she leaned in and whispered in my ear, "I'm bisexual. Will God still accept me?" At the time, I had not considered the nuances of sexual and gender ethics within Christianity, nor had I faced my own sexual identity. What I did know was the simple truth of Scripture that nothing can separate us from the love of God. I responded, "Linsey, please don't let your sexuality stop you from experiencing God's deep compassion for you. There is nothing about you that makes you less qualified to receive Jesus's favor." Then, without hesitation or question, Linsey's air of dejection melted away, and she proclaimed her newfound faith in Jesus. Since then, I've had the privilege of baptizing Linsey, watching her grow in faith, and exploring God's faithfulness within the beauty of her sexuality.

A few months after meeting Linsey, I received a text message from Vera, another young woman I had been meeting with; she requested we speak soon. She had something urgent to tell me. Vera grew up in the church with missionary parents, and although she was extremely active in ministry settings, unbeknownst to me and almost everyone, she did not identify as

---

the term is used within current LGBTQ vernacular and scholarship. This is out of respect, for the sake of representation of cultural language, and as an example of contextualized ministry.

2. All names have been changed to pseudonyms out of respect for the privacy of the individuals mentioned.

a Christian. Where onlookers saw a bright and wholesome twenty-one-year-old, a peek beneath her fragile facade would reveal a life of substance abuse, mindless sex, and deep depression. Even though I was unaware of Vera's lack of faith or secret life, it was evident that she struggled with something. She came to church and Bible studies eagerly engaged but always left visibly defeated.

After reading Vera's text, I met her, but what she needed to share was too heavy to express face-to-face. I left her with the invitation to reach out again when she was ready. Shortly after I left, I got a second message from Vera, which I later found out was sent while crying and dry heaving in a college bathroom stall. The message read, "I want to tell you I'm gay, and I've always known I was gay. I have a girlfriend. I want to believe in Jesus, but all I can hear in my head is my mother's voice saying God hates me and I am destined for hell. I trust you and need help understanding if God wants me as his child. I hope you don't hate me."

When I read Vera's message, I was filled with grief, but not about her Queer identity or relationship status. I was heartbroken over the lies she was fed, restraining her from coming into rest and security in Christ. We promptly set up a time to talk again that evening. We started a long and tenuous journey of dismantling her religious trauma and baggage of shame. Vera struggled to believe that God had any interest in her outside of disapproval because of her sexuality. What I offered Vera was friendship, a listening ear, and words of comfort. She needed companionship and even levity as she considered who God is and dealt with the weightiness of her depression and self-condemnation. Persistence and wrestling with God opened her eyes to the reality that her sexual identity did not stop her from having a loving relationship with God, nor did she need to figure out a dissertation-worthy explanation of biblical sexual expression before considering herself a Christian. All Vera needed to hear was that her simple faith was enough. Like Jacob in his wrestling with God, Vera wouldn't give up the fight until she experienced God's blessing, because she knew a life of depression was no life at all.

Linsey's and Vera's stories have stuck with me in such a profound way because they illustrate the ways the church has so inaccurately portrayed the gospel to those outside of the Christian tradition. For these women, and many other LGBTQ people I have encountered, the person of Jesus and fellowship of the saints are, at best, inaccessible and, at worst, conveyors of damnation. The prevailing, uninformed assumption that LGBTQ people are irreligious and preoccupied with self-indulgence shrouds the truly diverse nature of this community, where many are spiritual seekers searching for deep, authentic relationships with God.

Yet, the Queer community broadly doesn't look to Christians for care, camaraderie, or hope. They see a faith primarily concerned with drawing moral lines in the sand to preserve its wholesome status and favor with God. The gospel and its life-giving effects are reserved for those deemed worthy or those the church feels bad enough for while still ensuring their pity won't lead to moral compromise. We have lost sight of what the gospel and missions genuinely are and, as a result, have willfully abandoned the Queer community. We must sit with this discouraging reality honestly, facing its full force to hear the call to repentance emerging from this sad situation. It is a call to revisit our understanding of the church's mandate to be missional and ask how to share Christ's beautiful gift of salvation with the Queer community.

Rethinking Evangelism and Missions

One favorite aspect of my current evangelism ministry at Kaleidoscope[3] is meeting with groups of lay Christians aspiring to become deeper allies to the LGBTQ community. In a recent cohort, we discussed fears related to allyship. One member expressed that any allyship connected to the idea of mission felt unsettling. They felt it was wrong to build a relationship with someone or offer care with the ulterior motive of eventually pointing out their sins and "getting them saved." This concern is validated in the LGBTQ context, given the church's history of isolating and persecuting gay people. "Bait-and-switch" evangelism—in which the evangelist acts friendly and accepting toward someone only to later become forceful and condemning—is toxic and harmful. Still, we should not throw the proverbial baby out with the bathwater. After all, should we stop proclaiming the gospel because others have done it in harmful and disingenuous ways?

Mission and evangelism have, sadly, become historically charged acts of colonialism—that is, efforts to make people look and think like the White, heteronormative messengers of the gospel. One inspirational passage for early Western missions was the parable of the sower and the seed from Matthew 13. As ambassadors of the gospel, we are commissioned to "transplant" the seed of Christian belief, trusting it will sprout into a replica of its original source.[4] Unfortunately, many "sowers" have been as concerned with replicating their culture as they have with promoting Christlikeness. There is no regard for

---

3. Learn more about Kaleidoscope at KaleidoscopeUSA.org/about.
4. Bo C. Sanders and Randy S. Woodly, *Decolonizing Evangelism: An 11:59 p.m. Conversation* (Cascade Books, 2020), 50–51.

the soil itself. There is no permission to find value and beauty in the cultural richness in the lives of those we encounter, no interest in hearing about their actual needs, and, worst of all, no desire to preserve the gift of diversity offered to the kingdom of God. However, God's intention in missions and evangelism is more diverse and compassionate than we have been led to believe.

Though we could better use the Matthew 13 parable to create a more nuanced understanding of missions and evangelism, I believe Jesus's reading of Isaiah 61:1–2 in Luke 4:18–19 provides a powerfully rich understanding of God's missional mandate:

> "The Spirit of the Lord is on me,
>   because he has anointed me
>   to proclaim good news to the poor.
> He has sent me to proclaim freedom for the prisoners
>   and recovery of sight for the blind,
> to set the oppressed free,
>   to proclaim the year of the Lord's favor."

Jesus chooses to start his ministry by proclaiming God's continual desire and commitment to his people who have suffered from exile, oppression, scarcity of basic needs, and hopelessness.

Outlined in the words of Isaiah is God's mission, emphasized in four tangible expressions: good news, freedom, recovery, and favor. God's mission was and continues to be more than a convincing argument for belief or a desire for conversion and obedience. Instead, it provides abundance to those in need, recovers those imprisoned or exiled, and administers physical healing to the sick. This messianic prophecy is primarily a work of reconciling all things to a loving and generous God. And Jesus, the messianic catalyst, demonstrated this in his daily ministry of healing the infirm, feeding the hungry, and offering God's favor to the marginalized.

This passage encapsulates all Jesus offered his people during his time on earth and through his resurrection. He had an ulterior motive, which was blessing and reconciliation. Missions is the global and local movement of joining God in his reconciliatory work in the world. It is the diffusion of the good news that Jesus preached and demonstrated, the news that all things can be reconciled and restored because of his death and resurrection (Luke 4:17–21).[5] When we proclaim and demonstrate this message, we do the work of evangelism (Rom. 10:10–15).

---

5. Definition inspired by the Edinburgh Common Call. Daryl M. Balia and Kirsteen Kim, eds., *Edinburgh 2010: Witnessing to Christ Today* (Regnum, 2010), 23–29, Kindle.

This understanding of missions and evangelism should shape how we understand sharing the Christian faith in the LGBTQ context and beyond. To the aspiring ally who is concerned about making inroads into the Queer community, I recommend we always be motivated by the desire to join the work that God is already doing within LGBTQ people. This approach to evangelism shifts the focus from the task of conversion toward a fuller version of God's renewal of all things under his beautiful and gracious reign. It draws the Christian back into the exciting and re-creative promise of Christ that spans nothing less than the whole cosmos! And as a member of the LGBTQ community who is also a seasoned Christian minister, I know there is no shortage of the need for freedom and renewal.

Freedom and renewal are needed because there are still regular occurrences of hate crimes against LGBTQ people, particularly Queer folks of color. Both established and emerging realities of systemic oppression reinforce these acts of cruelty, which lead to the loss of life and leave surviving Queer people fearful and hopeless.[6] There are countless unhoused and displaced LGBTQ youth and young adults who have been rejected by their families.[7] And many in my community still suffer silently from HIV and AIDS. My LGBTQ siblings are searching for emotional health and spiritual hope, yet many fear bringing their whole selves and stories into religious spaces. We are hungry, sick, rejected, imprisoned by the system, and in desperate need of care. Like those listening to Jesus's declaration of corporeal and divine restoration, LGBTQ people are eager to see and receive "the year of the Lord's favor." With his heart for every tribe, tongue, and nation, God longs to see his restorative mission flourish within the Queer community, regardless of any theological position community members might hold on sexual or gender ethics.

The whole church can universally acknowledge that LGBTQ people are undeniably part of God's workmanship and included in his desire that all might know Jesus and be saved (1 Tim. 2:4). And in stories like Linsey's and

---

6. Homophobia and transphobia were the catalysts behind nearly a quarter of all reported hate crimes in 2020. See Delphine Luneau, "FBI's Annual Crime Report—Amid State of Emergency, Anti-LGBTQ+ Hate Crimes Hit Staggering Record Highs," Human Rights Campaign, October 16, 2023, https://www.hrc.org/press-releases/fbis-annual-crime-report-amid-state-of-emergency-anti-lgbtq-hate-crimes-hit-staggering-record-highs. In 2023, thirty-three transgender Americans were killed and 84 percent were minorities. See HRC Foundation, "Fatal Violence against the Transgender and Gender-Expansive Community in 2023," Human Rights Campaign, https://www.hrc.org/resources/fatal-violence-against-the-transgender-and-gender-expansive-community-in-2023.

7. In 2021, 28 percent of American LGBTQ youth battled houselessness or housing insecurity. For more statistics on the effects of LGBTQ homelessness, see "Homelessness and Housing Instability among LGBTQ Youth," Trevor Project, February 3, 2022, https://www.thetrevorproject.org/research-briefs/homelessness-and-housing-instability-among-lgbtq-youth-feb-2022/.

Vera's, I'm reminded of Paul's evangelistically motivated questions in Romans 10: "How, then, can they call on the one they have not believed in? And how can they believe in the one of whom they have not heard? And how can they hear without someone preaching to them?" (v. 14). There is still a need for gospel proclamation, and it should take place through authentic life-sharing, the giving of time and resources to LGBTQ people in need, and the declaration that God's favor is on this community. It must be encapsulated by God's desire for loving restoration.

Practical Evangelism within the LGBTQ Context

As much as we would like to sit back and wait for LGBTQ unbelievers to come into our churches, given the contentious relationship between the church and the Queer community and growing skepticism about Christianity, we cannot expect gay and trans folks to step into a setting that is neither their own nor reflects their daily realities. Additionally, the affirming/non-affirming debate threatens to further fracture the church from her God-forged unity, which Jesus intended as a spiritual reality demonstrating the inner unity of triune love to the world (John 13:35). We are so busy trying to figure out what to do with the LGBTQ believers within the church that we casually dismiss those LGBTQ neighbors outside of our church doors.

If we hope to engage in LGBTQ missional bridge-building, finding an authentic connection falls on the church. For many, that might seem like a difficult task because venturing into Queer spaces is foreign. However, the beauty of Queer evangelism is that trans, bisexual, and gay folks are integral members of our society. Queer people are our neighbors, siblings, children, and friends. To authentically reach Queer people with the gospel, I would like to pose a few principles for authentic and contextualized LGBTQ evangelism: acknowledging God's preceding presence within LGBTQ culture, remembering the power of compassion, and using contextual gospel presentation.

God Goes before Us

What is paramount in pursuing evangelism among the LGBTQ population is the acknowledgment of God's presence within Queer history and each LGBTQ story. Knowing that God longs to bring hope and resurrection to the Queer community is essential, but it is only the beginning of his relationship with LGBTQ people. He actively pursues and ministers to each Queer person through the work of the Holy Spirit.[8] Thankfully, the Lord never waits for the church to reveal him; he moves among LGBTQ people in both overt and subtle ways. I have seen this in many of my initial encounters with nonbelievers, and it always affirms that God's hand is on his Queer image bearers.

Rachel, a gay actress from Harlem, had been dating her girlfriend for a few months. Rachel's girlfriend, Gloria, was a Christian and desired to share her faith with Rachel but was often met with resistance. The day before attending a Pride festival in their neighborhood, Gloria and Rachel had a deep, heart-to-heart conversation about God. Rachel finally decided to consider Jesus if they could find an outlet to explore faith together. So it was no coincidence that on the day of Harlem Pride, Rachel and Gloria bumped into our Kaleidoscope ministry team giving out rainbow-colored popcorn and offering blessings to Queer festival goers. They were almost in tears when they arrived at our table and told our team they knew God must be doing something, and they were committed to pursuing him. We kept up with the couple and watched as Rachel drew closer and closer to Christ and now professes faith alongside Gloria.

It is important to recognize God's presence within the LGBTQ context because the work of evangelism should always be one of mutuality. The church can approach evangelism by looking and listening for the reconciliatory work God is already doing in the lives of our Queer neighbors. If God is near to the LGBTQ community, Christians should engage in missional opportunities with curiosity. I have seen God's faithfulness demonstrated in the ways trans young people have been adopted into Queer chosen families or God's creativity in the beauty of Queer art. The stories of LGBTQ folks, no matter their faith background, convey a picture of God's character and truth, and a practice of mutuality gives us eyes to see that. I am not implying religious relativism, because the Christian faith clearly positions Jesus as the exclusive means to the Father. Rather, God reveals himself in and through all good things, including the marvelous aspects of Queer culture.

As mission-minded Christians, we have an exciting task of identifying God's creative mark and walking with our Queer friends as they consider his presence in their lives. So, my mission field is gay and lesbian bars, drag shows, BIPOC Queer brunch hangouts, or Taco Tuesdays with a new lesbian couple next door. Before every hangout or event, my prayer is, "God, show me where you are already moving among my people. Reveal the ways you call them toward yourself, and teach me something about your character in our time together."

---

8. Debra Hirsch, *Redeeming Sex* (InterVarsity, 2015), 173–74.

LGBTQ folks are accustomed to others telling them what the church and God think of their queerness, so they are grateful when Christians ascribe dignity to them and recognize the spiritual value of their personhood. We can all come to the table and glean from one another, asking questions or unveiling valuable insights that point one another to the living God. And if we believe in the veracity of the good news, we can trust the Holy Spirit will draw each of us toward the fullness of the gospel in due time.

Compassionate Care

In my years in vocational missions, I have noticed the tendency to independently diagnose a population's spiritual needs and determine how to address them. There is an urgency for conversion, and many assumptions have been made about how to get people to that point. Unfortunately, the LGBTQ community is accustomed to this methodology. When potentially well-intentioned Christians offer unsolicited opinions about our sexuality to get us to repent for our very existence, we are saddened but not surprised. In his memoir, *Page Boy*, Elliot Page, a prominent transgender actor, described a flight to Los Angeles where a priest and his curate, who had been sitting behind Page, walked by and silently handed him a folded note. Elliot anticipated a friendly, encouraging letter based on the smiles on their faces. But the note turned out to be a presumptive chastisement. It began with a statement assuring Elliot they knew who he was, saying they "took the liberty of Googling" him, as if a quick Google search gave the relational license to speak into someone's life. It went on to diagnose the state of his soul, based entirely on Elliot's queerness: "Your soul is struggling. You need the arms of the Heavenly Father around you." And then, with the authority vested in them, they signed on behalf of "Your Heavenly Daddy."[9]

While I understand the pastor's desire to point people to God, this was done with little regard for the recipient and with many false assumptions. Would the priest be as emboldened to write this note if Google did not reveal Elliot's LGBTQ identity? Why assume that Elliot's queerness was God's most pressing concern? Where was the invitation for mutual dialogue or a compassionate acknowledgment of Elliot's journey of identity? It is in those kinds of exchanges that we need to practice compassionate evangelism, build trusted relationships within an understood cultural context, and administer care through the gospel. Without a heart of compassion for those to whom we are witnessing, it is nearly impossible to demonstrate God's character.

---

9. Elliot Page, *Page Boy* (Flatiron, 2023), 212.

Queer evangelism should flow from a place of compassionate availability, listening, and recognizing the felt needs in the lives of our Queer neighbors.

Much of Jesus's ministry was living among people and caring for those who approached him. Jesus often asked the petitioner a deliberate question: "What do you want me to do for you?" (Mark 10:36, 51). Of course, Jesus knew the nature of each person's situation, yet that did not stop him from dignifying people by allowing them to share their needs and tell their stories. He listened intently and, as we read in the Gospel of Matthew, was moved with compassion (14:14). His heart was moved by the honesty and faith his followers possessed, as well as their enduring burdens. With a posture of empathy and tenderness, Jesus healed and ministered, offering physical renewal along with spiritual freedom. Jesus exemplified the evangelistic skill of 1 Corinthians 13—namely, *love*. "If I . . . do not have love, I am nothing" (1 Cor. 13:2).

Dr. Brenda Salter McNeil, a pioneer in Christian racial reconciliation, illustrates the work of compassion when recounting a time that she accompanied a group of multiethnic college students on a tour of American Civil Rights sites. The purpose was to encourage the students to process historical evil together and discover ways to support one another in lamentation. After the tour concluded, McNeil watched a screaming match erupt between the Black students, who were filled with pain after encountering their history of enslavement, and the White students, who defensively distanced themselves from their ancestors' cruelty. Before she could break up the argument, a White student stood up and shared her sorrow over the brutality she witnessed. Though unaware of how to do so, she committed to fight against the vile forces that contributed to such wickedness and harm. Dissolving into tears, her sentiment was one of remorse. A Black student stood up and asked that everyone listen to this student's words because she was "crying Black tears."[10] Like Jesus, this White student saw the pain of the marginalized and suffering and aligned herself with their needs. Her Black tears brought healing to the students and became a vehicle for compassionate understanding.

This powerful illustration has challenged me to ask anyone interested in LGBTQ evangelism to cry Queer tears. Selfish motivations—like theological conformity or concern over how we are perceived—must be put aside, and we must adopt the hurt of Queer people. When we cry with the downtrodden, we encounter glimpses of their experience and offer a gospel that speaks to their deeply felt needs. This practice is something all Christians can participate in because it is not limited to one theological view of same-sex ethics.

---

10. Brenda Salter McNeil, *Roadmap to Reconciliation 2.0* (InterVarsity, 2020), 78.

Despite what you believe about same-sex relationships or gender expression, you can choose to cry Queer tears and present the truth of a compassionate gospel to all LGBTQ people. The evangelist's concern is not whether our LGBTQ friend will follow our interpretation of Scripture related to sexual ethics or any other nonsalvific theological matter. Rather, it is Christians' task to introduce LGBTQ nonbelievers to Jesus, who grants abundant life and transforms us into his likeness within our context and story.

Contextual and Reflective Gospel Presentation

No matter who we are or where we live, we interpret life and determine our worldview based on personal and sociocultural contexts. These contexts inform the way we navigate the world and help shape our values, convictions, and perspectives of spirituality.[11] God's intention for individuals is that they understand him from their own experiences, cultures, and stories. Our relational God desires to know and be known, which can occur only within our individual and corporate human experiences. Human diversity illuminates the glory of God's complex and diverse nature.

While context and culture are necessary frameworks for all understanding, their presence can be elusive, and they can easily be forgotten and disregarded. The danger in disregarding our distinctive lenses, particularly in the West, is that we presume our brand of Christianity is the exclusive way of understanding the gospel; therefore, we find little need for contextualization. Many are unaware of how much our gospel frameworks have been significantly altered to fit within our language, traditions, and values. We have forgotten the fundamental truth that God's reach is expansive, proving himself to be the God of all within the framework of every identity.

Many LGBTQ people, myself included, remember countless nights of pleading prayer, asking God to take away our attraction or gender incongruence. We wanted nothing more than to rid ourselves of our distinctive context, which others said was beyond God's reach. God graciously demonstrated his glory in others' experiences, but ours were too shameful and foreign. Our language, experiences, and values didn't compute within the nice and neat composition of the Christian faith. This is why many have disassociated with Christianity or never considered it an option. Since discarding our contextual realities was impossible, we could not see ourselves as recipients of the gospel. How could we consider Jesus if his church talked about us only as problems and liabilities?

---

11. Stephan B. Bevans, *Models of Contextual Theology*, 3rd ed. (Orbis Books, 2002), 3–15.

In addition to a contextual presentation of the gospel, the church must practice the skill of reflective gospel presentation. This means helping LGBTQ people see themselves within the gospel story; LGBTQ people should understand they are not essentially different from those with whom Jesus lovingly shared the message of salvation and eternal life. LGBTQ people have rarely been presented with the fullness of the gospel, including the idea that God cares about their interests or concerns. For meaningful evangelism to take place, it is imperative that the church show LGBTQ people how Jesus looks on them with care for their values and attributes.

Ultimately, Christians must help LGBTQ people behold themselves in the family of Christ. Jesus's method of evangelism—using personally and culturally relevant stories and examples, being attuned to the ways his audience processed their own experiences with God and the message of salvation, and inviting people into meaningful spiritual conversation by embracing their cultural context—reveals his relevant and deeply considerate usage of reflective gospel presentation.

Jesus was always conscious of the person he spoke with and to whom he relayed the universal message of salvation, using the social realities of his hearers to reveal himself in their contexts. For example, shortly after feeding the five thousand, Jesus taught those who received the loaves and fish that he was the "bread of life," using the materials of daily life to make a point. When he revived his beloved friend, Lazarus, Jesus preached that he was the "resurrection and the life." Even when participating in the Passover ceremony, Jesus used the symbol of the cup of wine and broken matzo, related to the redemptive sacrifice, to speak of his death and resurrection. Jesus was a master of speaking the people's language and using culture to convey his message, reinforcing the merit of culture as an important missional tool for self-understanding and spiritual reflection.

Jesus's portrayal of reflective gospel presentation should inform how we demonstrate LGBTQ evangelism. We cannot disregard the Queer community's identity, nor should Queer people be pulled away from every aspect of their culture and values, especially when some of those aspects already reflect the goodness of God, the author of life and creator of culture. Instead, the church should recognize and celebrate the unique vantage point Queer people have when observing and interacting with the gospel. The great theologian and missiologist Andrew Walls depicts the importance of the diversity of human perspective and cultural variants when thinking missionally in what he calls the "human auditorium."[12] He compares the world to an auditorium, where

---

12. Andrew F. Walls, *The Missionary Movement in Christian History: Studies in the Transmission of Faith* (Orbis Books, 1996), 43.

all of humanity, past and present, observe God's narrative within human history. Different people groups from different moments in time sit in differing sections of the auditorium, and those locational distinctions offer a multifarious interpretation and perspective of the life and ministry of Jesus—what Walls calls the "Jesus Act."[13]

Walls defends the importance of each group's place in the hall, recognizing that although everyone is seeing the same play, their diverse and equally valuable vantage points determine what is compelling to them within the narrative. It informs which aspects of Jesus's story stand out and which aspects of the gospel draw them in. Building on Walls's imagery, Queer people sit in their own section of the auditorium, seeing the stage differently than their cisgender or heterosexual counterparts. They offer a valuable theological vantage point; it is the missional task of the church to hear and learn from them as they interact with the mission of God.

As messengers of the gospel, we need to continuously look for ways to acknowledge the distinct context of LGBTQ people and contextualize the story of salvation as one directly speaking to shared LGBTQ culture. The church must dialogue with the Queer community and facilitate fruitful gospel awareness to help them see the value of their seats in the house.

The Missional Work of Kaleidoscope

Throughout the year, my team of ministers and volunteers at Kaleidoscope sets up outreach tables in historically Queer neighborhoods—or, as our community calls them, "gayborhoods." We give out hot coffee or Pride pins to demonstrate love and initiate conversations. At one of our outreaches in Greenwich Village, someone stopped and shared that they were a local drag queen on their way to a performance. After a brief but genuine conversation, I asked how I could pray for them before their show. I expressed interest in their context and culture and sought to introduce Jesus into the dialogue. They were shocked and couldn't believe that someone representing God would ever consider them and their art worthy of prayer. After that astonishment wore off, they asked if I could pray for their drag sisters' safety. Through tears, they shared how a few of their fellow drag queens had been attacked and seriously injured on their way home at night. Before praying, we shared a hug and a moment of lament—we both knew the prayer was meaningful, but we also realized more needed to be done. We cried Queer tears together.

---

13. Walls, *Missionary Movement*, 46.

I took this story back to some of our team and brainstormed about how we could support the safety and dignity of these precious members of our community; we are now working on distributing care packages to drag queens throughout the city that include personal safety alarms and emergency-contact phone numbers if they want someone to talk to on their way to their subway station. These packages will also include a spiritual message addressing the identity and culture of our drag friends. We want these messages to encourage them to experience God reflected in their artistic performance, social context, and language. Each package will also contain a contextualized prayer for safety to remind our friends that there is a God who is *serving* protection and sees their *fabulous* worth. (*Serving* is a commonly used term in the drag community, meaning "giving" or "demonstrating"—someone who looks great is "serving looks." *Fabulous* is also a common term within drag culture.) Lord willing, this prayer will allow each drag artist to truly see themselves in that prayer because it reflects their needs and recognizes their cultural context.

Offering hugs from Christian moms and dads has been another way Kaleidoscope has shared the gospel through community outreach. Borrowing from two other fantastic organizations called Free Mom Hugs and Free Dad Hugs,[14] we commission Christian parents, primarily parents of LGBTQ children, to distribute hugs at Pride parades. Our parents, hands full of free water bottles and signs like "This Mom Loves You" or "Jesus Loves You and So Do I," hug thousands of Queer youths and adults, many of whom have not been hugged by their families in years. With each hug our parents speak words of life, saying, "You are loved and seen!" It is remarkable how many people line up to be embraced by strangers. Without fail, some run up for a hug from not one but every parent present or come back to the same parent multiple times.

We have also learned the importance of diverse representation within our parents and have White, Black, Hispanic, and Asian parents present, which has made an enormous impact. One year, a Chinese mother recounted a time when a Queer person hugged her and, midembrace, said, "You look like my Asian mother who hasn't spoken to me in years." What a picture of the gospel and a demonstration of good news! We go out as reflective representations of our Queer community's ethnic culture as well as representing the familiar figure of an earthly parent and the heavenly Father, who offers ultimate warmth and ascribes decisive worth. In contrast to many other mothers or fathers, ours proclaim the unconditional love of Jesus in the streets of New York Pride.

This ministry is changing the narrative of what the LGBTQ community expects to hear from Christians. Another mother shared an exchange with a

---

14. See Free Mom Hugs, FreeMomHugs.org.

man who—after receiving a hug—asked her, "Are you with the people across the street?" Confused, she answered no. He explained that another group was representing God on the other side of the intersection, but their message was different than ours. They displayed judgmental messages, declaring that every Queer person there was going to hell. They lacked compassion and disregarded any loving ways the gospel could resonate with their audience. While they held signs of hate and condemnation, we held signs of love and invitation.

We were not there to intrude on LGBTQ sacred space or to unearth people's sins, mainly because we recognize that LGBTQ people are not inherently more sinful than heterosexual people. Furthermore, we recognize that such strident demonstrations of moralistic chastisement fail to move people closer to God. As Debra Hirsch has pointed out, focusing on people's sinful state is centering a "secondary truth" over the "primary truth" of their universal existence as images of a loving creator God.[15] We choose to be present as compelling and unexpected symbols of Christ, who came not to condemn but to save the world. These loving gestures open doors for further conversations where LGBTQ people can discover their stories and needs within the work of Jesus's ministry, death, and resurrection.

Conclusion

If we truly believe Jesus came to bring hope, healing, and salvation to all, we must obediently share the joy we have in Christ with our LGBTQ neighbors and friends. We cannot passively wait until we are fully convinced of one theological position or another or for LGBTQ unbelievers to miraculously see and experience the gospel by themselves. We must take seriously the words of the Great Commission to go and make disciples of all people from all cultures, expressions, and walks of life, teaching them and demonstrating everything Jesus shared with us (Matt. 28:18–20). And like Jesus, who spent his time with the most marginalized and forgotten, we too must share meals, offer aid, and restore dignity to those who have been rejected by the religious world.

We can build relationships with LGBTQ people, replacing the false gospel of an exclusionary, Western, philosophical faith with one that ushers all people into its enticing and applicable gift, proving this good news is for them too. LGBTQ lives are worthy of attention and can offer beautiful testimonies of Christ's transforming love. Though the work of LGBTQ evangelism can

---

15. Hirsch, *Redeeming Sex*, 169–73.

feel lonely and difficult, as it involves navigating largely uncharted waters, God continues to reassure me that these are his beloved children, worthy of intentional, missional attention and compassionate care. And, as in the Great Commission, he has promised he will be with his church as we seek to be present and demonstrate the good news. My prayer is, and will continue to be, that God's kingdom may come within the LGBTQ community as it is in heaven. May each of us humbly join in seeing this come to pass.

15

Black LGBTQ Ministry

Candace E. Hardnett

I was born in Fauquier County, Virginia, in a town called Remington. Remington is beautifully quaint, positioned on the border of rural Fauquier and Culpeper counties. When I think of home I think of corn fields, farm houses, mighty oak trees, and rolling hills. There was a train that ran through our town, separating the commercial area from the residential, and there was the beautiful Rappahannock River that ran along the border of the town. I lived just a mile from a place called Kelly's Ford. A ford is a shallow area in a river or a stream that allows people to cross the water safely, often on foot. Kelly's Ford is on the Rappahannock, which is one of Virginia's most dangerous waterways. That ford is arguably the most important river crossing of the Civil War. It gave passage to Union soldiers as they advanced their attacks on Confederate troops in southern counties. Without Kelly's Ford there would've been no direct route to the south because the Rappahannock River divides the entire northeastern part of Virginia. The river starts at the Blue Ridge Mountains and flows southeast almost two hundred miles into the Chesapeake Bay. Crossing at any other point would have taken troops miles out of their way and could have even cost them their lives.

Those of us from Remington know the dangers of the Rappahannock River. While its beauty is unsurpassed, there is a dangerous undercurrent that waits beneath its surface. As a child, I was warned not to swim in the Rappahannock because so many people had lost their lives attempting simply to swim to the other side. One of my first memories is the devastation of hearing that a church friend had lost his life to the river.

I can't help but draw a parallel here when I think of the LGBTQ Christians I know who have attempted to find safety in the loving arms of Jesus only to have to face the dangers of "the church" in order to get to Him. I can't count how many friends I've seen lose their faith because of the church, and even more devastating, how many I've seen lose their lives. So many LGBTQ Christians reach a point of hopelessness when it comes to their sexuality.

Finding Safe Passage

I was nearly one of the casualties of the church, as I denounced the Christian faith at a young age. I was raised in the church but found myself disillusioned by what I viewed as hypocrisy. I was young, but I was wise enough to recognize that certain people were treated differently within the church community. I recall conversations about the single mother, the wayward addict, and those who were "shacking up" (a phrase used to refer to people who were dating, living together, but not married). I was always intrigued by the fact that the same people who seemed to have so much to say about these wayward people were also the people secretly cheating on their spouses, perpetuating abuse in marriages, and gossiping. I recognized how hard it was to navigate the church for myself, and I left the faith for many years. However, I loved Jesus. I realized that I was not doing myself a service by distancing myself from Christ simply because I didn't like the institution that represented Him. I reasoned that if I could not find a church that was safe, I could provide one, and that's what I did.

I earned my bachelor's degree in religion and my MDiv shortly thereafter. I was determined to follow the call to ministry that had been given to me as a child. I was also determined to create a safe environment for people like myself, those who had questions that needed answering and who had made a decision to remove themselves from churches that could not provide security, safety, and grace. I was ordained in 2009, and my wife and I opened the first nondenominational, affirming Black church in Savannah, Georgia: Agape Empowerment Ministries.[1]

My pastoral call is to minister to all people, but most specifically to those who are lesbian, gay, bisexual, transgender, and/or questioning (LGBTQ) and to Black, Indigenous, and other people of color (BIPOC) at the intersections

---

1. Agape Empowerment Ministries can be found online at facebook.com/AEMSavannah.

of their particular life experiences and orthodox Christian faith and theology. In a way, I am the ford that offers safe passage to those from marginalized groups within the LGBTQ community, giving access to a faith with an otherwise impassable divide—that is, the *Black Church*. While I do not compromise the message of the gospel, I calm the fury of the traditions that often hinder people in their journey to Christ. After all, Jesus called everyone, not just those who fit a certain criterion. I offer a safe place of refuge for the BIPOC LGBTQ community because I know the importance of faith, particularly for Black people in America.

Black America and Church

Faith, spirituality, and church were instrumental in shaping Black American culture as a whole. There is debate regarding the percentage of enslaved Africans who were already Christian when they were brought to America during the transatlantic slave trade, but one thing is certain: Christianity was the religion of the slaver and therefore the only religion acceptable for the enslaved. African religions were prohibited, along with the use of African language, writing, and other rituals. Nevertheless, the entity that we now know as the Black Church derived from a combination of African spirituality, traditions, and the Christian faith. There are very few African American descendants of slaves in America who cannot trace their roots back to the church in some way. The importance of the church in Black communities cannot be denied, nor can it be overlooked.

The Black Church became a safe haven for those seeking freedom from enslavement before the Civil War, and it continued to be instrumental for Black liberation and equality throughout the Civil Rights Movement. That is why so many historical Black figures attribute their resolve to fight for freedom to their Christian faith. Notable men and women such as Sojourner Truth, Denmark Vesey, Harriet Tubman, and the Rev. Dr. Martin Luther King Jr. are all products of the Black Church. Even leaders such as Malcolm X, who was not Christian, was only a generation removed from the church. His father was a Christian minister. With the church being such a monumental influence on our liberation as Black people, we bear an extra burden when we are rejected by it, especially when that rejection is based on our sexuality (perceived or confirmed), gender expression, or gender identity.

This is especially painful for Black people living in the South. Here in Savannah, there are churches that were established in the 1700s. One of the oldest Black Baptist congregations in North America was founded here. The churches in Savannah have historical evidence of their contribution to equality and freedom. Great Civil Rights leaders delivered speeches and held meetings within the walls of these churches. Years prior, some of the churches in Savannah were used as safe houses for those traveling on the Underground Railroad pursuing freedom. Despite such an expansive history of fighting for human equality, some of these same churches now exclude the LGBTQ community from serving, being ordained, or being married.

I don't mention this to "call out" or slander churches in Savannah, but rather to show an example of how LGBTQ inclusion is not seen as an issue, even to churches that historically fought for human equality. Within the Black Church, being LGBTQ and being Christian are often seen as mutually exclusive. Being Christian is reserved for people who are heterosexual, or at the very least celibate. Those who are openly LGBTQ are assumed to be sinful and deviant, or struggling through a spiritual attack that can be healed or fixed through prayer, and therefore cannot be acknowledged or affirmed within the broader church community.

Within the Black Church there is a "Don't Ask, Don't Tell" policy. Similar to the military's restriction against gays serving openly, those who are gay in the church are expected to live their lives in the closet. They are expected to hide their sexuality and keep it to themselves. It's understood that no one will inquire as to one's sexuality, as long as it's kept private. Of course, people enjoy spreading rumors and having assumptions about others' sexuality, but as long as those rumors are never confirmed, there are no issues. The problem with that is, LGBTQ members are never fully embraced, never truly affirmed, and are often filled with shame. Don't get me wrong, sexuality is not the totality of a person, but to completely deny or hide one's sexuality can be damaging and stressful. People who hide who they are live in constant fear of being outed or exposed. This often leads to depression and illness, and sometimes even suicidal thoughts or attempts.

Helping to Heal the Hurt

I've ministered to so many hurting people who have been subjected to public ridicule and shame in front of congregations as church leaders prayed, spoke in tongues, and smeared holy oil on them in attempts to rebuke the "homosexual demons" that were thought to cause their attraction to members of the same sex. In other accounts, I've ministered to lesbian mothers who were told that spiritual attacks on their children were a direct result of their sexuality and that to "save" their child they must change. I've cried with male congregants who told me how the church forced them to marry women in an attempt to "fix" their sexuality and how, in the end, they ruined the lives of their wives and children when they could no longer live the lie. I've witnessed firsthand the depression of those who desired love and companionship but were convinced that they were crucifying their flesh and honoring God by suffering through loneliness. When offered an alternative, most were unwilling to even consider it.

In the early establishment of Agape, we found that many Black gay Christians in Savannah would rather attend traditional churches who preach condemnation and hell for LGBTQ people than attend our church. They felt that it was a burden they must bear and that they deserved to feel shame when at church. They had been erroneously convinced that their suffering was pleasing to God, and they were denying their flesh the freedom of attending an affirming church.

But, as the Bible teaches, the denial of one's flesh is not for the purpose of merely suffering; it should allow us to become alive in the Spirit and should lead us closer to God. Hearing messages of condemnation did the exact opposite. Living under the burden of condemnation is harmful both physically and spiritually. In my experience, those who continued to subject themselves to messages that condemned them were more likely to engage in drug and substance abuse, seek out dangerous sexual encounters, and ultimately decide to walk away from the Christian faith altogether. They didn't see how that type of environment could affect their emotional and spiritual well-being, and I think that's what I found most troubling in those early years.

Environment is important for every living and growing thing. The environment of a tree or a plant affects its growth. I learned this from my grandmother, who was a master gardener. There was nothing that she could not grow, so it seemed. One of the most amazing things about my grandmother was her ability to bring seemingly dead plants back to life. When my grandmother started to get older, her eldest daughter, my aunt Carolyn, decided that it would be best if her mother moved in with her. My grandmother was a country woman, but she agreed that she would live out her golden years with my aunt in the city of Baltimore, Maryland. I loved to spend the summers in Baltimore with my grandmother and aunt because I enjoyed visits to the big city, and I missed my grandmother when she moved.

It never failed, during each one of those summer visits, that one of my aunt's city friends would nearly kill one of their house plants and bring it to my grandmother for revival. On more than one occasion I remember watching my grandmother inspect the withered, lifeless twigs that were brought to her. I expected my grandmother to say that the plants were beyond help, but she rarely did. Even the most dried up and withered were accepted. What I didn't understand was that my grandmother was not inspecting the leaves or the stems of these plants, but rather, she inspected the roots. She looked for signs of life beneath the surface. She knew that if the roots were still alive, she could save the plant.

Once she had the right soil and the right pot, she'd go to work as a surgeon goes to work on a patient. She'd carefully remove the dying plant from its old soil and pot, prune its dead leaves and stems, and place it in the new soil within a new pot. She'd give it a little water and, depending on the plant, find the right area in the house to place it for adequate light. I remember questioning why she would change the pot. Why not just dump out the old soil and use the same pot? I'll never forget what she told me. She said that when something has death in it, you don't try to get life out of it.

She felt that if the plant was dying inside the old pot, to give it new life it needed an entirely new environment. It would not thrive if it were placed back into the pot where it was sick and dying. It needed something fresh and new, or it risked withering away again. I don't know if there was anything scientific or true about her method, but I can say that every plant my grandmother ever attempted to save survived and flourished. When the former owners would return to get their plant, my grandmother would give them a stern talk about plant care and would make them promise to be good stewards over the plant.

Often the plants never returned to their old environment. My grandmother would tell the owners that if they didn't think caring for the plants was something they could do, she'd gladly care for them herself. A lot of people took her up on that offer. They knew they couldn't give their plant the attention and care that my grandmother offered, so they opted to leave it and get a plant that required a little less maintenance.

I learned something very valuable from my grandmother's example that I have tried to apply to my ministry. When LGBTQ people are not affirmed, they wither, and some nearly die. I've seen the result of people trying to conform to heterosexual or cisgender norms, many of whom show very few signs of spiritual life. Some are addicted, some are careless in their sexual encounters, some are living lives that are not remotely healthy. But I learned that we cannot look at the outside to determine life; we have to consider their roots. We have to consider what is beneath the surface and look at the heart.

Sometimes it's the environment they are in that's killing them; but if they have living roots and are placed in a new environment, they can live and thrive—and unlike plants, *all* people have living roots. There is not one person who is beyond redemption. All people, if given the right information, support, and love, will thrive and grow. If only churches that don't intend on properly caring for these beautiful people would simply be gracious enough to release them into the care of a pastor who will love them and help them grow!

Love Covers All

Unfortunately, so many people are in harmful church environments that stifle growth and promote shame instead. Shame is not of God. Shame hinders faith and causes people to retreat into themselves, often hiding what is shameful, instead of addressing it. When God found Adam and Eve in the garden, they were ashamed and hiding. But God requested that Adam and Eve stand before Him, and He covered their nakedness in order that they would no longer feel ashamed. He convicted them for their disobedience, but He did not reject them. Regardless of how one may feel about LGBTQ people, shaming them is not godly. If God covered Adam and Eve, how much more should we cover our brothers and sisters, even if we feel that they are in error?

The Bible says that "love covers over a multitude of sins" (1 Pet. 4:8). We are told to love one another deeply. To deny love to one of God's children because we perceive them to be sinful contradicts the meaning of the passage. Yet this is exactly what happens in churches when it comes to LGBTQ people. There is no compassion, no love, no grace, no understanding—only judgment and condemnation. Church communities fail to seek Scripture for understanding when it comes to the passages that so many believe speak against same-gender love and marriage. Instead, they read them at face value, without seriously investigating the context, then hide behind them to mistreat LGBTQ people.

It never ceases to amaze me that Christians become theological scholars when it comes to the passages in Scripture that speak against things they want to do. Somehow, they are able to read those passages in context, give proper exegesis, and hermeneutically apply the text to fit our contemporary society to allow for all sorts of things. But they will read the story of Sodom and Gomorrah and still declare that it's all about homosexuality. None of their contextual critique is applied to Genesis 19. They don't bother to read the story again because they think they already know what it says, and their interpretation of the story gives them permission to be cruel toward LGBTQ people. At least that's what it feels like to LGBTQ people.

So many other issues found within the ancient text of Scripture are treated as matters of debate, and those who welcome scholarly discourse are happy to engage. Women in ministry is often seen as a matter of debate. Baptism by full immersion or sprinkling is a matter of debate. The use of certain instruments in church is a matter of debate. Regardless of the side a person falls on any of these issues, these matters are seen as secondary or tertiary, as having no bearing on whether or not the person has the right to be Christian. But LGBTQ inclusion is seen as inherently unchristian, and therefore those who affirm the LGBTQ community are declared not Christian at all.

To this I ask, When did Christians cease to reason with one another? Were the early church fathers not engaged in healthy debate? Why can't modern Christians come to different conclusions, especially when one can find substantial evidence in Scripture to support a theological argument? For instance, most evangelical Christians can argue for or against Calvinism or Arminianism without completely revoking another's Christianity because they come to a different conclusion. Is this not possible today when it comes to LGBTQ inclusion in the church?

There is a beautiful story found in the eighth chapter of Acts about a eunuch who was baptized into the faith. In those times, eunuchs were sexual minorities. They were often castrated men who could not marry, who often cared for queens and other women connected to the palace. The eunuch of Acts 8 had come from Ethiopia and was reading the scroll of Isaiah when Philip was led to him through the Holy Spirit. When he approached the eunuch, Philip asked if he understood the prophet Isaiah's words. The eunuch admitted that he did not have guidance to help him, and so Philip explained the passage, which was referring to salvation through Jesus. When the eunuch heard the good news about Jesus, he believed. As they were traveling, Philip and the eunuch came upon water, and the eunuch asked the question that so many people ask when they accept the gospel, "What can stand in the way of my being baptized?" (v. 36).

Unfortunately for LGBTQ people, when they hear the gospel and believe and ask, "What can stand in the way of my being baptized?" the church gives them a laundry list of changes they must make. They are told that they must change the way they dress, if they dress too feminine or too masculine. The church will tell them that they must somehow change their attraction to the same sex. The church will tell them that if they cannot change their attraction, they must hate that portion of themselves and pray to be delivered. They must vow to be celibate. They must remove themselves from friends and community. They must attempt to be straight and find someone of the opposite sex to date and eventually marry. Then, and only then, they can really be baptized.

This is a far cry from the answer that Philip gave the eunuch. When asked the question, Philip responded, "If you believe with all your heart, you may" (Acts 8:37). There were no qualifiers except that the eunuch believe that Jesus Christ is the Son of God. Philip did not consider the eunuch's sexuality, gender, or expression. Philip did not exclude or disqualify the eunuch, which was quite unique for those times. Philip was a Jewish man and would have been very aware of the prohibition against eunuchs joining the assembly of God (Deut. 23:1). Philip understood that the gospel was meant to tear down the walls of exclusion that prohibited certain people from reaching God. Philip, without hesitation, ordered the chariot to be stopped, and he baptized the eunuch upon request, based on the eunuch's belief.

As Christians, we must be keenly aware of our inclination to reestablish the walls of restriction that the death of Jesus eradicated, and we must fight to preserve the inclusive nature of our faith. There should be no person who believes that Jesus Christ is the Son of God who is denied access. No person should have to traverse the difficult waters of chaos that so often entrench church communities, especially when those waters are full of opposition to those with minority sexual orientations and gender identities. That is why churches like mine exist: to provide safe passage for believers to reach a loving God who is beckoning them to His arms. I believe that when people are allowed to experience God, He gives them new life. Those who are withering and dying are rejuvenated and revived when they are in His presence. Who are we to deny their access?

When a church mimics the love of Jesus, there is no condemnation or judgment; there is only love. Unnecessary rules and regulations that could serve as barriers to attendance are removed in order to create a safe space. For instance, at our church, we were intentional in removing dress codes for our congregation. Parishioners are free to wear whatever they are comfortable wearing to church. Church members wear everything from shorts, T-shirts, or jeans to full suits and ties on a Sunday morning. All are welcome, and no one feels out of place. This also provides a safe atmosphere for those who are experiencing homelessness, who may not have "dress clothes" to wear on a Sunday morning.

Another practical way to be inclusive is to encourage multiple Bible versions for study and review. Having grown up in a King James Version–only church, I know how difficult it is for the average person to read and understand the text, let alone engage with it. At our church, we use multiple versions of the Bible, encouraging people to cross-refernce them. No one version is held at a higher standard than another, and people are given the freedom to relate to the holy text as it best speaks to them.

These are easy ways I've found to create a safe place where people can learn and grow in Christ. Fostering a safe environment for God's people should be one of the most important things we do as Christians. In particular, as BIPOC people, we must not re-create the trauma of the church that traumatized us. Let us work to tear down the traditions that serve only to restrain us and release the chains of bondage to allow people to have a personal relationship with God. This is real freedom: to be at liberty to access God in full vulnerability and to allow God to heal us and make us new. Some people never fully have a relationship with God because they become lost in church tradition. They become consumed with creating an image of themselves that is palatable to the church.

As Christians, we must trust the Holy Spirit to do the work of the Holy Spirit. Jesus instructed His disciples that the Holy Spirit would come to convict the world of sin (John 16:8). The interesting thing about conviction is that it produces change without shame. Conviction, although it may not feel good, empowers one to be better. Consider the prodigal son, who had received his inheritance early, squandered it all on women and mischief, and was reduced to a pigsty. As a Jewish man, touching pigs was the ultimate disgrace, yet the son found himself among the filthy animals, longing to share their food. At some point the son became convicted; the Bible says that he came to his senses and decided to return home to his father. No one shamed the son. No one rejected the son. No one even attempted to rehabilitate the son. None of these things were necessary. If the job of the Holy Spirit is to convict the world, then we would do well to get out of the way and allow the Holy Spirit to work.

Only God can convict the hearts of people, and no amount of shame or guilt we attempt to heap on someone will ever result in the change of heart that comes about through the conviction of the Holy Spirit. Jesus left clear instruction for our job on this earth, and it's summed up in love: love of God and love of others. If our faith is real, and I believe that it is, God is the changer of hearts and minds—we are not. Perhaps our ultimate test of faith is whether we can relinquish our desire to control the portions of the ministry that belong to God and God alone. Do you trust Him enough to come into the lives of even the most egregious of sinners? Did God not meet Saul on the road to Damascus? How much more can He meet any one of us, especially those of us who earnestly seek Him?

Real Relationship Cultivates Real Love

It is impossible to form a real relationship with anyone, including God, while pretending to be someone else. If all we offer others is a version of who we want them to be, and not the authentic people they are, we are allowing them to fall in love only with a lie. True relationships are made when people share themselves and expose their innermost thoughts and ideas. Unfortunately, many LGBTQ people have been taught to hide who they are from everyone, especially God—as if it's possible to hide from God. Nevertheless, they love God from a distance because they have been convinced that there's something wrong with them that would prevent God's full acceptance.

Let us find healing from old messages that told us we were not qualified to be loved by Jesus, or that taught us we must be ashamed of who we love or how we express ourselves. Let us heal from the ideas that we must conform to gender and societal norms in order to be accepted by God. Let us walk in our uniqueness, in confidence, without apology, knowing that we are loved. Let us then create places of acceptance that offer refuge to others to walk in their authenticity. Let us be a ford for one another as we make our way to the God who loves us all, and who desires true relationship with us, whether gay, straight, cis, or trans. Let us make room for love not only in our hearts but in the pews of every church that proclaims Christ, as Christ makes room for us.

16

Cultivating a Shepherd's Heart for the Transgender Community

Amie Scott

Love God, love people. That's easy enough, right? According to John, "Whoever claims to love God yet hates a brother or sister is a liar. For whoever does not love their brother and sister, whom they have seen, cannot love God, whom they have not seen" (1 John 4:20). We are commanded to love God and to love people—that being the case, why do we still get this so wrong? To love well in our culture is extremely challenging. We tend to love one another conditionally, indeterminately, and superficially. Our love isn't always clear. On the contrary, it's vague at best. If we are really honest with ourselves, we often don't love well, and yet, we are commanded to love God and love people.

I know from experience that such love *is* possible. One of the first things I noticed before I ever became a believer was the authentic love that fellow believers had for one another. In my experience, the Christians I encountered knew how to genuinely care for one another. Even when believers had differences in their theological stances on certain topics, like eschatology, at the end of the day, they really knew how to love one another. I saw believers demonstrating mutual trust and friendship based on their shared commitment to Jesus. This specific kind of love that they had for one another was something I deeply longed for. It was something I didn't have in my life, and I wanted to experience it.

God used that love to bring me to a place where I, too, wanted a relationship with Jesus. The day I got saved, I experienced the *agape* love of God in a tangible way. It wasn't just that I saw this love poured onto other people; this was the first time I had ever experienced the *agape* love of God personally. I fell in love with God because he loved me, even though I had believed I was unlovable. He loved me when I felt like no one else would or could love me. He loved me and pursued me, even when I was lost. He loved me while I was still entangled in my sin. He loved me in my brokenness and rebellion. He simply loved me. Love was the catalyst that moved God toward me. Love was the reason God reached out and saved me from the despair I was in. God loved me simply because he chose to intentionally love me.

I came out as trans a decade or so after I met the Lord. As I wrestled with my gender identity and faith, I despised being trans. I saw it as a curse, not a blessing. I believed God merely tolerated my transness, rather than approved of it. I had not wanted to be trans. In fact, I didn't realize I was trans much of my life. All I knew was who I *wasn't*. I wasn't who people perceived me to be on the outside. Through pain and trial, through loss and devastation, I finally came to terms with the fact that I am indeed transgender.

I didn't know how to reconcile being a Christian and being trans. This tension was exacerbated through the exclusion I would suffer in my church community. When I came out as trans, even before I transitioned, I was no longer invited to social gatherings. The church family I deeply loved withdrew from me. If I walked into a group conversation, they turned their backs and walked away. I was ostracized and told that God has no use for a person like me. The pain from being treated like a modern-day leper was unbearable.

I started to doubt God's love for me. I started to despise the place that had brought me so much life, the church. So I left the church. Yet God never turned his back on me. I came to realize that his *agape* love never changes, and he never rejected me.

About five years after leaving church behind, I found myself wandering into a new church on the outskirts of Portland, Oregon. By this time, I had fully transitioned, and no one in my new life knew I was trans. As I became involved in this new congregation, I didn't tell them I am trans. I didn't want to deal with the pain of rejection again. I focused on building relationships and reimmersing myself in the church. But after several years with this faith community, the leadership found out that I am trans. Again, I was rejected and asked to leave the church family that I loved. The pain was intolerable. The very people I cared so much about wanted nothing to do with me. I found myself in a fetal position on my bed weeping inconsolably. In retrospect, I don't believe the church intended to be malicious; they just had never experienced someone like me. I challenged them in ways that made them uncomfortable. But the result was I began to feel God merely tolerated rather than fully embraced me.

A couple of months after being expelled from my church, I met a different pastor near where I lived. I decided to tell him right away that I was trans because I didn't want to experience the pain of rejection again. I figured if he pushed me away right off the bat, I wouldn't experience the trauma of investing in a relationship only to be discarded. But when I told him I was trans, he gave me the biggest hug. For the first time in my life, I felt hope for a trans Christian like me. He disarmed all of my reservations because he simply loved me as a human being, and he saw me as a sibling in the Lord.

I started going to his church, and I asked him if he was going to tell people that I was trans. I didn't want to be the person everyone looked and stared at. He said, no, that it was my story to tell. I said, "What if I tell them and they reject me?" He replied, "If they reject you, then I will walk out the doors of this church with you." His words made me cry. For the first time in my life, I had a pastor treat me with dignity and respect *as a trans person*. I was seen, heard, and cared for. It changed my life.

After being at this pastor's church for about six months, I was invited to their women's retreat. I asked the pastor if it was okay for me to go, and he said, "Uh, yeah. Why wouldn't it be?" At this point, no one knew I was trans except the pastor. I had no intention of telling anyone because I didn't want to be seen as a freak. I didn't want to experience the pain of total rejection again. As the retreat drew near, I was asked to speak at the event on Saturday night. So I decided to teach on the love of God. But during the Saturday morning session, one of the ladies shared about the pain she felt when her son came out as gay. This current church that we were both attending had split over it. The mother was devastated. She had been a part of this church for many years, and she felt like it was her fault that the church split, because she was unwilling to reject her son.

As she was telling this story, the Lord spoke to me. It was as clear as day. He said, "Amie, I don't just tolerate your being trans; I have called you to be trans." And then God gave me a Scripture: "I have made myself a slave to everyone, to win as many as possible. To the Jews I became like a Jew, to win the Jews. . . . To the weak I became weak, to win the weak. I have become all things to all people so that by all possible means I might save some" (1 Cor. 9:19–20, 22). This was the first time that I felt called to being trans. This was a game changer for me because it gave me purpose. I was here to win others like me to Jesus. But not just those like me—I was here to show others who are not like me how they can biblically love those perceived to be unlovable. This changed everything. Eventually, the Lord put me in the position of being the pastor of an incredible church, reaching out to other marginalized communities, including but not limited to transgender people.

It is not our job to determine who gets to receive love and who doesn't. We have all been invited as guests to the table of the Lord. We are guests at his table, not bouncers. It is not our job to exclude anyone from access to Jesus. Our job is to bring all who will come. Invite them all, and let Jesus sort out who's who. He's so much better at knowing a person's heart than we are.

If you know your Bible, you know there was a woman who anointed Jesus's feet with oil (Luke 7:37–39). Many speculate that she was a prostitute. And since oil was so expensive, what she gave was most likely her life savings that she earned through prostitution. The woman used her wages as a prostitute to offer a gift to the Lord. But that was an abomination according to the Torah, which prohibits a harlot from bringing her wages into the temple of the Lord (Deut. 23:17–18). Nevertheless, Jesus said, "'Therefore, I tell you, her many sins have been forgiven—as her great love has shown. But whoever has been forgiven little loves little.' Then Jesus said to her, 'Your sins are forgiven'" (Luke 7:47–48).

Just because someone is different doesn't give us the right to exclude them from being the recipient of genuine, inclusive love. Just because we disagree with someone's worldview or the way they choose to live doesn't give us the right to exclude them from access to the greatest love of all, Jesus. Love is patient, love is kind. Love endures. Love doesn't dishonor others, and it keeps no record of wrong. Love, genuine *agape* love, never fails.

We are so busy fighting the culture war that we have lost sight of loving God and loving people. Transgender people need authentic love poured upon them. We need you to love us, because truth be told, most people don't love us. We are the outcast and rejected people of this generation. We are attacked, mocked, assaulted, abused, mistreated, and murdered. We are hated by most on a regular basis. We are used as political pawns. We are despised and have no one who is willing to go out of their way to love us. We seek the one thing that all people seek: genuine, safe love.

Of the 4.2 million youth experiencing homelessness, as many as 40 percent identify as LGBTQ. Sexual and gender minorities "have a 120% higher risk of experiencing some form of homelessness."[1] More than 40 percent of

---

1. "LGBTQ+ Youth Homelessness," National Network for Youth, accessed March 7, 2024, https://nn4youth.org/lgbtq-homeless-youth/.

transgender youth have been bullied at school. Think about that. Almost half of trans youth who go to school have been bullied, compared to 18 percent of their non-LGBTQ peers. And 29 percent of transgender youth have been threatened with or injured by a weapon on school property, compared to only 7 percent of their non-LGBTQ peers.[2] Similarly, 47 percent of "all transgender people have been sexually assaulted at some point in their lives."[3]

Transgender people are significantly more likely to have a mood or anxiety disorder than the general population.[4] Depression rates are exceedingly high in people who do not identify with the gender they were assigned at birth. As many as 40 percent of transgender people have attempted suicide.[5] These issues are often rooted in lack of love. Trans people are not loved. They are abused, removed from churches, removed from homes, and seen as the lepers of our day. Many Christians have chosen to condemn and reject trans people. They argue that God created humans as male and female and that those categories are unchangeable and inherently tied to biology. But regardless of where you land in this debate, we are still called to love God and love people.

Removing Barriers and Opening Doors

If you feel like loving a trans person is an impossible task, then be encouraged because one of the greatest learning curves for me, as a trans pastor, was how to minister to the ostracized trans community. Just because I am trans doesn't mean I knew how to minister to trans people. In fact, as I began pastoring the congregants of my church, I had a lot to learn. But I have collected some nuggets along the way that have helped me to remove barriers and to open doors to minister the Word of God. And I hope these insights will be helpful to you as well.

---

2. Madeleine Roberts, "New CDC Data Shows LGBTQ Youth Are More Likely to Be Bullied Than Straight Cisgender Youth," Human Rights Campaign, August 26, 2020, https://www.hrc.org/news/new-cdc-data-shows-lgbtq-youth-are-more-likely-to-be-bullied-than-straight-cisgender-youth.

3. "Sexual Violence & Transgender/Non-Binary Communities," National Sexual Violence Resource Center, accessed March 7, 2024, https://www.nsvrc.org/sites/default/files/publications/2019-02/Transgender_infographic_508_0.pdf.

4. Jonathon W. Wanta et al., "Mental Health Diagnoses among Transgender Patients in the Clinical Setting: An All-Payer Electronic Health Record Study," *Transgender Health* 4 (2019): 313–15, https://www.ncbi.nlm.nih.gov/pmc/articles/PMC6830528/.

5. Ashley Austin et al., "Suicidality among Transgender Youth: Elucidating the Role of Interpersonal Risk Factors," *Journal of Interpersonal Violence* 37 (2022): 5–6, https://pubmed.ncbi.nlm.nih.gov/32345113/.

Risk Discomfort to Be a Friend

How can we love transgender people in a tangible way? We have such a beautiful example of what love looks like through the life of Jesus. Think about it: Jesus left heaven, he left perfection, he left the comforts of home to come to a people who were nothing like him. God the Son was served in heaven because he's the King of kings and Lord of lords. Yet Jesus didn't come to be served; he came to show us what love looks like through serving. Jesus came to a people who were entangled in all sorts of things—things like idolatrous worship, theft, sexual sins, brutality, selfishness, adultery, slander, rape, murders, and the list goes on and on. Jesus came and served people. He served sinners. He served the crude and the unrighteous. He served the prostitute and the outsider. Jesus came and sat with the leper, the prostitute, the tax collector, the marginalized, the sailors, and those who looked nothing like the polished religious leaders of the day. Jesus said, "I have set you an example that you should do as I have done for you" (John 13:15).

Jesus sat with many who were seen as heretics, and he loved them not with words only but with actions. Jesus fed them, counseled them, hugged them, led them. He opened up the Scriptures to them to show them that God is not unapproachable and scary but, rather, he is a loving Father who seeks to be in relationship with people who are on the fringes and outskirts of societal norms. He showed us the way to the Father, and the way to the Father isn't through beating our kin down and excluding them, but through embracing them and showing them the love that we have found through God's Son. Jesus showed us what true sacrifice looks like. True sacrifice is to lay down one's life for a friend. True love will, at times, lay down one's reputation for others. Jesus certainly had his reputation on the line often, so much so that he died a heretic's death.

Not only did Jesus serve and lay down his life, but he also does something so profound that it's worth mentioning here: he calls us his friends. Let that sink in for a moment. He called you his friend. He called me his friend. I don't know about you, but I do know about me: I know who I am. I know what I've done and where I have been. I know how much I have failed in my pursuit of holiness. I know how much sin has pursued me and just how often I have given in to the bondage that has enslaved me time and time again. And yet, God went out of his way—he left heaven to save that which was lost. "God demonstrates his own love for us in this: While we were still sinners, Christ died for us" (Rom. 5:8).

The question has to be asked: If Jesus loves people from all walks of life, if he laid his life down, and he calls us his friends, isn't this something that we should do too? Are you willing to do this? If you answered yes to this question, then let me get really personal and ask you another serious question. How many transgender people do you know who you would call your friends? I am not asking how many transgender people you are ministering to; I am asking how many are your *friends*? Sadly, that number won't be high for many. In fact, if we are honest, most of us would say zero. But if we are to serve as Jesus served, if we are to lay down our lives for our friends and love our neighbors as ourselves, then why don't we have trans people who are our friends? If you really want to love as Jesus loved, then this must change. If we really want to be effective in bringing people into a relationship with God, this has to change.

I want to encourage you to invite your transgender friends to dinner with you, and I do hope they are your friends. Invite them to go bowling with you. Invite them to hang out with you and your family. Invite them to be part of your life. Invite their opinions into your conversations. Many transgender people have no one in their lives. Many live alone and have very few friends, and the friends that they do have, oftentimes, are not believers. Many trans people have to suffer alone, so when they are sick, no one is there to care for them. When they are in the hospital, no one calls or visits or even checks in on them. When they are struggling financially, no one is there to give them a helping hand.

Most trans people will sit in church alone with no one sitting next to them. Many trans people have never received, or rarely receive, a genuine hug from another believer. How can we attract people to Jesus when we don't love like Jesus loves? Let us be a people who serve our neighbors. It shouldn't matter if they are LGBTQ; they are people, and they need love. Love is an action, a demonstration. And we are to love people the way that we want to be loved. We all want to be seen. We all want to be heard. We all want a voice and a place to belong. Trans people are no different.

I find it interesting that when COVID-19 hit, one of the symptoms that people struggled with the most, which got to a crisis level in the world and in the United States, was isolation. People just couldn't handle being without other people. They couldn't handle not receiving human touch, like a handshake or a hug. This led to extreme depression all across the world. Asim Shah says, "Human beings are wired to touch and be touched. When a child is born, that is how they bond with their mother—through touch."[6] Yet many trans people haven't received a genuine hug of friendship from anyone for much longer than

---

6. Asim Shah, MD, as quoted in Shanley Pierce, "Touch Starvation Is a Consequence of COVID-19's Physical Distancing," TMC News, May 15, 2020, https://www.tmc.edu/news/2020/05/touch-starvation/.

those who survived the pandemic. It has been years and years since they have been included and seen as a real soul, a real person who just needs to be loved.

So, go hug your trans siblings, but ask first because, after not being hugged for so long, there are trust issues. They have a real fear for their safety. There is trauma that may resurface for those who have been in isolation for so long.

Honor a Person's Chosen Name

Whether or not we agree on everything concerning gender identity, we can still take practical action to love trans people well. One important way to do this is by honoring a person's chosen name. This is similar to a practice we find in Scripture. Consider Barnabas: Was that his legal name? No, it wasn't. Barnabas's real name was Joseph. The apostles changed his name to Barnabas because they thought "Barnabas" better described his inner person than "Joseph" (Acts 4:36). Barnabas means "son of encouragement." Even the Holy Spirit honored this chosen name and explicitly used this new name (13:2). And if the Holy Spirit can honor a name change, then so can we.

We see name changes throughout Scripture. Abram became Abraham. Simon became Peter. Jacob became Israel. Naomi changed her own name to Mara, and it was honored by God. Saul also used the name Paul. My point is that God honors chosen names. He really does. Love honors a person's chosen name. Love respects the person by acknowledging what they want to be called.

Use a Person's Preferred Pronouns

An important way to remove a barrier and to show that you genuinely care about a trans person is to use their pronouns in prayer. Affirm their identity in personal and corporate prayers by using the pronouns and the name they request. You have no idea the impact this will have on the transgender person in front of you, but trust me, it's a game changer for them—for us. Also, use inclusive language. Using terms like *siblings in Christ* rather than *brothers and sisters* or *parents* instead of *mother and father* significantly helps because it shows that you are being intentional to love and include them. We trans believers want to be seen as Christians who love Jesus just like you, so acknowledging that we are believers and using inclusive language is a great way to show that you love us.

Invite Transgender Parishioners to Participate in Church Activities

Regardless of your church policy on inclusion, you can still invite us trans believers to get involved in ministry with you. Invite us to participate in as many things as possible. Let us help plan events, take part in productions, and share our stories in small groups. Include us like you would include anyone else. Trans people are complex image bearers, like anyone else, and just as capable of bringing God glory. I am evidence of this. I have been told over and over again that God can't use me because I am transgender. But I say, "Watch how he uses me for his glory."

God is able to do "immeasurably more than all we ask or imagine" (Eph. 3:20). He is bigger than we are. His thoughts are far above our thoughts. His ways are higher than our ways. We can try to limit the Lord, but he cannot and will not be contained or restrained by our views of who he is. What I am saying is, too often, we have limits where God doesn't place limits. God isn't bound by our limiting assumptions of what is possible. God can and does use transgender people for his purposes.

Create Accessible Spaces

Another way you can minister to trans people is to create physical and social spaces that incorporate trans people. Have a plan in place for bathrooms. Gender-neutral bathrooms are a major blessing for a trans person. Many trans people fear using the bathroom in public settings, which makes remaining in a particular place for a long period of time challenging. It's difficult for trans people to fellowship, worship, and pray if they can't use a bathroom. Sometimes, showing hospitality is as easy as a new sign on a bathroom door. Removing barriers to physical spaces is vital if we want to bring people into a relationship with the church and with Christ.

Other important spaces to make accessible to trans people are gender-specific small groups. Allow trans women to attend women's groups and trans men to attend men's groups. I know it may be hard for some of us to wrap our heads around these things, but love tries to accommodate. Love looks for new ways to pour itself out. I want to encourage you to be gender inclusive in your church activities. Make your men's Bible study group a group for all men and male/masculine-identifying people. Make your women's Bible study group a group for all women and female/feminine-identifying people. If that's not possible, then provide a support group for gender-diverse people. Love finds a way to include the outsider.

Support People Who Are Transitioning

Many people lose family, financial, and emotional support when they come out as trans. Provide a resource for trans people who need someone to accompany them if they have gender-affirmation surgery, or consider creating a fund to help trans people who need financial support, whether for gender-affirming care or housing assistance or gender-affirming clothing.

Not all trans people are the same. Some love being trans; others hate it. Some see it as a blessing; others see it as a curse. When we choose to transition, it is usually out of desperation, and in the process, we lose people in our lives. I have never met any trans person who has not lost important relationships when they transitioned. You can make a difference by staying connected during the transitioning process.

Stand Up for Transgender People

Defend us when we are bullied. Defend us when people are out of line and say things to us that are inappropriate. Defend us publicly and privately. Correct people when they stereotype us. Even though you may or may not agree with a trans person's ideology, you can agree that no one should be mistreated or insulted.

The hate we have received from various people in our lives has caused us trauma. Help us work through our trauma. Sometimes we just need you to listen to us and love us, even if you don't understand and can't relate to us. Listening goes a really long way. Take our pain seriously. The trauma that trans people have experienced is real; and as uncomfortable as it is to acknowledge, some of this trauma and pain has come from the church. Some comes from the congregation, but more often it comes from leadership in the church. About 72 percent of Protestant pastors "believe that it is morally wrong for an individual to identify with a gender different than the [biological] sex they were born."[7] Not surprisingly, the majority of LGBTQ Americans believe religious institutions are unfriendly toward transgender people.[8] Churches have historically caused more harm than good to this community.

Yet, if you want to understand and defend trans people from mistreatment, then start with just listening to us. Even if you believe that gender dysphoria is a result of the fall, any brokenness that trans people experience deserves deep compassion rather than moral blame. The reality is that the transgender person is your neighbor, and we are commanded to love our neighbor in the same way that we want to be loved. No one wants to be excluded. No one

---

7. Aaron Earls, "U.S. Protestant Pastors See Gender Change as Immoral," *Lifeway Research*, March 16, 2021, https://news.lifeway.com/2021/03/16/u-s-protestant-pastors-see-gender-change-as-immoral/.

8. Aleksandra Sandstrom, "Religious Groups' Policies on Transgender Members Vary Widely," Pew Research Center, December 2, 2015, https://www.pewresearch.org/short-reads/2015/12/02/religious-groups-policies-on-transgender-members-vary-widely/.

wants to be mistreated. No one wants to be invisible or disrespected. Love believes all things and covers a multitude of sins.

Consider Attending or Recognizing LGBTQ Events

Finally, attend relevant events such as the Transgender Day of Remembrance (TDOR), National Coming Out Day, Pride Month, and LGBTQ History Month. This shows that you genuinely care about all people, and it shows that you have taken an interest in things that are important and relevant to them.

Conclusion: The Bottom Line

At this point you might be thinking, *Wow, this is a bit much. Why do we have to do all these things? Other people don't need these things to feel loved.* But remember, love has a cost attached to it. To love well means there will be sacrifice. When you love a transgender person, it will cost you. People will start to baulk and complain. Some will call you out. Others will talk behind your back. Some will write you nasty emails letting you know just how horrible you are for loving the unlovable. Just like they did in Jesus's day when a leper came to town, people will move out of the way to avoid contact.

Loving well means serving as Jesus served. So, yes, there will be a cost to loving well. At the same time, there is great reward when we bring people into the kingdom of God. The reward far outweighs the cost; it outweighs the sacrifice. Don't ever forget that. Our love has a purpose. It is designed by God to bring people into a relationship with Jesus. So, yes, the cost is high, but the rewards are greater than the costs.

The bottom line is that many trans people have no hope. Can you be someone who gives them the hope that they need? Can you show them the hope of glory and the reason you have hope? Can you love them and show up when no one else does? Will you show them what love looks like? When you love them as God loves you, they will experience the love of Jesus. This is what it is all about. So let's be those who love God and love people.

17

Supporting Parents of LGBTQ Children

Staci Frenes

Imagine living in a house most of your life where everything is in its rightful place: familiar, tidy, orderly. Then, one day, a package arrives at your door from someone you love. A package so unexpected, unwieldy, and large, you don't know where to put it, or whether it will even fit through your door. Suddenly, you're faced with the difficult choice of either rearranging everything in your house to make room for this mystery package or turning it away.

In my case, the unexpected package was my sixteen-year-old daughter coming out as gay, and the house was the conservative Christian belief system I'd grown up in my entire life. During an otherwise uneventful morning drive to school, my daughter tearfully revealed to me the secret she had been keeping for years, while I tried desperately to make room for it. Though I managed to reassure her in the moment that I loved her and we would "get through this together," my mind and heart were thrown into a panic. *How can my child be gay? What does this mean?* I had nowhere to put this information in my social or religious framework. It didn't fit anywhere. And yet, she was my daughter, and there was no way I would turn her away at the door. I knew, somehow, I would need to make room for this new reality.

Like so many Christian parents whose child comes out as gay, lesbian, or transgender, I found myself overwhelmed with questions, doubts, worries, and sometimes downright existential terror in the days and weeks after that morning drive to school. My particular conservative evangelical upbringing had in no way prepared me for parenting a gay child. I was introduced to Jesus at a junior-high Young Life camp, then a few years later to a preacher's kid at an Assemblies of God church, and I gave myself, wholeheartedly, to both of them. I went on to attend an evangelical Bible college, and eventually, my passion and gifts led me to a career and ministry as a singer/songwriter, worship leader, and Christian conference speaker. I had been singing and speaking in evangelical faith spaces for over twenty years when my daughter came out to me. I didn't know how I could ever reconcile the faith I'd been brought up with and my fierce love for my child.

As a parent, I shared the same hopes and prayers for my daughter as every other Christian mother I knew: I wanted her to be safe and happy and to have a future in which God "blessed" her. As I envisioned it, that meant having a husband and a family. I never imagined grappling with the complexities of a future that included a child who was gay. In fact, before our daughter came out, I didn't give much thought to the topic of homosexuality at all, beyond a limited understanding of what I had been taught to believe the Bible said about it. And in the evangelical circles I moved in, little else *was* said about it other than it was a sin. After Abby came out, the topic took on levels of intricacies I couldn't have imagined. Suddenly, it was all I could think about, pray about, obsess over. My doubts and fears multiplied into a constellation of uncertainties and questions for which I had no answers.

Determined to learn more, I embarked on a roller-coaster process that took months—and for some aspects, years—to better understand and accept my daughter's sexuality. I wrote about the experience in a memoir, *Love Makes Room*, and since then I have received countless emails, texts, and private messages from other Christian parents of LGBTQ children, echoing many of the same fears and doubts I have had. In these messages, from ministers and laypeople alike, parents of children across the spectrum of sexual orientation and gender identity, common themes showed up again and again. Among them are the following:

"I feel so alone."

"I don't know who to turn to with my questions."

"Is my child going to be okay?"

"I'm confused about what the Bible says about this, but what resources can I trust?"

"My friends/family don't understand our desire to understand and accept our child."

"My church doesn't welcome or accept my LGBTQ child. Should I stay?"

Reading the heartache in these messages from fellow parents, it became clear to me that there is a growing number of casualties of what our media calls "culture wars" sitting in our churches week after week who desperately need compassion, understanding, and support. These include not only the LGBTQ youth among us who are hurting (experts tell us young people who come out in religious homes experience higher-than-usual rates of depression and suicidal ideation) but also their parents. These parents often feel pulled between loving their child and honoring their faith, and they don't know where to turn for guidance. Whether we're aware of them or not, these parents of LGBTQ kids are suffering in our churches, many of them silently. Regardless of where we land in the "affirming" or "non-affirming" debate, we have a clear mandate as followers of Jesus to reach out to these hurting parents and make room for them with compassion and kindness.

I believe making room for these parents in our faith communities involves several things: seeking to better understand their situation, offering to walk alongside them in their pain, and being instrumental in their healing. It involves rising above the divisive rhetoric around this topic and examining where we have failed to care for these parents and their children as members of our family. It involves asking, How can we do better? And while every parent with an LGBTQ child has a different story, with needs that are unique to each family, I believe we can apply some basic principles as we seek to love them in a more Christlike manner. What follows is a discussion of four ways we can learn to "make room" for parents of LGBTQ children—in our churches, in our homes, and in our hearts—and by doing so, demonstrate compassionate, Christlike acceptance.

Make Room for Comfort in the Midst of Grief

One of the most overwhelming emotions a Christian parent experiences when their child first comes out is that of grief. On discovering their child is gay, lesbian, or transgender, many feel a massive shift in perspective, separating the familiar "what was" from the daunting and sometimes terrifying "what is," and the chasm between those two worlds is often so wide and deep that it can feel like a complete loss, even like a death for some.

To understand this, we must recognize that these parents are mourning the loss of many things in that moment, including the person they thought their child would become and, in some cases, their child's gender identity. Perhaps the most difficult to acknowledge and accept is the loss of their own dreams for their child's future. Depending on the child's age (many LGBTQ youth come out in their late teens or first year of college), parents also face the prospect of their child leaving home for the first time. While grappling with these losses, parents often experience a profound sense of isolation from their faith communities, particularly evangelical churches, where there typically aren't "safe" spaces for conversations around this topic. That isolation compounds the sense of loss, as it now includes people with whom they once fellowshipped, prayed, and gathered together on a regular basis.

The day my daughter came out to me, I vividly remember staring down at my phone with intense dread and wondering, *Who can I call that would understand what I'm going through?* In any other situation—financial hardship, sickness, even mental-health issues—there were a number of people within my faith community I knew I could talk to, pray with, confide in. But there was no one in my church, friend group, or ministry network who had ever spoken of their LGBTQ child coming out. This, I knew, was something altogether different—it was controversial, divisive, taboo—and instinctively, I felt the need to keep it a secret. Unfortunately, I am not alone. Most parents I've talked to in similar situations experience the same sense of loneliness on top of already enormous grief. They feel isolated, unsure of who to trust with this information, and because of this, they often keep it within the walls of the family home, where it becomes a heavy secret everyone in the family is expected to bear.

In my case, the secrecy and grief led to prolonged depression, during which the only person I felt I could talk to about it was my husband. And while he did his best to process the implications of our situation with me, he was dealing with his own doubts, questions, and grief. Rather than talk about it, his response was to set it aside and focus on work. Our son, the eldest of our two children, seemed to take the news of Abby's coming out in stride, which at the time was a relief, as neither my husband nor I had the emotional capacity to have many meaningful conversations with him about it. We moved through the first few days and weeks in a kind of shell-shocked disbelief. It was a disorienting and strange time for all of us. We were not just a churchgoing family; we were worship leaders, small-group facilitators, prayer-team members. And now, we were mourning the loss of something we didn't even fully comprehend—and we were doing it mostly alone, without our church family.

What might it look like to walk alongside parents of LGBTQ children in our faith communities who are experiencing grief? For me, staring at my phone that day in a turmoil of emotions, it would have looked like someone on the other end ready to listen with compassion, without judgment. Someone willing to shed tears with me and share their own experiences of loss. Someone who could simply sit with me, right where I was, their presence alone offering comfort. We find the theme of comfort for those who grieve woven throughout the Old and New Testaments. In Psalm 34:18, we read that God is "close to the brokenhearted." Jesus acknowledges in the Beatitudes that grief is a "blessed" state in which we can experience God's comfort on a deeper level (Matt. 5:4). And Paul urges believers in his Letter to the Romans to "weep with those who weep" (Rom. 12:15 ESV).

Yet, even with these reminders in Scripture that grief is a common human condition that we are invited to share with one another in the family of God, we're typically not very comfortable with comforting others. We find it difficult to be present with people in their pain, especially when we don't understand the particularities of their situation, or feel awkward or ill-equipped to talk about it. The truth is, however, most of us have experienced grief similar to the type parents of LGBTQ children feel. We've all been touched by the pain of letting go of a beloved, long-held dream we've had for ourselves or someone we love. When we remember how that felt, we can, at the very least, offer our presence and a compassionate listening ear to parents who are grieving. We can say, "I understand your pain," even if we can't fully comprehend all the implications of their specific loss.

As Christ's body, we can extend this practice of compassionate listening outward, not just as individuals, but as churches and even entire denominations. We can offer parents like me, who felt they had nowhere to turn within their faith communities, a safe place to bring their pain. Many churches already provide small-group settings to support people going through a whole host of life situations, from addiction recovery and divorce to postpartum depression, teen pregnancy, adoption, and many others. Acknowledging that parents of LGBTQ kids also need support, and offering a place for them to share their experiences in a kind, nonjudgmental space, is a tangible way to live out a tender, necessary function of the church.

Make Room for Peace in the Midst of Uncertainty

For most Christian parents, the personal and spiritual implications of having a child come out as LGBTQ are so big, so much to deal with, that initially there are many questions along with the grief, none of which seem to have clear answers. The questions I poured out to God when my daughter first came out bubbled up from a place of deep fear within me, each one more urgent than the last:

"What kind of future will she have?"
"Who will keep her safe, take care of her?"
"Will she ever have children?"
"How will she be treated—at school, at church, at work?"
"What will I tell my friends, our church, our extended family?"
"How did this happen? What caused Abby to be gay?"

This last question in particular fueled many late-night Google sessions and book purchases from Amazon and my local bookstore. Over time and much research, I learned that even the best theologians, psychiatrists, and scientists who have been studying this subject for decades couldn't say conclusively what caused a person to be gay. The uncertainty of that didn't sit well with me for a long time. I wanted cut-and-dried answers about her sexuality, but also about the far-reaching implications of what being gay meant for her eternal soul, and there didn't seem to be any. This lack of certainty was new to me. Baked into my evangelical upbringing was the notion that certainty is not only possible when it comes to matters of faith, it is downright essential. And to be sure, I still believed certain aspects of my faith were foundational, unchanging truths. But when it came to the spiritual, moral, and emotional complexities of my child's sexual orientation, the Bible didn't seem clear at all, and I realized I had much to learn.

In conversations with other Christians, I discovered how quick many were to dismiss those complexities with simple explanations and shallow platitudes. The so-called clobber verses were often quoted to me, as though I hadn't studied them from every possible angle, or read countless books about them in my attempts to better understand their context and meaning. The surface-level assumptions my Christian friends made about "the gay lifestyle" and other such notions didn't begin to scratch the surface of the intricacies in human behavior I observed in my own child. "Love the sinner, hate the sin" became especially problematic as my understanding of Abby's same-sex attraction deepened.

When I witnessed my daughter fall in love for the first time, I saw how naturally the relationship developed from a friendship to something different altogether. It reminded me of the ways in which I grew to love my husband, her father, at nineteen years old. Though I was all too familiar with the Bible verses that mentioned homosexuality, I didn't know how to separate the sin from the sinner in my daughter's case. Just as there was no point at which, when I was Abby's age, I willfully chose to develop feelings for my future husband, there wasn't a point at which Abby willfully chose to sin against God by developing feelings of affection for someone of the same sex. It simply unfolded in the most innocent and natural way possible. What I once thought was so simple was not so at all.

One incident stands out in my mind as my husband and I grappled with this need for certainty. Not long after Abby came out to us, my husband and I were finishing up dinner while having a difficult conversation. I told him I had begun to experience peace by meditating on Psalm 139:13, as it helped me to understand that God knew Abby better than I did; he had knit her together in my womb and saw her just as she was. This was comforting, as I'd been wrestling with so many questions about her spiritual destiny. My husband listened, then shook his head like he wasn't having it. He wanted rock-solid, biblical proof that embracing our daughter as gay was the right thing to do.

We couldn't find middle ground that night, and I went to bed early, unsettled. When I woke up the next morning, I saw that he hadn't come to bed, so I crept downstairs and found him pacing the living-room floor. Bleary-eyed, hair a mess, he looked like he'd been at it all night. I gave him a questioning look, and he stopped pacing for a moment and said, "I don't have any control over the next life, . . . but as long as she's my daughter, she'll never be loved by anyone outside this house more than she's loved by me." I was grateful for this declaration of love. I knew what it had cost him. I knew he had sacrificed his need for certainty on the altar and exchanged it for unconditional love. We didn't have answers yet, but we could love her. That we could do.

When we're willing to prioritize love over our questions and step into the uncertainties that life sometimes presents, we can be a source of great comfort to parents of LGBTQ children. People who moved beyond wanting to "fix the problem" of my daughter being gay and were open to accepting her, even though not every aspect could be explained, were the ones who most modeled the love of Christ to me. If every one of us is "fearfully and wonderfully made," as Psalm 139:14 states, by a God whose ways and thoughts are "higher" than ours (Isa. 55:9), then perhaps we can make room for complexities and mysteries about the human experience that we don't yet, and may never fully, understand. May we echo the apostle Paul in this matter, declaring that we know only "in part" (1 Cor. 13:12). In doing so, we might have more humility and grace in our encounters with those parents in our faith communities who are wrestling to better understand and love their LGBTQ children.

Make Room for Grace in the Midst of Differences

While it's tempting to hope that, someday, every one of my Christian friends, family members, and ministry colleagues will come to an agreement regarding LGBTQ acceptance and inclusion within the body of Christ, chances are they won't. There seem to be as many opinions and beliefs about this topic as there are people. The challenge, then, is how to make room for these differences in a way that aligns with Christ's teaching on unity within the church and, more importantly, on loving our neighbors as ourselves. For the parent of an LGBTQ child who is wrestling with their own set of beliefs while navigating life within a faith community, that question has life-changing implications.

There is a saying among parents of LGBTQ kids that goes something like this: "When a child from a Christian home comes out of the closet, their parent goes into it." That parent then experiences their own "coming out" when they make the decision, if they ever do, to acknowledge publicly that they have an LGBTQ child. For me, that decision was an extremely difficult one, as I feared it would impact my life's work—singing and speaking in evangelical churches—in irrevocable ways. But the potential threat of losing work isn't the only consideration parents have in deciding whether to share about their situation with others. Whether they reveal it to their small group at church or to their Facebook followers online, a big consideration, and a very real fear, is that of being shunned or shamed by their community, particularly if their views differ from those held by the leaders within that community. This fear was proven justified in my case, time and again. One particularly humiliating and painful example remains instructive to me about the ways in which we handle our differences as siblings in Christ.

I received a call from a women's ministry director of a large evangelical church where I had been welcomed as a featured guest singer and speaker multiple times over several years. This particular time, however, she was calling to *uninvite* me from an upcoming event I had been booked for months earlier. She had been made aware of a blog post I wrote in which I revealed my daughter's coming out, my struggle in coming to accept it, and what I was learning about God's love in the process. She felt that since some of the thoughts I shared in the piece didn't align with their church's stance on homosexuality, my presence would disrupt the "sense of unity" they hoped the event would foster, and I was asked to step down from the engagement.

The rejection I experienced in that conversation hit me on two levels. First, as a ministry professional, I felt dismissed and devalued, not for a lack of gifting or skills but for reasons that had nothing to do with my ability to do my job well. I had spent years developing a professional relationship with the leaders of this church, and in one conversation, I felt it being destroyed. At a deeper level, as the mother of a daughter who had played and gone to school with children of other mothers from this church, I felt ostracized because I chose to see my child differently than how they saw her. And on both of those levels, the notion of my presence threatening the unity of this group was especially painful. These were my people, my "church family" in the largest sense—fellow followers of Jesus, serving one God, our heavenly Father, together. Yet, I couldn't help but feel like an "other," the outsider no longer welcomed in the inner circle.

I wish my story was an outlier, but sadly, it happened more than once to me, and it's often the norm with other parents. I have friends in evangelical church ministry who, when their children came out as gay or transgender, were subsequently forced, in one way or another, to step down from their positions. One parent of a troubled trans child went to his senior ministry team asking for help and guidance only to be told he would need to take a sabbatical to work out his "family problems." He was eventually forced to resign and told not to speak about the matter to anyone in the church. Rather than supporting and walking alongside him and his family in this painful situation, his church chose to abandon him.

Another friend works for an evangelical nonprofit organization training ministry leaders overseas, and since her child came out as gay over a year ago, she has been navigating the precarious waters of loving and accepting her child as gay while staying silent about the matter in the presence of work colleagues for fear of losing her job. Another ministry leader of a large evangelical church told me she had to be careful not to "like" any social media posts that advocated for loving and accepting the LGBTQ community, as her job would be jeopardized if she did. Stories like these are plentiful among evangelicals: parents and loved ones of LGBTQ people feeling forced into secrecy for fear of being ostracized.

Thinking back to the conversation in which I was directly uninvited by that church ministry leader, it occurs to me that her reasoning likely came from a place of fear. It's the same fear that has motivated people throughout history to tighten their circles and exclude others according to their differences—be those differences of skin color or of how to interpret certain verses in the Bible. Within Christ's body there exists a vast array of opinions, beliefs, and doctrines regarding homosexuality and the acceptance and inclusion of LGBTQ people. Parents of LGBTQ children don't need everyone in their faith communities to agree with their views. In fact, many parents will admit they themselves are still on a journey of discovery when it comes to reconciling their faith with their child's sexual orientation or gender identity. What these parents desperately need, and should expect from their siblings in Christ, is a safe space to share their experiences and feel loved and supported, whatever our differing beliefs and opinions.

I have resigned myself to the fact that some people won't ever make room at God's table for the LGBTQ community. A much harder truth for me to accept is that, as the mother of a gay child who also happens to be a member of God's big family, I have to make room for *them*. I am compelled to show grace when I'm tempted to write off folks who believe differently than me. What I usually discover, when I sit down and have conversations with them, one on one, is that most are kindhearted people who would never intentionally hurt anyone, even if I see the ways in which their beliefs and practices inadvertently do just that. Allowing for differences on all sides of these divisions that threaten to separate us, especially when they hit us close to home, is one of the most difficult, and most gracious, things love asks of each of us.

Make Room for an Expanding Faith

Another important step in understanding and supporting Christian parents of LGBTQ children, parents who are grappling with the complexities of loving their children in the context of their faith, is acknowledging their need for an expanding theology. As parents wrestle with scriptural passages that reference homosexuality, trying to make sense of them within the framework of their faith tradition, the implications become more and more difficult to reconcile with the reality they see on a daily basis. The sense that "something's got to give" often propels parents to push beyond the boundaries of their present belief systems.

In my case, I began to see the importance of a lived theology, one that is best understood in the context of real life. As a parent raising a teenage daughter who happened to be gay, what I saw on a day-to-day basis was, for the most part, normal teenage behavior. In the months leading up to her coming out, my daughter had been isolating herself, getting poor grades, and in general acting depressed. After coming out to us, she seemed to flourish, no doubt relieved to be free of the burden of keeping such an important secret from us. Of course, she experienced ups and downs like other kids her age. But nowhere in her personality or behavior did I see signs of the sort of destructive, rebellious behavior those familiar Bible verses talked about. Reading them, I felt a disconnect, a fault in their logic: that label did not match this behavior I was seeing. It wasn't that I was trying to change Scripture to fit what I wanted to believe about my daughter—a common misconception some

Christians have of parents of LGBTQ children—it's that my lived reality, the one I witnessed on a daily basis, was demonstrating a different truth: my child was healthy, happy, normal.

Many Christian parents of LGBTQ kids experience this conflict between what their faith has taught them about homosexuality and what their day-to-day reality demonstrates. It's in this tension where many parents become curious and begin to examine more closely what they've long held to be true. I began to approach my reading of Scripture differently, trying to better understand it in the light of my lived experience as the mother of a gay child. To do so, I found it helpful to seek wisdom outside of my familiar ecumenical boundaries. I began to consume books, podcasts, and articles from people who were exploring biblical interpretations that I had never heard before. I discovered the work of Matthew Vines, Karen Keen, David Gushee, Kathy Baldock, and other thought leaders who had done a lot more research on this topic than I had. Their informed voices helped me parse out some of the complexities of language and culture reflected in those familiar Scripture passages on same-sex relations that I had never been taught in my church. I found great comfort in discovering more expansive ways of thinking about the Bible.

As Christ followers, if we can look at Scripture with new eyes, seeking to understand God's love in the context of caring for and supporting those who are marginalized, we find no judgment or condemnation. In Jesus, we see the Son of God more concerned with restoring, healing, and reconciling people than pointing out their sin. To the religious leaders who called Jesus out for eating with outcasts and "disreputable characters," we hear him say, "Go figure out what this Scripture means: 'I'm after mercy, not religion'" (Matt. 9:10–13 MSG).

To his closest followers, we hear Jesus say, "Love each other as I have loved you" (John 15:12), and "Everyone will know that you are my disciples, if you love one another" (John 13:35). In Jesus's words we see that the defining characteristic of the family of God—and dare I say, of our human families—is not a set of beliefs or doctrines that we all agree on but, quite simply, how well we love one another. While this may seem like a fundamental truth, even obvious, it's a revolutionary, life-changing one to parents like me, whose greatest fear was that I would somehow get all of it wrong—the parenting part and the following Jesus part. Allowing love to have the final word, not a set of rules or religious practices, brought me indescribable peace both in my theology and as the parent of a gay child.

Many Christian parents of LGBTQ children come to the realization that the love they have for their child and their desire to encounter the truth of how God sees their child are not, as they might have feared, in direct opposition.

They discover, in Scripture and in the wisdom of their own lived experience, that there is room for both. This can be a growing process that is equal parts painful and beautifully expansive. To the extent that we understand this journey of discovery is not simply an academic exercise, or a spiritual-discipline practice, but a necessary endeavor to survive and thrive as parents and members of Christ's body, we can provide loving, supportive, and safe places for these parents to land along their way.

Last Thoughts

I often wish that people in my faith community had made room for my family and me when our daughter came out as gay. If they had, I'm convinced we would have felt less alone, less ostracized, less misunderstood. The damage done by church leaders (knowingly or unknowingly), the pain of isolation we experienced as a family, the loss of my vocation as a result of choosing to share my story publicly—all of this has profoundly affected my experience of both church and *the* church, Christ's body of believers. I would be disingenuous if I characterized my relationship with it today as completely healed. And yet, even as I write these words, I have hope for change. As more and more faithful, Spirit-led LGBTQ people and their families bravely share their stories of God's grace and unconditional love, I believe the church must, and will, learn to make room for them.

18

Christlike Acceptance in Practice

Moving from Enmity to Integrity

Marcus George Halley

Paul instructs the faithful in Rome, "If possible, so far as it depends on you, live peaceably with all people" (Rom. 12:18 NET). I take this exhortation seriously, even when it comes to those who possess different theological, ethical, or political commitments. This personal value arises from a negating motivation, wanting to undo the corrosive effects of ethical purity that destabilize everything, from our families to our body politic. It also arises from an affirming one, a desire to fulfill what I believe to be the fundamental vocation of the church—reconciliation. By reconciliation, I do not mean the mere papering over of human hurt, brokenness, and pain. Such a posture lacks the robust call of repentance that the Gospels claim is the gateway to the reign of God. "Repent," John the Baptizer says, "for the kingdom of heaven has come near" (Matt. 3:2). Instead, reconciliation requires both the confession and the accountability of the guilty, as well as mercy and forgiveness on the victim's part. Accountability and mercy become possible when we possess the humility to understand that, due to the complexity of human nature and existence, each of us stands in need of mercy and is called to offer forgiveness. "Forgive us our trespasses," we pray, "as we forgive those who trespass against us."[1]

This personal commitment to live peaceably also emerges from a more mundane belief: people are endlessly complex and interesting, and much of who we are is shaped by forces larger than us. The more we can contextualize our disagreements through proximity and relationship and explore our beliefs about ourselves and the world, the more we can find room for shared connection across ideological, theological, and ethical differences. In *Differ We Must: How Abraham Lincoln Succeeded in a Divided America*, National Public Radio host Steve Inskeep argues that the through line he discovered in the Great Emancipator's political career was his ability to meet people where they were and to move them just far enough on important issues while leaving more progress for later.[2]

Lincoln did so because he understood that everyone is motivated by self-righteousness and self-interest. His approach infuriated both those committed to slavery and those committed to its abolition. Still, Lincoln knew something about human nature. He understood that people are shaped by systems and circumstances larger than they are. He once told critics of Southern enslavers that "they [the Southern enslavers] are just what we would be under similar circumstances."[3] It might seem odd that I, a descendant of enslaved people from Kershaw County, South Carolina, am writing such words, and I make no apologies or defense of the brutality of American slavery. But the nugget of wisdom is that we are all shaped by forces larger than us. The zeitgeist of our time is more potent than we readily give it credit.

Paul reflects on this when he writes, "I do not understand what I do. For what I want to do I do not do, but what I hate I do. . . . For I do not do the good I want to do, but the evil I do not want to do—this I keep on doing" (Rom. 7:15, 19). The inner struggle to which Paul writes reveals that we are trapped in a web of sin and brokenness, and that it is impossible, but for the grace of God, to find freedom and release. The Gospel presents us with God's invitation to be free from this slavery and, rather than being formed in the image of the world around us, to be "transformed by the renewing of [our] mind[s]" (Rom. 12:2). In Christ, we trade our self-righteousness and

---

1. "The Lord's Prayer," in *The Book of Common Prayer*, according to the use of the Episcopal Church, 336, BCPonline.org. Hereafter cited as BCP.

2. Steve Inskeep, *Differ We Must: How Abraham Lincoln Succeeded in a Divided America* (Penguin, 2023).

3. Abraham Lincoln, "First Debate with Stephen A. Douglas at Ottawa, Illinois, August 21, 1858 (excerpt)," George Mason University, https://mason.gmu.edu/~zschrag/hist120spring05/lincoln_ottawa.htm.

self-interest for God's righteousness and the interests of others. Rather than taking on the evil forms of this world, we are called to grow up into the full stature of Christ (Eph. 4:13).

Thus, the struggle for LGBTQ acceptance into the full life of Christ's church is not a struggle between individuals—it is a struggle against what Paul refers to as "the rulers, against the authorities, against the powers of this dark world and against the spiritual forces of evil in the heavenly realms" (Eph. 6:12). This is a crucial distinction. The Christian gospel calls us beyond the fraught relationship between enemies and into the redemptive and salvific relationship of members of one body—Christ's body. I may disagree vehemently with other members of the body—and I do with those who see me and other LGBTQ members of Christ's body as deficient and evil—but I am also called to the second greatest commandment: to love them as I am called to love myself (Mark 12:31). To borrow from Audre Lorde, "The master's tools will never dismantle the master's house."[4] Othering, shaming, and disposing of others will never bring about the vital community life to which the church is called to bear witness. This is not easy. Hence our call to continue the Christian journey, daily growing in charity and compassion, until we all see the fullness of God's eternal glory face-to-face.

In nearly every community where I have served as a priest, I have initiated a story-sharing ministry in one form or another. The practice began as something I learned while facilitating antiracism training workshops. The workshops included sharing information and one-on-one conversations to help students process and integrate the new learning into their own experiences. I quickly discovered that many people I met through this work needed to be more familiar with being listened to. They were accustomed to being talked at. They were also adept at talking toward someone else, a practice that looks like speaking, but with little faith that one will be genuinely understood and affirmed. However, when participants were asked to reflect on the experience of talking about themselves for two minutes based on a series of reflective prompts, they often shared how hard it was to fill two minutes because they were unaccustomed to speaking without interruption. Likewise, they would share how hard it was to listen without interrupting. The more people talked, the more they often discovered the nuances in their own stories and perspectives and those of others.

Years later, in a parish setting, I started a story-sharing ministry after discovering that two longtime parishioners who had sat in the same pew for

---

4. Audre Lorde, *The Master's Tools Will Never Dismantle the Master's House* (Penguin, 2018).

decades didn't know basic information about each other, things like their favorite movie or something that made them afraid, or what motivated their involvement in church. I have found that whenever I am experiencing a breakdown in a relationship, it's because there is something in the story of another that I have not fully understood or appreciated. It often stems from not taking the time to know their story. This is especially important now in my ministry as a college chaplain amid the current Israel-Hamas war, with both Jewish and Arab students feeling misunderstood and unheard, both accused of callous inhumanity, both striving for a world of peace and security. As I stand between these communities, I do so as a listener and a learner, hearing how deeply they feel the pain of the war and how difficult it is to adequately convey this pain to people who don't share their identity or perspective. The world is hungry for spaces where we can be seen and affirmed. This starts with listening to the stories of others and sharing our own stories—stories that reveal our endless and beautiful human complexity.

The issue of LGBTQ acceptance in the church has surfaced deep divides in families and congregations, both within and between Christian denominations. These divisions further imperil the witness of the one church to the one God, and they ignore Jesus's prayer that his followers "may become completely one" (John 17:23 NRSV). I am not suggesting that storytelling is the answer to all that ails us; instead, I am suggesting that much of what contributes to our division is a failure of relationships—an unwillingness to be sufficiently human. Stories help to humanize us to ourselves and to one another, thus enabling us to build durable relationships across perceived lines of difference.

If I can learn to appreciate my flawed beauty, perhaps I can learn to appreciate the imperfect beauty of another. This is more than simply agreeing to disagree, which often only heightens passive aggression, even while formally signaling the cessation of active aggression. This is about pluralism, a word Eboo Patel, founder of Interfaith America, defines as "the proactive and positive engagement of difference."[5] Pluralism is not relativism. It does not suggest that all truths are the same. Rather, pluralism suggests that we need one another to discover and live into truth. As Frank Griswold, former presiding bishop of the Episcopal Church, writes, "Truth of its nature is dialogical and involves a willingness to engage together in a common search. . . . The only way I can enlarge my truth is by being exposed and open to the dimensions of truth expressed in the experiences and understandings of others."[6] Plural-

---

5. Eboo Patel, *We Need to Build: Field Notes for Diverse Democracy* (Beacon, 2022), 51.
6. Frank T. Griswold, *Tracking Down the Holy Ghost: Reflections on Love and Longing* (Church, 2017), 102.

ism is at the heart of God's dream for creation and is central to the vision of God's redeemed world. God calls us to move from enmity to integrity, being gathered by God's grace as the many members of the one body of Christ. This requires us to make room for one another and to practice a different way of being in community together.

Coffee with Michael: A Case Study in Christlike Acceptance

Many years ago, while serving a parish community in the Midwest, I came across someone who would teach me a lot about what it means to practice Christlike acceptance, even if he didn't know that God was teaching me through him. For the sake of this exploration, we will call him Michael. It began after I gave a sermon on God's grace and hospitality where I reflected on my journey to the Episcopal Church and the incredible welcome I experienced—a welcome I didn't expect, because I am gay. A few Sundays later, after shaking hands following the morning eucharistic service, I stuck my hand into the pocket of my cassock and found a folded-up photocopy of an article from a prominent Christian magazine blaming the decline of the Episcopal Church on its "liberal theology" and "apostasy." I couldn't quite remember how the piece of paper had gotten there, but I assumed that I had somehow picked it up, put it in my pocket, and just forgotten about it.

The mystery was solved a few Sundays later when Michael shook my hand after service and put a copy of the same article in my hand. He looked me squarely in the eyes, with a stern look, and then walked away without saying anything further. I noticed a few things in the following weeks. Michael avoided me during coffee hour after services; he repeatedly visited the vesting sacristy before services to deliver more articles similar to the one he had given me a few weeks prior; and he refused to take communion from me, even when I was the priest assigned to preside. These actions caused deep pain for me. At a fundamental level, I was reliving all the pain and rejection I had felt growing up gay in a church that equated non-heterosexual identity and practice with sin.

A wise colleague encouraged me to contact Michael and invite a conversation. After mulling it over, I emailed Michael, asking him to meet with me over coffee. He responded and agreed to meet. We met at a local coffee shop. At first we exchanged pleasantries, stumbling to find a way to enter the conversation we both knew we had agreed to have. So many years later, I am unsure how we finally entered the conversation. What I do remember is how vulnerable it felt. I shared with Michael how the Episcopal Church had saved my life, shown me the wideness of God's love and mercy, and allowed me to step into my vocation with a sense of integrity. Michael shared with me the welcome he felt—particularly in the liturgy—and the grief he feels because he believes his beloved church is abandoning the centrality of the Scriptures that saved his marriage and guided him through an addiction that almost cost him his life.

Michael and I shared more, which we will explore below, but I remember an overwhelming sense of connection in that moment. Neither of our minds was changed then, but I believe our hearts began to grow. I know this because a few months later, on my last Sunday as a priest in this community, Michael knelt at the altar rail in front of me during communion. When I pressed the bread into his hand, he grabbed mine—an eternity passed in that moment. So much that needed to be said was expressed in a wordless, attentive act of love—God's love that holds space for us to step out of isolation and into the community to learn to love one another. I have not seen Michael since, but my interaction with him has taught me more about Christlike acceptance than any other exchange.

Christlike Acceptance and the Pursuit of Truth

A few years ago, while researching for a presentation I was invited to give at the Prayer Book Conference, held at the School of Theology at the University of the South in Sewanee, Tennessee, I rediscovered a concept that I had first encountered in my days growing up as a Baptist: *Sola Scriptura*. This doctrine is the belief that the Bible is the supreme authority in Christian theology. It is not that I forgot about the Bible's authority. After all, not only are an Old Testament lesson, a psalm, and two New Testament passages read each Sunday in a typical Episcopal church, but 70 percent of the Book of Common Prayer is lifted directly from the Bible. Rather, through my research on the need for the Christian community to experience liturgy as a communal activity,[7] I discovered a nuance that I had not sufficiently appreciated before.

Much good can come from the personal study of the Scriptures. In *Being Christian: Baptism, Bible, Eucharist, and Prayer*, Rowan Williams reminds us both that we Christians are "people who expect to be spoken to by God"

---

7. Wherein the *ekklēsia*—the community gathered by the power of the Spirit for the sake of God's purposes—participates in God's saving work for the sake of the world.

and that the primary way we hear from God is through the Scriptures.[8] But *Sola Scriptura* is often misinterpreted as individualistic biblical interpretation, wherein *I* determine what these Scriptures mean *for me* apart from what they mean for the church and the world. Williams goes on to remind us that the primary location for Christian engagement with the Scriptures is the *ekklēsia*, writing that it "would have been quite strange in many parts of the Christian world for many centuries" for Christians to have the kind of ready access to the Scriptures that we now enjoy, such as through personal Bibles and even phone apps.[9] Thus, when Reformed Christianity (I consider myself Reformed *and* Catholic) promotes *Sola Scriptura*, it is not putting biblical interpretation into the hands of the individual; instead, the doctrine places biblical interpretation in the hands of the *ekklēsia*. To put it differently, as hard as this is to live into, we need one another in order to discover the truth of God in the Scriptures.

When I met with Michael, I assumed my job as his priest was to convert him to my point of view. I had my argument all ready to go. I would begin by naming how his actions hurt me. After that, I would connect his hurt to all the times the church inflicted pain on me growing up, thereby proving his guilt by association. Following that, I would provide him with the latest scholarship on LGBTQ theology, and then call him to repentance. If I succeeded, there would be "joy in heaven" for a repentant sinner, and I could come away justified.

This argument went out the window when I looked into Michael's eyes and saw someone scared but eager to connect, even if he was closed off to any new revelation. Perhaps he had the same goal as I: to convert the other. What we both discovered in that shared encounter was our mutual love of the Scriptures: its cadences, its complexity, its beauty, its difficulty, its invitation to pursue wisdom and truth. I also learned that my desire to convert Michael had closed me off to some wisdom or insight that he might possess. I can't say what Michael might have discovered in me, but I saw someone desperately searching for God in a secular age.

The church often cites ordinations as evidence that "things which were cast down are being raised up, and things which had grown old are being made new, and that all things are being brought to their perfection by him through whom all things were made."[10] There is some truth to this. It is also true that the resurrecting power of God is at work in the hearts of all who earnestly

---

8. Rowan Williams, *Being Christian: Baptism, Bible, Eucharist, and Prayer* (Eerdmans, 2014), 21.
9. Williams, *Being Christian*, 23.
10. BCP, 291.

seek God, including Michael. We may come to different conclusions on some matters, but we shared in that moment a conviction of the truth that is Jesus, the Son of God, and our mutual earnest desire to find him and be found in him.

One of the reasons schism harms the church is because it prevents us from listening deeply to the Spirit. When we decide that we have no need for a fellow sibling in Christ because we disagree with them—even on important and weighty matters—and that we are unwilling to associate with them until they repent, we neglect the reality that the same Spirit that is at work in us, bringing us to perfection, is also at work in them. If we genuinely seek Christ, we will find ourselves in the company of all those who truly seek him, even those we despise. This is the true scandal of the wideness of God's grace, the scandal that causes us to abandon the reign of God that comes near to us. We affirm that God has room for *us*, but not that God has room enough for *them*.

Toward the end of C. S. Lewis's *The Last Battle*, the final volume of his Chronicles of Narnia series, the Narnians find themselves in Aslan's Country after the destruction of Narnia, along with Emeth, one of the Calormenes, the servants of the evil, false god Tash. When Emeth asks Aslan how he now finds himself in Aslan's Country, despite living his whole life in supposed opposition to him, Aslan tells him, "Beloved, . . . unless thy desire had been for me, thou wouldst not have sought so long and so truly."[11] The earnest seeking of truth and love will bring us into the arms of Christ, though at times it may seem like we are far from him. As much as we claim this truth for ourselves, it is just as important that we claim this truth for others, for only then can we begin to open our hearts to the connections that we need in order to discover more of the truth of God.

Christlike Acceptance and Christian Hospitality

Contemplating the wideness of God's mercy makes particular claims on us. As I have already shared, my theological journey to joining the Episcopal church as a young adult was based on my discovery of the ever-expanding nature of God's love and mercy. This is shown throughout the Scriptures. In Romans 5:8, Paul explores God's love, writing, "God demonstrates his own love for us in this: While we were still sinners, Christ died for us." Similarly, John recalls an expansive vision of the reign of God, writing, "You ransomed for God saints from every tribe and language and people and nation; you have

---

11. C. S. Lewis, *The Last Battle* (HarperCollins, 2005), 206.

made them to be a kingdom and priests serving our God, and they will reign on earth" (Rev. 5:9b–10 NRSV). There is a welcome to the whole world at the heart of the gospel.

Yet, as much as this welcome presents us with an opportunity, it also gives us a challenge. If there is room for *us*, there is also room for *them*. Each of us has a margin across which it is increasingly difficult to see the image of Christ in the face of another. This is not a moral judgment but a statement of reality. In the fight-flight-or-freeze world of our ancestors, we developed an evolutionary bias in favor of people who resemble us and against those who do not. With the opportunity of God's welcome comes its challenge: to overcome this evolutionary bias against people different from ourselves and to see God's welcome as extending to them.

When I first sat down with Michael, I thought my job was to convert him to my way of thinking and seeing. I thought this was the only way for me to see him as just as much a member of God's kingdom as I believed myself to be. I began to shed this prejudice when I heard him speak of his love for the church and the Scriptures that saved his life and marriage. In the place of conversion, I adopted the posture of *companion*, a word that means "one who shares bread," though in this case, it was coffee and probably a croissant.

As Michael shared his journey with God, I heard him talk about how unworthy he felt to be welcomed into the church because of the shame he carried around from his addiction to alcohol. My shame was not around addiction, but it was shame nonetheless. He and I both connected, and in that moment I saw something of the wideness of God's love and mercy in our exchange. In the words of the "Prayer of Humble Access,"[12] neither he nor I saw ourselves as worthy "so much as to gather up the crumbs" under God's table, and yet God's character is always to have mercy.

Michael taught me much about the ministry of faithful, Christlike hospitality, which is at the heart of Christlike acceptance. As Jesus brings the reign of God near to people throughout the Gospels, he isn't embodying a colonial "convert or die" paradigm; rather, Jesus embodies the reign of God in such a way that the environment is set for transformation to take place. Christlike acceptance has, at its heart, a belief that when we can learn to be in community with one another despite our different theological, political, and ethical commitments, we can learn more about what it means to live the life of Christ. In *Being Christian*, Rowan Williams writes,

---

12. The Anglican Pastor, "The Prayer of Humble Access," Anglican Compass, October 14, 2019, https://anglicancompass.com/the-prayer-of-humble-access/.

Jesus is not only someone who exercises hospitality; he draws out hospitality from others. By his welcome he makes other people capable of welcoming. And that wonderful alternation in the Gospels between Jesus giving hospitality and receiving hospitality shows us something absolutely essential about the Eucharist. We are the guests of Jesus. We are there because he asks us, and because he wants our company. At the same time we are set free to invite Jesus into our lives and literally to receive him into our bodies in the Eucharist. His welcome gives us the courage to open up to him. And so the flow of giving and receiving, of welcome and acceptance, moves backwards and forwards without a break. We are welcomed, and we welcome; we welcome God, and we welcome our unexpected neighbors.[13]

Michael moved from being my enemy to being my "unexpected neighbor" when I opened myself to the possibility that the reign of God was coming nearer to me through him. Hebrews 13:2 reminds us, "Do not forget to show hospitality to strangers, for by so doing some people have shown hospitality to angels without knowing it."

Christlike Acceptance and the Reign of God

Ultimately, all of this is meaningless apart from God's saving work—the redemption and restoration of God's creation. In *After You Believe: Why Christian Character Matters*, N. T. Wright elucidates the importance of developing the virtues of the Christian faith, likening them to a language we will need to speak fluently in the world to come. He writes, "The New Testament's vision of Christian behavior has to do, not with struggling to keep a bunch of ancient and apparently arbitrary rules, nor with 'going with the flow' or 'doing what comes naturally', but with the learning of the language, in the present, which will equip us to speak it fluently in God's new world."[14] One of the virtues Wright explores in his book is love. He says love is not mere tolerance, which costs us nothing. Love, for Wright, is rooted in our complete humanity, which will be restored at the end but is accessible to us now in Christ, and is thus teleological by nature.[15]

In other words, love sees beyond our present reality, the hostility between us based on contemporary realities, and points toward a reconciled future, one where enmity has been destroyed and the very status of "enemy" has

---

13. Williams, *Being Christian*, 42–43.
14. N. T. Wright, *After You Believe* (HarperOne, 2010), 78.
15. Wright, *After You Believe*, 189.

been ground to dust by the power of God. Howard Thurman speaks to this in his seminal work *Jesus and the Disinherited*, where he stresses that "love of enemy means that a fundamental attack must first be made on the enemy status."[16] For Thurman, this attack takes the form of moving closer to one another and sharing something together, something that is prohibited within the framework of enemy.

Coffee Is a Great Place to Begin

Again, Michael was my enemy when I sat down for our coffee meeting. He was every person who told me I was evil, who bullied me, or who told me I would go to hell. When my colleague counseled me to invite Michael to coffee, he instructed me to move beyond the framework of enemy and into our true natures as members of the one body of Christ. He didn't assume that there would be a dramatic change of heart from either of us; instead, he knew that by sharing something—coffee—we could dream of more.

The author of *Emergent Strategy*, adrienne maree brown, writes astutely about the dream of God from a non-Christian background, challenging social movements to consider the connection between their means and their vision. She asks, "When we imagine the world we want to shift towards, are we dreaming of being the winners of the future? Or are we dreaming of a world where winning is no longer necessary because there are no enemies?"[17] The former, a world of winners—and, thus, losers—is our current reality where we justify the mistreatment of one another in the service of some perceived greater good or in the name of "justice." This is the world of prisons, war, and schism, where we discount the value of the lives of other people, seeing them as expendable, not essential parts of our world.

The latter world, where there are no winners and losers "because there are no enemies," is the reign of God. It is a world where we have learned how to live deeply from our values and hospitably, making room for others to show up with their perspectives. This is the world of Isaiah's "feast of rich food for all peoples" on the mountain of the Lord (Isa. 25:6) and John the Revelator's "new heaven and . . . new earth" (Rev. 21:1). This is what we glimpse in the Eucharist when we receive the Lord's body into our own bodies, confirming our identity as members of the one body of Christ and strengthening our

---

16. Howard Thurman, *Jesus and the Disinherited* (Beacon, 1976), 97.
17. adrienne maree brown, *Emergent Strategy: Shaping Change, Changing Worlds* (AK, 2017), 132. Author intentionally uses lowercase names.

connection and union with Christ and everyone else who seeks this intimacy. I glimpsed this future when Michael and I shared space together, setting aside the false security of self-righteousness and choosing instead the open-hearted vulnerability of Jesus.

Conclusion

In *How to Know a Person*, David Brooks suggests that building a community "involves performing a series of small, concrete, social actions well," among them being "disagreeing without poisoning the relationship," "being a good listener," "knowing how to ask for and offer forgiveness," "knowing how to sit with someone who is suffering," and "knowing how to see something from another's point of view."[18] As someone who has just been married, I can share that these social actions are key for my husband and I as we seek to keep our vows to each other in holy matrimony. The church could learn a lesson or two from this list.

I was not of age, or even part of the Episcopal Church, when the conversations around human sexuality split the church, resulting in the formation of the Anglican Church in North America. But I engaged in similar discussions in seminary with classmates from a variety of Black Protestant denominations, and I can say clearly that these "small, concrete, social actions" were not in play. I wonder how the conversation would change if everyone committed to them. What if we saw our connection to one another in the body of Christ as a vow that we cannot break? I am not suggesting that this work is easy or comes naturally. That it does not come naturally to us is all the more reason why we ought to practice it. The call of God is to die to what comes naturally to us so that we can be raised into the life given to us by grace.

What a witness the church would make to a broken and atomizing world if we learned how to live together in love despite our vast differences in theology and ideology. We could teach the world how to speak the truth with humility, hold space for complexity and mystery, and love unconditionally. We haven't yet arrived at the reign of God, but there are moments of reconciliation and healing where this reality becomes more apparent and where the body, broken by division, is healed.

---

18. David Brooks, *How to Know a Person: The Art of Seeing Others Deeply and Being Deeply Seen* (Random House, 2023), 8.